INITIATIVES IN COMMUNICATIVE LANGUAGE TEACHING

A Book of Readings

Edited by
SANDRA J. SAVIGNON
and
MARGIE S. BERNS

ADDISON-WESLEY PUBLISHING COMPANY
Reading, Massachusetts
Menlo Park, California • Don Mills, Ontario
Amsterdam • London • Manila • Singapore • Sydney • Tokyo

THE ADDISON-WESLEY SECOND LANGUAGE PROFESSIONAL LIBRARY SERIES

Sandra J. Savignon
Consulting Editor

HIGGINS, John and JOHNS, Tim
Computers in Language Learning

SMITH, Stephen M.
The Theater Arts and the Teaching of Second Languages

SAVIGNON, Sandra J.
Communicative Competence: Theory and Classroom Practice

VENTRIGLIA, Linda
Conversations of Miguel and Maria

WALLERSTEIN, Nina
Language and Culture in Conflict

Library of Congress Cataloging in Publication Data
Main entry under title:

Initiatives in communicative language teaching.

(Second language professional library)
Includes index.
1. Languages, Modern—Study and teaching.
2. Communicative competence. I. Savignon, Sandra J.
II. Berns, Margie S. III. Series
PB36.I585 1984   418'.007'1   83-21529
ISBN 0-201-06506-1

ISBN: 0-201-06506-1
ABCDEFGHIJKL-AL-8987654

Contents

iii

Introduction

Sandra J. Savignon

Communicative language teaching means many different things to different people. For some it means the adoption of a "functional" syllabus, or the use of "notional-functional" teaching materials. For others it means a learner's increased participation in decisions pertaining to course content, along with a more "humanistic," learner-centered style of teaching. Still others view communicative language teaching as the expansion of audiolingual-type programs to include small group activities, role-play, and "games" in which learners are given the opportunity to use grammatical structures that have been previously presented and drilled. (For a discussion of these interpretations, with examples, see Savignon 1983). Largely because of the diversity of the many frequently voiced opinions concerning the nature of a communicative approach to second- or foreign-language (L2) teaching, it is probably safe to say that many teachers remain unsure just what communicative language teaching in fact is, and how it differs, if at all, from what they are now doing.

Initiatives in Communicative Language Teaching is a resource book for classroom teachers and program administrators who want to know not only *what* communicative language teaching is all about but *how* the goal of communicative competence is being met in teaching contexts similar to their own. While theoretical discussions of language and language learning are helpful in clarifying goals and issues, examples of ongoing developments in teaching and evaluation often provide the incentive needed to make changes, to modify or redesign inadequate programs and materials. The emphasis in this volume is therefore on accounts of programs that are working, on reports of initiatives that are being pursued on local, regional, and even national levels to make the goal of communicative L2 use a reality.

The authors of individual chapters are all intimately involved with teaching and/or program development and evaluation, and they describe initiatives in many different parts of the world. Moreover, the deliberately international scope of the volume shows that communicative language teaching is not a British, Canadian, European, or American phenomenon, but rather a universal effort that has found inspiration and direction in the *interaction* of initiatives, both theoretical and applied, in many different contexts. Linguists, methodologists, and materials writers around the world have contributed to this effort, for which it is all the richer.

The nature as well as the importance of this interaction will become clear as the themes of communicative language teaching are expanded from one chapter to the next. These themes may be summarized briefly as follows:

1. Language learning, like language, is a human activity, and the approaches, methods and techniques used should reflect the concerns of the learners and the teacher alike. Programs depend in a very real sense on the support of those they serve as well as those who implement them.

2. Teachers and program administrators are challenging evaluators to develop approaches to testing and evaluation that more clearly reflect communicative L2 use; and evaluators in turn are responding. The attitude is no longer "We will teach what we can test," but rather, "We will find ways to evaluate those skills that are important for learners to develop."

3. The search for alternative teaching strategies is principled, not random or "eclectic" in the sense of no overall design or objective. Observation of language learners in both natural and formal settings, as well as insights from linguistic, communication, and education theory have all contributed to the elaboration of a framework for communicative language teaching, a framework that takes into account the learning/teaching context.

The fourteen chapters that comprise this volume are grouped into three major sections: *Background Perspectives*, *Methods and Materials*, and *Evaluation*.

Section I, *Background Perspectives*, includes discussions of some of the theoretical issues related to functional and communicative approaches to language teaching. In Chapter 1, "Functional Approaches to Language and Language Teaching: Another Look," Margie Berns reviews the linguistic foundations of the functional approach to language teaching and clarifies the original, restricted meaning of the terms *notion*, *function*, and *context of situation*. As she shows, the divergent use of these terms by applied linguists, methodologists, and authors of teaching materials has often led to misunderstandings and frustration for classroom teachers who would like to meet their students' communicative needs. This review of the functional approach to language and language teaching concludes with a critique of selected textbook exercises, providing criteria that teachers can use to evaluate materials as either functional or communicative, or both.

In Chapter 2, "Contextual Considerations in Communicative Language Teaching," Sauli Takala draws on his long experience with the development of a communicative curriculum for Finnish schools to look at language teaching as it relates to language education policies and to education policies in general. If reforms are to be meaningful and lasting, educational programs have to be seen in their social context, as social institutions serving fundamental social desires, needs, and functions. Time and effort are required to launch any new approach, and all interested parties should be consulted and given an opportunity to participate in the process.

Discourse, input, and "natural" language have become familiar terms in discussions of second-language learning. In Chapter 3, "Intake, Communication, and Second-Language Teaching," Elizabeth Guthrie reviews the research in second-language acquisition that highlights the importance of *experience* in communication (as opposed to conscious attention to linguistic rules) in the development of functional proficiency. She shows how formal classroom learning environments not only differ but are often *made* to differ from natural environments, in terms of the nature of the L2 experience they provide. These insights in turn suggest ways in which teachers can adapt their own style of speaking to the level of the learner in order to achieve a maximum amount of communication, or meaningful discourse.

At the heart of any discussion of communication is the matter of mutual intelligibility. People learn languages to be able to communicate appropriately, that is, in a socially acceptable manner, with others. Sociolinguistic contexts of language use, social attitudes that determine preference for one or another linguistic norm, or language variety, and attempts to impose norms—to provide "linguistic watchdogs"—are among the topics addressed by Braj Kachru in Chapter 4, "Regional Norms for English."

Kachru points out that the socially acceptable variety for a growing number of English language users in the world today is neither RP (Received Pronunciation, or "BBC English"), nor GA (General American), but one of a number of other regional norms. In such a case, adherence to external as opposed to local norms is attitudinally undesirable. Moreover, as the number of speakers of English as a second, third, or even fourth language continues to grow, the validity of the concept "native speaker" itself becomes doubtful. Matters of comprehensibility, acceptability, and tolerance of "error" take on important new dimensions in a world where non-native varieties of English are used increasingly for communication across cultures and across languages. This example of the global spread of English provides a perspective on the nature of language use and language change in general, a perspective important to an understanding of the concept of communicative competence.

Section I concludes with Chapter 5, "I Got Religion!—Evangelism in Language Teaching." Alan Maley, a representative of the British Council in Peking who confesses to being "locked in unequal combat with Mandarin Chinese," looks at the dazzling complexities of language learning and the disconcerting, if human, tendency for some teachers to see convenient solutions to the problems of language teaching in the often doctrinaire, almost evangelistic, promotion of one or another method or model. He notes the fascination exerted by methodological approaches and their creators and goes on to illustrate the incompatibilities of the more prominent among them: *Silent Way*,

Suggestopedia, and *Community Language Learning*. Maley's view is not that we should abandon our search for better solutions, but rather, that we should exercise our independent judgment and not be too ready to adhere to this or that system or approach without carefully considering the claims that are made for it.

Section II, *Methods and Materials*, and Section III, *Evaluation*, are collections of case studies that provide examples of ways in which teaching is becoming more reflective of the goal of communicative competence. These case studies are drawn from second- and foreign-language programs at both school and college levels in the U.S., Canada, and Europe. Their unity of focus, despite the diversity of the contexts they represent, offers compelling evidence not only of the gains that have been made for communicative language teaching, but of the vitality and imaginativeness of the language teaching profession. In their descriptions of teaching and evaluation programs, methods, and materials, they provide very practical guidelines to those who would like to bring about similar changes in their own programs.

The creation of a classroom environment that allows for learners' personal as well as linguistic development is the focus of Chapter 6, "Beyond Notions and Functions: Language Teaching or the Art of Letting Go" by Günter Gerngroß and Herbert Puchta. Through two sample lessons developed as in-service demonstrations for secondary school teachers of English in Austria, the authors show how communicative language teaching goes beyond attention to the more technical side of language to involve the "inner world" of the teacher and of the learners.

Teacher training is also the focus of Chapter 7 by Pearl Goodman, "Preparing ESL Teachers for a Communicative Curriculum—American Style." The author, a teacher/trainer of long experience who has learned to adapt to new directions in language teaching without losing sight of her own goals and purposes, describes a project in communicative curriculum design that she has incorporated into a practicum for ESL teachers-in-training. Her chapter concludes with examples of some of the results.

In Chapter 8, "Teaching Strategic Competence in the Foreign-Language Classroom," Elaine Tarone illustrates the nature of strategic competence as a component of communicative competence and gives examples of classroom activities that provide learners with practice in using what language they do know in order to communicate their intended meaning. Strategic competence, she is careful to note, is not the same as sociolinguistic competence, and involves skills that should be given conscious attention in language programs.

Chapters 9 and 10 look at the uses of new classroom technology. In Chapter 9, "Teacher-Made Videotape Materials for the Second-Language Classroom," Tony Silva shows how teacher-made videotapes can capture a communicative act in its entirety and illustrates some of the many possibilities for the use of such videotapes in the classroom. These include analysis of discourse features (paralinguistic as well as linguistic) and follow-up activities. Chapter 10, "Computer-Aided Instruction: Language Teachers and the Man of the Year," is written by Fernand Marty, a teacher/researcher well-known for his experimental work in computer-aided language learning (CALL). He describes the potential as well as the limitations of the machine that *Time* magazine (1982) has dubbed "Man of the Year," and provides some very practical advice for neophytes regarding features to look for in a computer system.

The final chapter in this section, Chapter 11, "Immersion and Other Innovations in U.S. Elementary Schools," is written by Helena Anderson, foreign-language curriculum specialist for the Milwaukee public schools, and Nancy Rhodes of the Center for Applied Linguistics in Washington, D.C. They describe and document the spread of immersion programs in elementary and secondary schools across the U.S., a reflection of the willingness of American taxpayers to support programs that provide learners with the opportunity to develop functional L2 skills. Many of these programs are modeled on the successful immersion programs in Canada and have produced impressive results in terms of both learner achievement and community support.

Section III, *Evaluation*, includes three chapters, each reporting on initiatives in the evaluation of language proficiency in a specific context. Together they span testing efforts at secondary and college/university levels in Canada, Britain, and the U.S. In each case, the interrelatedness of teaching and testing for communicative competence is emphasized. All three authors stress the fact that tests of functional proficiency are valued as much for the influence they have on classroom teaching methods and objectives as for the assessments they yield of learner achievement.

In Chapter 12, "Large-Scale Communicative Testing: A Case Study," Merrill Swain describes the testing units that she and her colleagues in the Modern Language Centre of the Ontario Institute for Studies in Education have developed for use in province-wide assessments of the communicative performance of immersion students. Her discussion includes an outline of several general principles of communicative language testing that guided their test development and a description of the process they are following in developing scoring procedures for the test's large-scale administration.

The focus on Chapter 13, "Testing Performance in Oral Interaction" by Keith Morrow, is the examination set by the Royal Society of Arts (RSA) in the communicative use of English, an examination that is becoming widely established in Britain as a measure of what candidates can actually *do* in English. Morrow provides descriptions of three different levels of performance (Basic, Intermediate, and Advanced) with samples of the tasks required of candidates.

In Chapter 14, "Proficiency in Context: The Pennsylvania Experience," Barbara Freed reports on the replacement of a long standing college requirement of four semesters of foreign-language study by a proficiency requirement. She cites as impetus for this change the recognition by faculty of many students' failure to attain a meaningful level of communicative ability in a foreign language, even after four semesters of study, and the need to establish a common set of standards against which student achievement can be measured. The ACTFL (American Council on the Teaching of Foreign Languages) Provisional Proficiency Guidelines, which served as a basis for describing proficiency requirements in both oral and written skills, are included as an appendix to this final chapter in the volume.

The interrelatedness of the initiatives reported in these second and third groups of chapters is clear. For example, the immersion programs that are appearing in communities across the U.S. owe their inspiration and structure to the successful experience with immersion in Canada—programs that have in turn prompted the development of more communicative approaches to evaluation of L2 achievement. Efforts by ACTFL to develop functional proficiency guidelines for U.S. school and college programs parallel European Council of Europe efforts to establish proficiency guidelines for adult learners of English and other languages used in the Common Market. In turn, European programs have looked to some of the learner-centered interaction activities developed in U.S. classrooms as models of teaching strategies that involve the learner in communication.

Together with the background perspectives provided in Section I, these reports give a sense of the nature of communicative language teaching and of the directions being pursued as increasing numbers of programs respond to the goal of communicative competence.

REFERENCE

Savignon, S. 1983. *Communicative competence: theory and classroom practice.* Reading, Mass.: Addison-Wesley.

Section I

Background Perspectives

Chapter 1

Functional Approaches to Language and Language Teaching: Another Look

Margie S. Berns

Margie S. Berns writes EFL and ESL teaching materials and has presented numerous papers on the topic of materials development and evaluation at state, regional and international conferences. After receiving her M.A. degree in TESL from the University of Michigan, she taught English in Germany for several years. She is currently completing a Ph.D. degree in Linguistics at the University of Illinois, Urbana-Champaign, where she teaches a special oral communication course for foreign teaching assistants.

INTRODUCTION

Communicative language teaching, or the teaching of language for communication, has been the center of language teaching discussions for the last decade or so. Dozens of books, journal articles, and conference papers, in addition to an array of teaching materials, have been written under the banner of this movement. Communicative language teaching has grown out of the realization that mastering grammatical forms and structures does not adequately prepare learners to use the language they are learning effectively and appropriately when communicating with others.

The functional approach to language teaching is intimately related to the communicative approach and in recent years has enjoyed considerable attention. Initially there was optimism about the promise of functional language teaching to overcome the inadequacies of largely structural course materials, and publishers and textbook writers were quick to respond with so-called functional materials.

While *functional approach* has been largely understood as a cover term for the underlying concept that language is used for communication, and while most interpretations have emphasized the communicative needs of learners and the explicit presentation of language functions and the linguistic structures associated with them, there has been no standard interpretation of the terms *function, notion,* or *communication.* For some a function has been as general as "describing a person or place" or "describing mechanical processes"; for others it has been as specific as "requesting help with baggage" or "answering questions about what people have been doing." The multiple usages of the terms *functional/notional, communicative functions,* and *communicative notions* have reflected and also have contributed to uncertainty about precise meanings on the part of textbook writers, publishers, and educational administrators, not all of whom are aware of these terms in their more original and restricted meanings.

This uncertainty and lack of uniformity often has resulted in materials that are neither functional nor communicative. In one instance the selection of a particular set of materials means beginning with grammar and delaying any introduction to the functions of language until later in the course. In another, communicative functions are taught from the very beginning, with no systematic treatment of grammar or consideration of context. The net result of such divergent interpretations of the functional approach to language teaching has been disappointment and frustration on the part of the teachers who wanted to respond to their learners' needs but discovered that functional materials could not keep the promises their supporters had made for them.

Another look at the theoretical foundations of functional approaches and their relationship to communicative language teaching will help to resolve this confusion about the terms and concepts they have introduced into discussions of second-language learning and teaching, and, in so doing, suggest a more coherent, reasoned application to materials development.

Such a review properly begins with a summary of the linguistic tradition from which this approach grew, the long tradition which is that of the British school of linguistics. Following this summary, we will look at applied linguistic research within the tradition and, subsequently, teaching materials and exercises based on this research. An assessment of the viability of these materials and their linguistic bases concludes the review.

THE FUNCTIONAL APPROACH: THEORETICAL FOUNDATIONS

The functional approach to language can be identified with the linguistic tradition of Sweet (1899), Jones (1917, 1918), and Firth. This tradition is variously referred to as British linguistics, the London School, or Firthian linguistics, none of which, however, are precise labels.

This tradition has flourished not only within Britain but also in various contexts outside of Britain. For example, it has influenced linguistic study in Canada (Gregory and Carroll 1978), and in Germany where it is known as "British contextualism" (Geiger 1981). However, it is little known in the United States, where Chomskyan transformational linguistics has dominated linguistic inquiry during the last twenty years, preceded by the earlier dominance of American structuralism.[1]

In essence, a functional approach to language is based on an interest in performance, or actual language *use*. It is thus in decided contrast with the Chomskyan concern with the linguistic competence of the ideal speaker-hearer (Chomsky 1965). J. R. Firth (1930, 1937), the founder of the British school, viewed language as "a way of behaving and making others behave" (1951). Language in the Firthian view is interaction; it is interpersonal activity and has a clear relationship with society. In this light, language study has to look at the use (function) of language in context, both its linguistic context (what is uttered before and after a given piece of discourse) and its social, or situational, context (who is speaking, what their social roles are, why they have come together to speak).

If we accept this Firthian view of language, three concepts that are part of this linguistic tradition become useful in establishing a framework to serve as a reference point in the development and evaluation of language teaching materials. The first is *context of situation*. Firth used this construct, which became an important part of his view, to frame the analysis of language events in the social context. He borrowed the term from Bronislaw Malinowski (1923, 1935), an anthropologist who shared Firth's view of language as a mode of human behavior. Malinowski held that if language is active, it is most appropriately studied as part of activity, an approach he illustrated in his own study of the Trobriand Islanders. Malinowski used the term *context of situation* to designate the physical environment in which a linguistic activity is performed. It proved particularly useful to him as a procedural concept in solving problems of equivalence in the translation of texts from the Trobriand Islands into comprehensible English.

In borrowing the term, Firth interpreted it more abstractly than Malinowski. He used it to refer to general situation types, the features of which are established by a set of broad and general categories.

1. The relevant features of participants; persons, personalities
   a. Verbal actions of participants
   b. Nonverbal actions of participants
2. The relevance of objects
3. The effect of the verbal action

In this way, the context of situation does provide a first approximation to the specification of the components of the communication situation and hence a step towards answering both the question "how is it that, in spite of a lack of perfect and consistent correlations between language and situation, the native speaker, given the text alone (a tape recording say) is often able, with a considerable degree of accuracy, to reconstruct the situation?" and conversely "given a situation, how does such a person produce language which is appropriate?" (Firth 1951).

This view of language as interaction, as use in context, requires that authentic language, not idealized language, be the object of the analysis. This is necessary in order to understand or interpret the uses to which the language is being put, since no direct correlation exists between form and function, except in such highly ritualized functions as greeting and leave-taking. This last point is more fully developed by Michael Halliday, a student of Firth, who is especially interested in the social functions of language and the way in which language fulfills these functions.

Halliday's work in systemic linguistics focuses on the second important concept in a functional approach to language teaching: *function*. (The term *systemic linguistics* is used to refer to Halliday's linguistic theory and will be explained more fully below.) In systemic theory, function has a dual status. It is referred to as both a micro- and a macro-concept. The micro-functions are those that a child learns in the early stages of language development. At the beginning, function is equivalent to *use* for the child in six broad functions, which Halliday observed in his son's development of English: the regulatory ("do as I tell you") function, the instrumental ("I want") function, the personal ("here I come") function, the imaginative ("let's pretend") function, the heuristic ("tell me why") function, and the interactional ("me and you") function (1973). As Halliday describes it, these micro-functions give way to the macro-functions as the child's language more closely approximates the adult system, a system that has only three, more abstract, functions. As the child learns to *combine* functions, he is able to speak about objects (and persons, places, etc.) while at the same time relating his attitude toward the listener—that is, whether he expects some kind of response or not. Halliday calls these two kinds of meaning the *ideational* and *interpersonal* functions of language. These two functions in themselves, however, are not sufficient for the construction of texts, or discourse. A third function, the *textual* function, serves this purpose of language by providing means for the formation of coherent texts. Any linguistic unit is the simultaneous realization of these three functions.

Within the theory on the whole we can see these functions as serving language (1) to express "content," to give structure to experience and help to determine the speaker's way of looking at things (ideational); (2) to establish and maintain social relations, to delimit social groups, to identify and reinforce the individual (interpersonal); and (3) to provide for making links with itself and with features of the situation in which it is used, to enable the speaker (or writer) to construct passages of discourse that are situationally relevant (textual) (Halliday 1973). By providing a means of accounting for the complexities of language in actual use, Halliday's Firthian view of language and his view of function have informed the thinking of many concerned with language teaching, as we will see below.

The third concept offering a useful insight into language is *meaning potential*. Halliday, like Firth before him, refuses to recognize any dichotomy between *knowing* (competence) and *doing* (performance); he sees them as inseparable. Meaning potential captures both the knowing and doing. The potential is what is available to the speaker, what is known. From the potential, choices are made for use of the language, for performing. This concept is seen as comprising what the speaker can *do* (in terms of choices in social behavior), what the speaker can *say* (in terms of the formal choices the language provides), and what the speaker can *mean* (which is related to the other two).

Meaning potential is an integral part of Halliday's theory because it embodies the range of possibilities and open-ended sets of options in behavior that are available to the individual. These options can be organized into sets of options that form *systems*, the concept lending its name to systemic linguistics. System, as a technical term, specifies the potential in terms of the options and their relationship to one another. It can be represented schematically as:

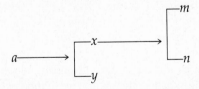

and read as follows: There are two systems, *x/y* and *m/n*, the first having entry condition *a*; if *a* is chosen (over not choosing anything at all), then the choice is between x and y; the system m/n has entry condition x; if x is chosen over y, then either m or n has to be chosen, and so on (Halliday 1973).

An example of how such a system works is an illustration from a "regulatory context" in which a parent and child are the participants. This is a semantic system, showing which possibilities are open to the parent in a situation of regulation, or control. The parent has opted for "physical threat" over doing (saying) nothing; the choice of physical threat is related to further choices, the systems of agency and condition, which are, in turn, the entry conditions for further choices:

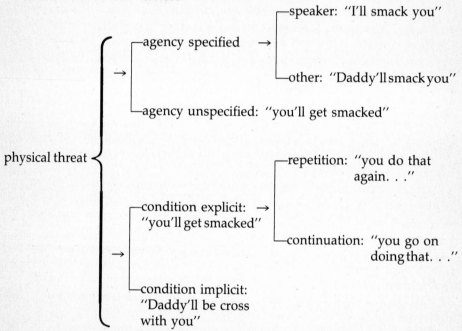

physical threat

agency specified →
- speaker: "I'll smack you"
- other: "Daddy'll smack you"

agency unspecified: "you'll get smacked"

condition explicit: → "you'll get smacked"
- repetition: "you do that again. . ."
- continuation: "you go on doing that. . ."

condition implicit: "Daddy'll be cross with you"

Although the system presented here is adapted and simplified (Halliday 1973), it illustrates what is involved in language use and specifically how the speaker begins with meaning, as in this case with the semantic option of "physical threat."

We come full circle when we consider the source of the semantic options, the social context. It is the social context that determines which behavior options, both verbal and nonverbal, are available to the speaker—for example, whether it is even appropriate in a given situation for the speaker to choose physical threat. It is the features of Firth's context of situation that would guide in the selection of options in the particular situation. These features include those on the level of meaning associated with the *context of culture*. This is the larger framework for the situations, the range of which is actually determined by the culture in which they occur. This implies that situations of control, for example, are not necessarily found across cultures, and therefore that the related linguistic forms may serve different functions in another culture.

This concern with appropriateness and generalizability will become an important consideration as we examine and discuss language teaching materials and exercises.

SYSTEMIC LINGUISTICS AND COMMUNICATIVE COMPETENCE

Before moving on to a discussion of the practical application of the concepts, it is important to establish the relationship of systemic theory to communicative competence.

Halliday's meaning potential can be considered compatible with this concept if we follow Savignon's (1983) interpretation of communicative competence: the *expression, interpretation,* and *negotiation* of meaning involving interaction between two or more persons, or between one person and an oral or written text. This compatability is supported by Breen and Candlin's (1980) description of meaning potential as that which allows us to participate in a creative and meaning-making process and to express or interpret the potential meanings within spoken or written discourse.

It is not to be inferred that the use of the term *communicative competence* in any way implies tacit acceptance of Chomsky's competence/performance distinction. Communicative competence as understood here reflects the sociological and linguistic insights of Hymes (1971) and Halliday (1978), both of whom reject the notion of linguistic rules divorced from social contexts.

APPLICATIONS OF SYSTEMIC/ FUNCTIONAL THEORY

It is the applied linguist's task to draw upon linguistic insights and apply them to areas of social concern where language is involved. Education and the teaching of languages is one such area. Systemic theory has proved to be a viable reference point for those linguists—e.g. Candlin, Widdowson, and Wilkins, among others—who have applied it to the teaching of English. Each of them has developed different areas of language teaching, but their similar theoretical heritage is evident in their work and provides a consistent frame of reference from which the models they propose can be evaluated.

Candlin's work (Candlin, Bruton and Leather 1976, Candlin 1981, Breen and Candlin 1980) ranges from the particular concerns of doctor-patient interaction for foreign doctors and their British patients to the specification of criteria for the development of communicative teaching materials. His more recent work has stressed the sociological as well as linguistic aspects of language learning. He sees the social conventions that govern language form and language behavior, for example, as central to the process of learning language for communication (Breen and Candlin 1980). Candlin also addresses the relationship of teacher responsibility and the social implications of communicative language teaching. The need for discoursal insights into human interaction, he points out, involves the teacher in the manipulation of human behavior (1977). The establishment of language norms is a particularly critical aspect of this issue. For example, the acknowledgement of the legitimacy of language varieties, which some purists may consider substandard (Prator 1968), constitutes a challenge to the supremacy of mono-model language teaching and to existing norms of traditional education, which are seen in terms of a set stock of information, simple skills, and static conformity to a code.

Widdowson (1978) has also applied systemic theory to problems of language teaching. He is known for his work on materials for ESP (English for Specific Purposes). His interest is not in the teaching of functions, but in the teaching of discourse—the process of deriving and creating meanings (ideational, interpersonal) through text. One well-known illustration of his approach is the coherence of the following exchange:

> A: That's the telephone.
> B: I'm in the bath.
> A: OK.

He points out that while there are no grammatical markers to indicate the relationship of these utterances to one another, this brief exchange is accepted as coherent when a context is established.

In spite of the range and depth of the work of Candlin, Widdowson, and others, it is Wilkins' work that has had the greatest impact on current materials for language teaching. Wilkins was among a group of specialists faced with the task of providing the Council of Europe with an organized program for foreign-language teaching in Western Europe. One of the first steps was an analysis of existing syllabus types (grammatical and situational), which Wilkins found to be wanting for the particular needs of this group of learners. In place of the existing syllabus types, Wilkins proposed a notional syllabus that would have a semantic and behavioral prediction of learner needs as its starting point (1976). In this context "notional" was to be understood as meaning-based—that is, this type of syllabus was to specify what the learners were to *do* with the language, what meanings they would need to communicate through language. *Notional Syllabuses* contains three components of meaning: semantico-grammatical, modal, and communicative function. A notional syllabus would consider all three of these; a functional syllabus would consider the communicative functions alone, but would then be "the weakest application" of his proposal (1976:68).[2]

The notional syllabus was to be an improvement over a situational syllabus, which is broken down into units with a heading, such as "At the post office." The problem with situational organization is that a language learner does not automatically generalize a grammatical lesson learned in such a unit to other situations. In addition it is unlikely that all the possible significant situations in which a learner might find himself could be listed.

A notional syllabus was also to be an improvement over a grammatical syllabus because it would provide the context of *function* for a grammatical form. That is, a learner would not only learn the forms of the language, but would also learn forms appropriate to his or her immediate needs. Rather than all of the forms of the language, only those forms relevant to the necessary functions, or uses, of language would be learned.

Wilkins' link to the British linguistic tradition is thus apparent in his stress on meaning and uses of language. He considers the communicative functions his most original contribution to syllabus design; it is this variously defined concept that has had the most impact on language teaching and that has probably been the least understood.

Van Ek (1975), also a contributor to the Council of Europe project, used Wilkins' concept of a notional syllabus as a basis for the "threshold level," a specification of an elementary level in a unit/credit system for Europeans who from time to time have professional or personal contacts in European community countries. Van Ek's usage of the terms *function* and *notion* differ somewhat, however, from Wilkins'. In place of communicative function he specified language function, although referring essentially to the same kind of meaning—that is, what people *do* through language.[3]

Wilkins and Van Ek each had specific language teaching contexts and objectives in mind when they made their proposals. These proposals reflect one of the primary concerns of applied linguistics in Europe—the need for a framework in meeting the demands of the rapid growth of foreign-language learning and teaching in the context of the European Community (Strevens 1981).[4]

NOTIONAL SYLLABUSES AND MATERIALS DEVELOPMENT

Wilkins' application of linguistic theory to syllabus design was accepted by teachers, administrators, publishers, and materials writers. As already mentioned, the result was an array of materials and publications claiming a functional base. In fact, because of its pervasiveness it has unfortunately become equated with communicative language teaching, instead of rightfully being seen as *one* kind of syllabus for programs which have the development of learners' communicative competence as their goal.

In 1964, Halliday, McIntosh, and Strevens, in writing about the applications of linguistic knowledge and insights to language teaching, saw textbook writers as consumers of these applications. These consumers, they emphasized, should clearly perceive and understand these applications since it is the nature and quality of textbooks that exert a powerful influence on the way the subject can develop. A look at the materials on the market reveals that not all textbook writers have always clearly perceived and understood these applications.

Those materials that claim a communicative and/or a functional base make their claims directly or indirectly—for example, "The functional approach of this material is based on the ideas of David Wilkins . . ."; "The purpose of this text is the communicative function of language"; ". . . meaningful interaction is facilitated by communicative uses (functions)"; "The later units shift emphasis from a grammatical to a functional starting point"; "Our teachers include Joos, Coulthard, Wilkins, and Van Ek . . ."; ". . . the second part deals with the language appropriate to a particular *function* . . ."; "The communicative approach to language teaching is the fundamental concept of these materials." But making such claims is not enough, as some of the exercises that follow show.

Each of the following exercises is taken from a text that claims a functional base. While they share features that classify them as functional, we will find that their representation of the theoretical framework that their authors claim informs them ranges from adequate to inadequate.

If we accept the assumptions of systemic linguistics as viable for the linguistic basis of communicative language teaching, we should be able to evaluate materials as communicative if they are consistent with these assumptions. By the same token, if functionally based materials also claim to foster the development of communicative competence, they too should be subject to evaluation in the same manner.

In the following, the criteria applied in the evaluation of the adequacy of these exercises as representative of a functional and/or communicative approach are based on assumptions of systemic linguistics:

1. Utterances are presented with sufficient context for the interpretation of meaning.
2. The relevant contextual features are identifiable—that is, persons, objects, verbal and nonverbal behavior, and effect.
3. The insight gained into an instance of language use is generalizable— that is, the learner can make predictions/interpretations of meaning in similar situation types.
4. All three macro-functions are taken into account—that is, the ideational (conceptual), interpersonal (behavioral) and textual (formal).
5. Texts are authentic—that is, if not taken from original sources,they are believable as representations of actual use of English.

6. Options are provided for the expression and interpretation of meaning.
7. More than formulaic functions of language are illustrated.
8. The interdependency of formal and functional meaning in context is explicit as opposed to simple equivalency of form and function.

Of course, not all of these criteria are equally relevant for the following five exercises. Criteria not given might also reveal something about the adequacy or inadequacy of each selection as a representation of language as interaction. However, for the purpose of illustration, the discussion will be limited to those criteria listed. It should be noted at this point that one exercise or page from a set of materials is not necessarily representative of the complete set of materials. A critique should not be interpreted as judgment on an entire work, but rather as an illustration of how an exercise can be evaluated in terms of its usefulness in developing a learner's communicative competence.

EXAMPLES OF EXERCISES

ACCEPTING

1 KENJI:	Do you think you'll be able to?
2 FRANCESCA:	Yes. It sounds fine.
3 KENJI:	That's great.
4 FRANCESCA:	Thanks for asking me.
5 KENJI:	You're welcome. I'm glad you can make it.
6 FRANCESCA:	So am I.
7 KENJI:	Okay. We'll see you then.
8 FRANCESCA:	Right. I'm looking forward to it.

CONTENT ANALYSIS

Francesca might be accepting:

  a dinner invitation

  a babysitting job

  a substitute-teaching job

  an invitation to meet his family

  a tennis date

  a ride in a car pool

What else?

a skiing invitation

_____

_____

_____

_____

_____

Source: C. Akiyama, *Acceptance to Zeal.* (New York: Minverva Books, Ltd., 1981), p. 3.

The dialog in Example #1 reveals little about the identity of Kenji and Francesca other than their names. We do not know if they are peers; if so, we need to know their ages. And since Francesca is female, it might be helpful to reverse the roles to determine if the same forms are appropriate for males in "accepting." We can also raise the question about the appropriateness of females extending invitations, a form of behavior that may not be acceptable in some contexts. (It seems to be the case in most examples of "inviting" that it is men who do "inviting," not women.)

Asking the students to provide for different "invitations" does not seem like an activity that helps in understanding why Francesca chooses the forms she does. It seems likely that the forms chosen would depend upon just what it is she is accepting. For example, the appropriateness of the given dialog if Francesca is accepting a substitute teaching job is questionable.

The focus on the individual function of "accepting" directs the students' attention away from both meaning in general and the *potential* meaning of a given form. Forms given are also representative of other semantic contexts— e.g., thanking. A line-by-line analysis might reveal that this exchange is exemplary of a number of functions, with the sum of the parts actually contributing little to the whole—that is, accepting. (See Silva, this volume, for an example of a line-by-line analysis of functions in a dialog.)

The generalizability of these forms is also called into question for cultural reasons. In order to interpret the meaning more fully, we need to know the cultural context of this exchange. If Kenji and Francesca are students in the U.S., the language presented is generally acceptable; if they are in Japan or Italy, where English is learned as a foreign language or is used for international communication, the language they use will most likely differ in tone and form from that shown here.

By focusing on form as if it is identifiable with a particular function, this exercise misleads students and does not provide them with everything they need to know to *interpret* and *express* meaning effectively. This is a result of an inadequate representation of language as interaction.

In Example #2, "study these language functions" gives the impression that functions, like forms, need only be studied sufficiently to be learned. If the learner does study these functions, what is gained? Are the guides "very formal" to "informal" generalizable? Context will determine the appropriateness of a formal form, yet formality is a relative term. Will a Chinese student who considers informality with one's professor rude recognize a professor's informal forms as a gesture of cordiality?

The form "That would be fine" may also serve in functions other than "accepting an invitation." It may be an expression of approval or of a choice. This entire chart illustrates the dangers of equating form and function, as if such equivalences are reliable or even possible.

How to Say It

Study these language functions.

	VERY FORMAL →	INVITING → → →	INFORMAL
INVITING	Would you like to join me for coffee?	Would you like to go out for coffee?	Want to go out for coffee?
ACCEPTING INVITATIONS	Certainly. I'd like to very much.	Thank you. That would be nice.	Sure. (or) Okay.
ASKING FOR INFORMATION	When would you like to go?	When do you want to go?	When?
INVITING	Would after class be a good time?	Would after class be all right?	How about after class?
ACCEPTING AN INVITATION	That would be fine.	Fine.	Good. (or) Okay.
CONFIRMING AN INVITATION	So, we'll meet after class.	See you then.	See you.

Source: J. Bodman and M. Lanzano, *Milk and Honey.* (New York: Harcourt, Brace, Jovanovich, 1981), p. 83.

While examples #1 and #2 seem sorely inadequate and even misleading in their representation of language as interaction, example #3 provides a richer view of language. Part iii, for example, allows for the openness and unpredictability involved in actual speaking. The notion of someone's refusing to honor a request is entertained and the learner is called upon to formulate appropriate responses.

In 4 i) the learners are asked to define the situation and the participants, thus providing for consideration of the context of situation.

4 i)   Who says these things? In what situations?

a) It would help if you could hold the torch for me a second and I'll see if I can find it.	Hold ....?
b) I wonder if you could move your head a little. I can't see.	Could you ....?
c) I want you to run round and tell John to come back home immediately.	Run ....?
d) As it's raining, I thought you might collect him by car.	You couldn't ....?
e) What *is* the time? Mine's stopped.	Could you ....?
f) I like it better over there. Do me a favour and move it for me, dear.	Move ....?
g) I wonder if you could change it. I like to have a clean tablecloth.	You couldn't ....?
h) Let me borrow yours, George. I've only got a pencil.	Could I ....?

ii) Make new sentences using the words on the right.
iii) How do you think the other person replies? They don't say yes all the time. Maybe they can't help.

Source: K. Morrow and K. Johnson, *Communicate 1*. (Cambridge: Cambridge University Press, 1979), p. 69.

While these two features enhance the communicative nature of the exercise, one aspect is troublesome in terms of generalizability. The language models seem distinctly British (upper?) middle class; they are very polite and well formed. The learners are asked to provide less formal forms, but no attention is drawn to the differences in appropriate contexts, or to the implications of deliberately choosing an inappropriate form over the appropriate form in terms of conforming behavior. Also, this exercise falls under the rubric "asking people to do things," yet is not necessarily a request. It may be a command or an example of "telling people to do things." The actual effect, or function, of each of these could be determined only by placing them in a text.

Example #4 illustrates the concept of choice and the effect of choices on the response of the next speaker. The interactive nature of language is conveyed by the form this exercise takes: the first student makes a choice from the two options given; another student makes an appropriate choice from "2"; the first student, or yet a third student, chooses a response from "3", or even "2." It is theoretically possible that all choices be exhausted if the activity went on long enough and if utterances selected produced coherent discourse.

Since this exercise provides for the production of a coherent text with grammatically accurate forms provided, learners concentrate on meaning, not

14 **Chatter Chain:** I Wouldn't Go to New York City

1 I wouldn't go to New York City for
a million dollars.

I'd love to go to New York City.

2 I sure would. I love big cities.

Why not? It's supposed to be
the most exciting city in the world.

Why?

Are you crazy? Don't you watch TV?
Not me. New York's full of gangsters.
I wouldn't. There's nothing to do there.
Me, too. My . . . says it's fantastic.

But big cities are | loud.
| dirty.
| ugly.
| crowded.

3 New Yorkers are supposed to be the
unfriendliest people in the world.

You call | concrete | exciting?
| skyscrapers |
| traffic jams |

Do you believe everything | you see on TV?
| you read?

New York is full of | interesting sights.
| theaters.
| stores.
| museums.
| interesting people.

That's not true.

(Because) I'd like to see | Harlem.
| the U.N.
| the World Trade Center.
| the Empire State Building.
| Central Park.

Source: H.E. Piepho et al., *Contacts.* (Bochum, W. Germany: Ferdinand Kamp, 1979),
p. 8.

form, and perhaps in the process even express their own views about New York City. It thus appears especially adequate as representative of the assumptions of systemic linguistics.

While you are driving alone through the desert on vacation, your camper breaks down late in the afternoon, and you cannot fix it. You discover that the road you are traveling on is closed to traffic. There is little hope of anyone driving by to help you. There are no telephones nearby.

Your best solution is to walk back to a service station which you remember passing. You calculate that you have driven about one hour and fifteen minutes at an average speed of eighty kilometers (fifty miles) per hour. You will have to travel only at night because of the intense heat and burning sun.

The camper has the following items in it:

- roll of toilet paper
- mess kit
- dozen eggs
- box of powdered milk
- canteen of water
- sleeping bag
- book of matches
- dozen flares
- portable radio
- wool blanket
- can of gas
- first-aid kit
- large utility knife

- insect repellent
- tent
- flare gun
- flashlight
- thermos of hot coffee
- camping stove
- compass
- fresh vegetables
- beach umbrella
- fresh fruit
- canned food
- can opener

ORAL INTERACTION

1 Because of the limitations of space and weight, you can only carry five items.

a. Decide which five items to take.

b. Arrange these five items in order of importance.

2 Most of the items in the camper can fit into two categories: (1) camping gear, and (2) food. Put these items into their categories.

3 Calculate the distance and the approximate amount of time needed to walk that distance.

4 What other alternatives are there for solving this situation, other than walking back to the service station?

5 Can you think of any items missing from the list that you might need? Name them.

Source: D. Byrd and I. Clemente-Cabetas, *React/Interact*. (New York: Regents, 1980), p. 23.

Problem-solving exercises such as Example #5 are becoming increasingly popular in language classes. They respond to the need for learner-centered activities, but do more than that. They also provide the opportunity for learners to express meaning, using the meaning potential they have developed up to that time, about a specified content. Thus, the ideational, interpersonal, and textual functions of language come together in the activity. In a problem-solving situation the learners also have to focus on meaning and have to contend with the possibility of not getting their meaning across. In addition, the unpredictability of discourse and the variable relationship between form and function are accented by this exercise. Because of these features, this exercise, if done without teacher intervention to correct errors (except those that are obstacles to the expression of meaning), provides for interaction among students to an optimal degree.

As this limited sample of exercises illustrates, the inclusion of what might be classified as a function in the title of a unit or exercise does not guarantee that the authors fully perceive what it means for language teaching to be communicative, or that they fully understand the role of "function" in the interpretation and expression of meaning in a discourse.

CONCLUSION

If language as interaction, and all it implies, is not taken into account, materials will continue to fall short of developing a learner's communicative competence. While both the functional aspect and the formal features of language are necessary considerations in determining what to teach, they are not sufficient. It is *context* that gives meaning to form and function and makes it possible for us to make sense of any instance of language.

Systemic linguistics provides a framework for integrating these components of language use. Application of the insights this view of language provides not only has consequences for materials development as has been illustrated here, but also has implications for other areas that touch upon communicative language teaching, such as techniques, methods, and teacher training. A theoretical base that can serve as a point of reference in our attempts to develop learners' communicative competence is available; we need only exploit it.

NOTES

1. American structuralism differs from the European structuralist tradition. In the United States the term is used with special reference to Bloomfield's emphasis on segmenting and classifying physical features of an utterance. British "structuralism" on the other hand is interested in finding social explanations for the structures that are used by speakers.

2. Wilkins' 1976 book is the synthesis of working documents for the Council of Europe and of conference papers written from 1972–1974.

3. *Notion* has two meanings in the Threshold Level, neither of which refers to an overriding principle as it does in *Notional Syllabuses*. Instead, there are general notions which refer to the "concepts which people use in verbal communication (1979:39)"—for example, the property of space or the quality of importance. Specific notions are the particular lexical items relating to a topic. For example, under the topic of "personal identification," Van Ek lists *name, surname, address, telephone number,* and *age* (1975:41).

   These different usages may partially explain the confusion and misunderstanding reflected in materials and discussions of the functional approach to language teaching. These differences notwithstanding, Van Ek's work is important because it is the first concrete example of teaching objectives specified in notional terms for an actual group of learners.

4. Specifications have also been complete for German (M. Baldegger et al. 1982. *Kontaktschwelle.* Munich: Langenscheidt.), French (D. Coste et al. 1976. *Un niveau seuil.* Strassbourg: Council of Europe.), and Spanish (P. Slagter, 1980. *Un nivel umbral.* Strassbourg: Council of Europe.)

REFERENCES

Breen, M. and C. Candlin. 1980. "The essentials of a communicative curriculum in language teaching." *Applied Linguistics* **1**: 89–112.

Candlin, C. 1977. *Preface,* In M. Coulthard. *An introduction to discourse analysis.* London: Longmans.

———. 1981. "Discoursal patterning and the equalizing of interpretive opportunity." In L. Smith (ed.). *English for cross-cultural communication.* New York: St. Martin's Press.

Candlin, C., C. Bruton, and J. Leather. 1976. "Doctors in casualty: applying communicative competence to components of specialist course design." *International Review of Applied Linguistics* **14**: 245–272.

Chomsky, N. 1965. *Aspects of the theory of syntax.* Cambridge, Mass.: M.I.T. Press.

Firth, J. R. 1951. "Modes of meaning." *Essays and studies of the English Association,* N.S. **4**: 118–149. Reprinted in *Papers in Linguistics 1934–1951.* London: Oxford University Press.

———. 1964. *Tongues of men/speech.* London: Oxford University Press. Reprint of works first published in 1937 and 1930, respectively.

Geiger, A. 1981. "Application of 'British contextualism' to foreign-language teacher training." *English Language Teaching* **35**:209–216.

Gregory, M. and S. Carroll. 1978. *Language and situation: language varieties and their social contexts.* London: Routledge & Kegan Paul.

Halliday, M. 1973. *Explorations in the functions of language.* London: Edward Arnold.

———. 1978. *Language as social semiotic: the social interpretation of language and meaning.* Baltimore, MD: University Park Press.

Halliday, M., A. McIntosh, and P. Strevens. 1964. *The linguistic sciences and language teaching*. London: Longman's.

Hymes, D. 1971. "Competence and performance in linguistic theory." In R. Huxley and E. Ingram (eds.). *Language acquisition: models and methods*. London: Academic Press.

Jones, D. 1977. *An English pronouncing dictionary*. London: Dent. 14th edition, first published in 1917.

———. 1976. *Outline of English phonetics*. Cambridge: Cambridge University Press, 9th edition, first published in 1918.

Malinowski, B. 1923. "The problem of meaning in primitive languages." In C. Ogden and I. Richards (eds.). *The meaning of meaning*. London: Kegan Paul, Trench & Trubner.

———. 1935. *Coral gardens and their magic I, II*. New York: American Book Company.

Prator, C. 1968. *"The British heresy in TESL."* In J. Fishman et al. (eds.). *Language problems of developing nations*. New York: John Wiley and Sons.

Savignon, S. 1983. *Communicative competence: theory and classroom practice*. Reading, Mass.: Addison-Wesley.

Strevens, P. 1981. "Notional—functional—communicative: links between theory and practice." In J. Esser and A. Hübler (eds.). *Forms and functions*. (Papers in General English and Applied Linguistics presented to Vilem Fried on the occasion of his sixty-fifth birthday) Tübingen: Gunter Narr Verlag.

Sweet, H. 1964. *The practical study of languages*. Oxford: Oxford University Press. First published in 1899.

Van Ek, J. 1975. *Threshold level English*. Oxford: Pergamon Press.

Widdowson, H. 1978. *Teaching language as communication*. Oxford: Oxford University Press.

Wilkins, D. 1976. *Notional syllabuses*. Oxford: Oxford University Press.

Chapter 2

Contextual Considerations in Communicative Language Teaching

Sauli Takala

Sauli Takala is a researcher at the Finnish National Institute for Educational Research, University of Jyväskylä, specializing in curriculum construction and evaluation in foreign languages. From 1981–1983 he was at the University of Illinois, Urbana-Champaign, as Coordinator of the IEA International Study of Written Composition. He has published extensively in the areas of language planning and testing, curriculum construction, and language teaching methodology.

INTRODUCTION

That language teaching throughout the world has undergone several abrupt pendulum swings is a common observation. In the process, dichotomies are often introduced to conceptualize a very complex phenomenon: behaviorist/ cognitive, discrete-point/integrative, formal/informal, learning/acquisition.

Thus, language teaching may appear to undergo quite a number of changes without necessarily making any significant advance. What look like promising new ideas often lead to disappointment. Many are in fact not new at all; they are simply revised versions of old approaches, marking yet another change in the direction of the pendulum.

Why should this be so? The philosopher Alfred North Whitehead once observed that the art of progress is the ability to maintain order amidst change and the possibility of change amidst order. Progress is possible therefore only if we know how to manage the factors that contribute to it. In the case of language teaching, our inability to demonstrate clear theoretical and practical progress would seem to lie with the inadequacy of our theoretical conceptualization of language teaching in relation to both language education and to education in general.

If this premise is valid, one implication is immediately obvious. In order to make meaningful progress, we need to have a better understanding of education, teaching, and learning; we need a comprehensive model of these basic concepts.

This chapter briefly outlines one such model. It is based on my experience with foreign-language curriculum construction and evaluation in Finland, where we have spent the last decade redesigning our programs to give them a communicative orientation. Because of the importance of foreign-language instruction in Finland—all students study at least two languages, and language studies comprise some 20–45% of available class hours—this reform was not a responsibility to be taken lightly.

THE NEED FOR MODELS IN EDUCATION AND LANGUAGE TEACHING

Education and language teaching as systems and processes are so complex that we need models to help us:

1. Understand and explain how they function
2. Guide and inform our thinking, planning, and actions without determining them in detail
3. Evaluate their performance and make required changes
4. Foresee problems and developments

In Finland we have in recent years been particularly interested in macro-level models. This has been a natural consequence of extensive reforms at all educational levels from preschool to higher education. The need for national planning was recognized in late 1976 when the Ministry of Education set up a committee to draft a plan for a national language teaching policy eventually submitted to the Ministry in February 1979. While models are obviously needed in planning and administration as well as in research, teachers also should be familiar with them if they do not wish to relinquish a legitimate interest in how the language teaching system operates and how it should and could be improved.

A major development in education in general, and in language teaching in particular, seems to be a growing awareness of education as a social institution, a social system serving fundamental social desires, needs, and functions. Thus, language teaching serves basic communication needs, and as its importance grows it increasingly acquires the characteristics of any institutionalized process. This means, among other things, that language teaching is becoming (1) more organized—roles and role relationships are specified in more detail; (2) more systematized—tasks are specified; and (3) more stabilized—language teaching does not depend on particular individuals.

Language teaching is therefore not only the activity of individual teachers; it is a system of many activities. To understand it as a system, we must realize its boundaries, its central purposes, and its level in a larger context. We must be aware of its various subsystems and their interrelationships. For all this we need models to describe and work out the practical consequences of different approaches (see Takala 1983).

The preceding discussion implies that education in general, and language teaching as one aspect of education, is an "artificial" science (Calfee 1981). "Artificial" refers to the fact that education, schools, curricula, etc. are the products of the human mind (artifacts), not natural phenomena (natural objects). Another way to express the same idea, without the possibly unfortunate connotations of the term "artificial," is to characterize education as one instance of the "sciences of design" (Simon 1981), which deal with the interaction between the inner and outer environments—in other words, how goals and intentions can be attained by adapting the inner environment (human mind) to the external environment. One of the major consequences of this view of education is that educational phenomena must be seen in context if our aim is to improve current practices. Decontextualized reforms are bound to fail or to result in only limited success.

A GENERAL MODEL OF
LANGUAGE TEACHING AS
A SYSTEM

Having made the claim that educational phenomena are subject to human judgment, we should try to see what implications this view has for language teaching. What kind of model could we have of language teaching as a complex system of a great number of different activities? One possible model is presented in Figure 2.1 (Takala 1980). It is an adaptation of similar models proposed by Stern (1974) and Strevens (1977).

Formal language teaching in a school-type context takes place in a complex setting consisting of a number of levels. At Level 1, the societal level, the need of languages is manifested in a more or less clearly defined language teaching policy and is recognized in the form of societal support for language teaching. At Level 2, the school system level, we are concerned with the foundations of language teaching, its infrastructure: the organizational and administrative framework and the traditions of language teaching. At Level 3 we are concerned with the definition of the general approach or strategy of language teaching. This is usually expressed in a curriculum (syllabus). Syllabus construction is a demanding task in which a number of disciplines can and should be drawn upon. The written curriculum (the *intended* curriculum) is carried out to a smaller or greater extent (the *implemented* curriculum) at the level of teaching (Level 4). This teaching takes place in a complex setting, where the teacher must make many tactical decisions every day. However, the curriculum is ultimately realized by the pupils (the *realized* curriculum).

Evaluation data are mainly collected from the teaching and learning levels to get feedback to other levels as well. All parties involved in education (teachers and their students, principals, superintendents, school boards, state educational authorities, and national or federal educational agencies) consider data on student performance as the ultimate criteria of how teaching works. The motives and uses of data vary, but there is no substitute for actual student performance data.

The model presented in Figure 2.1, which is based on the Finnish situation, shows that the curriculum plays an important part in teaching. Some modifications may have to be made to it to suit other contexts, but it is likely that on the whole the model is applicable to most countries whose school systems provide systematic teaching of foreign languages.

FACTORS AFFECTING
CURRICULUM CONSTRUCTION
IN LANGUAGE TEACHING

Curricula (syllabuses) are among the most important factors that guide the construction of teaching materials, tests, and teaching itself. As the importance of knowing what guides teachers' activities has increased along with a growing awareness of teachers' crucial role in carrying out the educational objectives, a special line of study called curriculum research has emerged. After more than ten years of work on various aspects of the curriculum, I have come to the

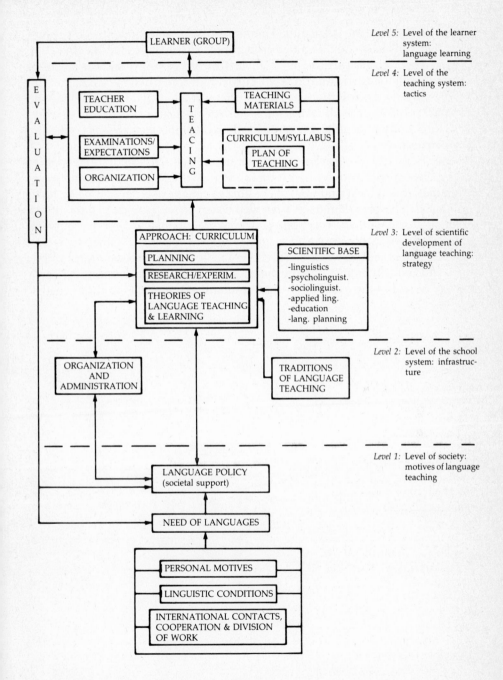

Figure 2.1. General model of the language teaching system (Takala 1980)

conclusion that *how* the curriculum should be constructed depends on a number of factors. These are illustrated in Figure 2.2 (Takala, 1980: 59).

Who constructs the curriculum? Is it constructed centrally so that teachers only work *with* the curriculum? Or will curriculum construction be a hierarchical process—that is, will there be contributions at all levels, from the federal/national level to the individual teacher level? Are the teachers expected to work *on* the curriculum interpreting it to suit local circumstances, as well as work *with* the curriculum?

The subject matter also has a definite impact as such. We do not expect a mathematics curriculum to resemble a foreign language curriculum, but even within the same subject a number of possible varieties exist, depending on how the subject, in this case language, is viewed. What is our *perspective*, our view of language? As Halliday (1974) points out, a comprehensive view of language requires that we recognize it as a system (linguistic focus), as behavior (sociolinguistic focus), as knowledge (psycholinguistic focus), and as a form of art (literary focus). Differences in how the language teaching profession sees each of these aspects—for example, a predominantly formalistic or functionalist

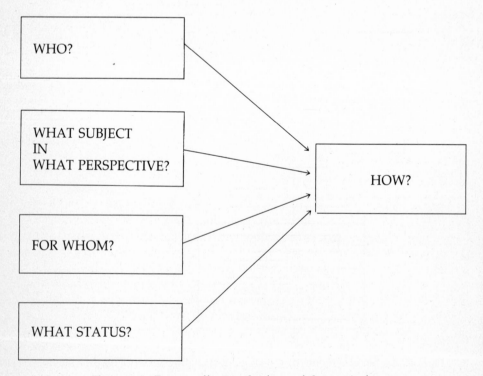

Figure 2.2. Factors affecting the form of the curriculum

view of language—have brought about changes in curricula and will continue
to do so in the future. (See Berns, this volume.)

Because it is very important in all human communication to take into
account the communication partner(s), it is necessary in syllabus construction
to remind ourselves of our possible target groups. *For whom is the curriculum
intended?* There are several possible target groups: political decision makers,
general public, employers, writers of teaching materials, teacher educators,
examining boards, teachers and students. There are also many different kinds
of students with different needs and expectations. For different target groups
we need different versions with varying degrees of specificity. We cannot
expect to be able to communicate properly with such diverse groups unless we
tailor our message to suit each group.

The way in which we should construct the foreign language syllabus also
depends on the *status* it is to have. Will it be binding in terms of what should be
taught or even what should be learned, or is the curriculum only a guideline, a
road map, to help teaching proceed in a desired direction? It makes quite a
difference if a detailed curriculum is a binding document or only one possible
exemplification of the general objectives of teaching. In the latter case the
curriculum would be a kind of yardstick or point of reference for teachers and
textbook writers.

Thus we can conclude that there is not, and *can never be*, a definitive
curriculum or any one best curriculum for all times and for all circumstances.
As there are no universally valid tests, there are no universally valid curricula.
Both tests and curricula are valid only under specific circumstances and for
specific purposes. Here again the contextual dependence of educational phenomena is demonstrated.

A NEW COMMUNICATIVE
FL SYLLABUS FOR THE FINNISH
COMPREHENSIVE SCHOOL

Syllabus construction is a very important task in a country like Finland where
all schools have to follow the national syllabus and where textbook publishers
have to make their textbooks congruent with the syllabuses if they wish to have
them approved for school use. The syllabuses are also used as a basis for
teacher training, tests, and examinations. Thus syllabuses are potentially very
powerful instruments for guiding what goes on in schools. It is thus imperative
that they be based on the best expertise available.

In Finland the 1970s were hectic years of syllabus construction because all
levels of the national school system were reformed during that period. More
than twenty syllabuses were constructed for foreign/second-language teaching
(English, Swedish, Finnish, German, French, and Russian). During this period
syllabus construction became a more institutionalized process in which repre-

sentatives from the teaching profession, staff inspectors from the National Boards of Education, and researchers participated. (For further discussion of some aspects of this work see Takala 1983b).

A new communicative FL syllabus prototype was constructed in 1975–76, revised in 1979–1980, and approved in 1981. This prototype, which included English and Swedish, subsequently served as a model for syllabus work in several other languages.

One practical problem on communicative curriculum construction is that such curricula tend to become very long and unwieldy, and the initial version of one Finnish syllabus was no exception. For this reason, it was considered necessary to provide an overview of the objectives. After several attempts, it turned out that a procedure called "facet analysis" (Guttman 1970; Millman 1974) provided a useful method for such a concise statement of objectives.

Facets are central dimensions of a phenomenon, something like the factors in factor analysis. In the new Finnish FL syllabus, the facets are (a) language functions, (b) language skills, and (c) topics and notions. The following excerpts from the new syllabus for teaching foreign language in the Finnish comprehensive school illustrate this system. This overview, which is followed by detailed accounts of each facet, has been favorably received by teachers. It is cognitively manageable. It also appears that the systematic juxtaposition of the facets helps in seeing the links between them.

(1) **Language functions**	(2) **Language skills**	(3) **Topics and notions**
The aim is that the student can understand, respond to, and produce language in oral and written discourse for the following purposes.	The following communication skills are practiced.	The following topics and notions are dealt with.
Social interaction	**Oral communication**	**People and their immediate environments**
addressing persons	*Listening comprehension*	self
greeting, taking leave	The student can	family, relatives, friends
presenting oneself	understand short expressions	other people
thanking	understand simple conversations	home, everyday tasks and chores
apologizing	understand complete discourses spoken at almost normal tempo and based entirely on familiar language structures and vocabulary	food and eating
complimenting		clothes and accessories
making an offer		parts of the body, health, illness, hygiene
making an invitation	understand complete	
conversational gambits		

Directing activity
ordering, exhorting
forbidding
warning
requesting
advising
suggesting
persuading

Expressing opinions, attitudes, and feelings
like/dislike
agreement/disagreement
pleasure/displeasure
approval/disapproval
surprise
sympathy
wish/persuasion
intent/purpose
certainty/uncertainty
necessity

Imparting and seeking information
labeling, categorizing
asking and answering
stating something
correcting statements
describing and reporting

discourses that may contain also some unfamiliar structures and vocabulary which can easily be inferred from the context

Speaking
The student can
produce expressions needed in oral communication
take part in simple conversations
produce short complete discourses

Written communication
Reading comprehension:
The student can
understand written expressions and respond to them
understand short texts with familiar structures and vocabulary
understand the gist in new short texts containing familiar structures and vocabulary
understand the gist in texts that may contain also some unfamiliar structures and vocabulary, easily inferred from the context

Writing:
The student can
write short messages in accordance with a model or instructions

perceptions and feelings
thinking

Activities
being and possessing
doing things
moving about
school and study
world of work and occupations
leisure time and hobbies/interests
shopping, running errands
traffic and travelling
mass media

Nature, countries, and peoples
nature and weather
country and town
Finland and the Finns
English-speaking countries and peoples
other countries and peoples

Quantity and quality
number and quality
age
money and price
attributes: color, size, shape, quality

Time
point of time and contemporaneousness
present time

write short answers
to written or oral
questions

write short messages
independently

write descriptions, re-
ports and stories
according to prompts
and independently

the past

the future

frequency

duration

Place and manner

location and direction

method, means,
instrument

Relations

qualitative relations
(comparisons)

temporal, spatial and
referential relations
(time: now-then;
place: here-there;
reference to persons
and things: pro-
nouns)

order and dates

quantitative relations

cause, effect, condi-
tion

combination, discrim-
ination

definiteness: indefi-
nite/definite

CONCLUSION

Systematic work on how new ideas in foreign-language teaching might be
approached in Finland began towards the end of the 1960s. Several versions of
FL curricula were developed and tried out at different levels of the school
system (Takala 1980, 1983). New revised versions were officially approved
some ten years later. This ten-year lag is not due to lack of effort. On the
contrary, a massive effort was required to develop the first drafts, to inform
teachers about them through pre-session and in-service education, collect
feedback from teachers, textbook writers, university departments, etc., and to
incorporate this feedback in the revision. Now, after ten years of work, new

textbooks also exist which are in line with the communicative syllabuses. In retrospect, I am convinced that it requires about ten years of systematic hard work to introduce any new idea in education. In some cases, even that estimate may be optimistic.

One outcome of this intensive work in curriculum construction was a growing realization of the complexity of language teaching, which led to work on models of the system of language teaching. One of the merits of comprehensive models like the one presented in Figure 2.1 is that it shows the complex interdependence of various aspects of educational phenomena. Thus, in language teaching we should not overestimate the role of curricula in guiding teaching. As Level 4 in the figure shows, teaching is influenced not only by the curriculum but also by the available teaching materials, the training that teachers have received, the expectations of various interest groups, tests and examinations, and the organization of the school system. The conditions for change are optimal if all these have a similar orientation.

It follows that due consideration should be given to all contributing parties, and all should be consulted and encouraged to help in implementing new ideas. Of crucial importance are tests and examinations. Since, as mentioned earlier, they are used to get feedback for a variety of purposes, they are probably the single most important factor in education. Thus, it is an advisable strategy to devote early and considerable attention to tests and examinations when a new approach is launched. In fact, new approaches are most efficiently introduced if tests and examinations embody their central ideas. Such partly test-driven educational improvement also has the practical advantage of requiring less time and effort to produce good tests than to produce good curricula and textbooks. Educators should not underestimate the positive contributions of evaluation, as they should not underestimate the possible negative washback effect of evaluation that is not congruent with teaching objectives and the teaching itself.

REFERENCES

Calfee, R. 1981. "Cognitive psychology and educational practice." *Review of Research in Education* **9**: 3–73.

Guttman, L. 1970. "Integration of test design and analysis." *Proceedings of the 1969 Invitational Conference on Testing Problems*. Princeton, N.J.: Educational Testing Service.

Halliday, M. 1974. *Language and social man*. London: Longman.

Millman, J. 1974. "Criterion-referenced measurement." In W. J. Popham (ed.). *Evaluation in education: current applications*. Berkeley: McCutchan.

Simon, H. A. 1981. *The sciences of the artificial*. 2nd ed. Cambridge, Mass.: MIT Press.

Stern, H. 1974. "Directions in language teaching theory and research." In J. Qvist-gaard, H. Schwartz, and H. Spang-Hansen, (eds.). *AILA Third Congress Proceedings. Vol. III: Applied Linguistics: Problems and Solutions.* Heidelberg: Julius Groos Verlag.

Strevens, P. 1977. *New orientations in the teaching of English.* London: Oxford University Press.

Takala, S. 1980. "New orientations in foreign language syllabus construction and language planning: a case study of Finland." Institute for Educational Research, University of Jyväskylä, Bulletin No. 155 (Also in ERIC ED 218 925).

———. 1983a. "New orientations in foreign-language syllabus construction in Finland in the 1970s." *Studies in Language Learning,* 4:56–97.

———. 1983. "The need for theoretical advance in education and language education." *The Rackham Journal of the Arts and Humanities* **II:** 105–120. (This issue contains the papers presented at the Ann Arbor Symposium on English and Education.)

Chapter 3

Intake, Communication, and Second-Language Teaching

Elizabeth M. Leemann Guthrie

Elizabeth Leemann Guthrie has taught French in the United States and Canada, and English as a second or foreign language in the United States, France, and Switzerland. She holds an M.A. degree in TESL and a Ph.D. degree in Second-Language Acquisition and Teacher Education (SLATE) from the University of Illinois. She is presently the coodinator of undergraduate French language instruction at the University of California at Irvine.

Formal methods of language instruction have generally been based on the assumption that the development of language competence in a classroom requires different activities, a different kind of interaction, and different constraints on behavior from those of the informal second-language acquisition environment. To some extent, of course, such differences are unavoidable: a natural acquisition environment normally includes one learner and an unlimited number of native speakers, whereas in the classroom there is one fluent speaker with a large number of learners; a natural acquisition environment typically includes a wide variety of times and places, while the formal environment begins and ends on schedule and (in most cases) at the classroom door. On the other hand, there are many ways in which the classroom environment is *made* different from the natural one because of our assumptions about how people learn languages in a formal environment. The natural environment, for example, entails no formal practice exercises, no syllabus, little or no explanation of grammar, and no homework.

Attempts to make classroom learning (and the kind of language learned) more similar to non-classroom interaction and language use have led in recent years to instructional methods that emphasize interpersonal communication, contextualized and personalized practice, in-class discussion of topics of current interest, etc. It is undeniable that such trends have wrought genuine improvements in the quality of language instruction we are able to offer, and that they represent a healthy and exciting trend away from lock-step methodologies and towards more humane education. Nevertheless, they touch only indirectly on an aspect of the acquisition environment known to be vital in non-classroom situations—the way in which language is used in daily interactions between fluent and non-fluent speakers, as a way of providing the data from which the learner constructs a coherent sense of grammaticality and meaning in the second language.

The enormous handicap that hearing impairment places on language acquisition demonstrates just how essential some form of input data is for language acquisition. For small children, these data are available through the speech of adults and older children; for adults in a foreign-language environment, they come through interaction with native speakers of that language. In both cases, it has been shown that the fluent speakers regularly adjust their language to the listening competence of the acquirer by speaking more slowly, pronouncing clearly, using less complex structures, etc. (Krashen 1980). It has also been shown that children respond to this adjusted register of speech rather than to normal adult-to-adult discourse (Snow 1971).

In the case of children learning their first language, psycholinguists' explanations have differed on how input affects the acquisition process; but no one has ever seriously argued that first-language acquisition, under normal circumstances, depended on any variable condition beyond the normal day-to-day verbal interaction that is a part of a child's normal environment. This view of language acquisition is generally extended to include children's second-language acquisition. For adults learning a second language, however, popular and professional notions of the conditions required for minimal success are much more varied. Success in formal language learning has been seen, in general, as a function of some combination of intelligence, talent, motivation, effort, and the "right" teaching method—meaning, usually, the way in which linguistic rules are ordered and presented and the way in which student practice is organized. The target language samples used in everyday classroom interaction have received very little attention.

The view of adult second-language learning as a function of conscious intellectual effort has been seriously challenged in recent years. Numerous studies of adults learning a second language have revealed that the sequences of linguistic development in adults closely resemble those of children learning a first or second language (Bailey, Madden, and Krashen 1974; Perkins and Larsen-Freeman 1975). In detailed studies of the utterances of German students learning English in school, Felix (1981a) has shown that the "natural" developmental sequence occurs in many structural areas in the formal learning situation, even though the natural order is different from the sequence of instruction. Furthermore, Felix (1982) notes that formal—that is, classroom—learners do apply certain complex rules of structure that are not taught in language classes, even though the same learners may fail to apply other rules that they "know" in the intellectual sense. Although considerable debate still rages over how clear a distinction can be made between explicit (or "learned") and implicit (or "acquired") knowledge of a second language, the point remains that the performance of second-language learners cannot be satisfactorily explained as a function of consciously learned linguistic rules.

An alternative view of adult second-language learning is that it depends only in part, and in very limited contexts, on understanding of linguistic principles. Researchers like Krashen (1977), Bialystok (1981), and Felix (1981) have suggested that real language competence depends on a kind of intuitive sense of grammaticality which is not consciously learned, but which develops through a regular progression of stages (like first-language acquisition) as a function of an innate human language-acquiring capacity in the presence of appropriate conditions. The learner's involvement in linguistic interaction appears to be among the most critical, if not the single most critical, of these conditions.

This raises the question of why "direct" teaching methods and immersion experiences are not uniformly successful in producing fluent speakers of foreign languages, since both do make extensive target-language samples available to the learner. The answer may lie in the distinction between language *input* (all language samples that the learner hears) and *intake* (language samples that actually influence the learner's evolving sense of the language). Although many questions about how intake influences language development are still unanswered, it is now generally agreed that a crucial feature of intake is the listener's active involvement in decoding linguistic signals. This implies that intake must be appropriately adjusted in such a way that it falls within the range of the listeners' comprehension but demands their active effort to identify and use the linguistic clues to meaning. Indeed this is the kind of adjustment that has been found in parents' speech to children (Newport 1975) and in native speakers' language addressed to foreigners (Freed 1978).

It is clear that in a second-language environment, the learner does not attend to many linguistic signals, either because of fatigue, lack of interest, or a preoccupation with some other line of thought. Those who have attempted to follow a prolonged native-speaker conversation in a language in which they are not fluent can attest to the effort required for sustaining their attentiveness to the discourse; if the language is not consistently tailored to the listeners' level of understanding, their attention soon begins to drop and their minds wander to other concerns. The range of discourse to which an individual attends and the degree of tailoring that he or she requires probably fluctuate with mood, fatigue, etc. Even at the same level of language proficiency, the nature of optimal discourse is also likely to vary from one learner to another, depending upon a variety of psychological, affective, and social factors. Not surprisingly, then, we have yet to discover the ideal language-learning environment in which every learner will predictably achieve fluent command of a foreign language.

With these conditions in mind, it is not difficult to understand why different individuals in an immersion environment—reputedly the best possible situation for language acquisition—may derive very different kinds and degrees of benefit from it. For example, some learners seize every opportunity to communicate in the foreign language by enrolling in leisure-time classes, seeking out the company of native speakers, and actively trying to initiate conversations with taxi drivers, shop clerks, waiters, classmates, and co-passengers on trains and buses. Others interact less—they associate with speakers of their own language if possible; they learn the minimum number of stock phrases for ordering meals and buying necessities; they shop in self-service stores to avoid sales clerks; they use a map instead of asking directions.

But beyond controlling the number of situations in which they will need to interact in the language of the country, foreigners can also do a great deal within interaction situations to limit the amount and the complexity of the language samples addressed to them. Numerous studies of "foreigner-talk" discourse (e.g., Freed 1978; Tarone 1980; Long 1981; Scarcella and Higa 1981) have demonstrated that when native speakers talk to foreigners, their language is simpler than the language they use with one another, but more complex than the language used by their non-native interlocutors. In other words, the foreigner's language is tailored to the listener's ability to understand rather than to his or her speaking ability. In order to decide whether to simplify further, to restate a question, to go on to another topic, etc., it seems probable that native speakers depend on a range of subtle clues from the foreign conversational partners—eye contact, facial expression, hesitation, nodding or shaking the head, gesture, etc.—as well as explicit verbal signals like "Yes, I understand" or "Please repeat." This means that with only a minimum of demand upon their limited linguistic skill, non-natives can exercise considerable control over the pace and complexity of the interaction, simply by manipulating the level of comprehension perceived by the fluent speaker.

At present, we cannot say precisely what function linguistic intake plays in the development of second-language fluency. It may be that the second-language samples heard by the acquirer serve in some sense as models against which hypotheses about the form of the language can be tested. They may serve a more general function, simply by helping the acquirer form a sense of the limits on possible combinations of words and sounds in the second language. Or perhaps linguistic interaction may serve as a sort of neurological "trigger" that activates the psychological structures responsible for language acquisition. Whatever the truth of its role may be, however, linguistic intake is clearly a *sine qua non* of language acquisition.

Given the importance that linguistic intake appears to have in non-classroom language acquisition, surprisingly little attention has been given to determining its role in the foreign-language classroom. Intuitively, one would expect the classroom to provide an excellent environment for linguistic intake, with the teacher furnishing appropriately adjusted linguistic forms corresponding to the meaningful content on which the students' attention is focused. But whereas these conditions—meaningful content, appropriately tailored linguistic forms, and their coincidence in the learner's attention—occur more or less spontaneously in ordinary conversation between foreigners and native speakers, the problems specific to foreign-language classrooms may make the same conditions less likely to occur there.

Even in highly "communicative" classrooms, teachers and students do not address each other in the target language *primarily* because they have important things to say, but because practice is part of foreign-language learning. Conversely, second-language learners outside of classrooms do not often set out to practice; they set out to get information or to buy something or simply to establish human contact. There is no way to avoid the fact that *foreign-language instruction aims at teaching the language rather than at communicating.* Inevitably, however, this fact imbues the formal learning situation with a kind of artificiality that is rare beyond the walls of a foreign-language classroom.

Foreign-language courses, like most academic programs, are usually based on an ordered sequence of material, and this too adds to the problem of "natural" target-language use in class. The sequential steps around which the course is organized may vary with the teacher, the program the syllabus, and the textbook; they may be explicitly stated or not; but to some extent they are always arbitrary, if only because our present knowledge of language acquisition has not made it possible to define an educational sequence known to be consistent with the natural acquisition process. But since textbooks and course syllabuses provide the basis for testing and grades, teachers and students quite naturally see them as the main business of the course. This makes it difficult to establish the importance of activities that do not directly train students to proceed along the defined (usually structural) sequence.

The problem is compounded by the fact that the vast majority of foreign-language teachers share a native language with their students, so that "covering the material" is considerably more cumbersome in the target language than in the native language. Using the target language for everyday communication can therefore be experienced as an artificial constraint that simply impedes the class's progress. Indeed, research in this area (Moskowitz 1976; Wing 1980) suggests that very few language teachers use the target language for as much as 80% of their discourse in class. When the target language is used, it may be reserved for functions where it is the least likely to interfere with the pace and direction of the class—that is, for routine functions that fall *below* the students' level of speaking ability rather than *above* it.

Another problem that faces foreign-language teachers and students is a long-standing emphasis on the productive skills, to the virtual exclusion of the receptive ones. (One might object here that the principle of "listening before speaking and reading before writing" was a cornerstone of the audiolingual method and has remained a tenet of most contemporary approaches in public schools. However, as Asher (1981) points out, the "listening" of the audio-lingual method was listening for repetition rather than for comprehension.) Behavioral objectives for language classes are generally stated in terms of oral or written performance; "oral participation" is frequently a component in the evaluation of students: and teachers, during their methods courses, are instructed to see that every student speaks regularly in class.

This overriding concern for eliciting production from the students creates a situation very unlike that of the informal environment. If we learn a second language by living in a foreign country, we follow a sequence of learning something like this: As we learn to decode language samples in our day-to-day interactions, the linguistic forms begin to take on meaning for us until we ourselves are able to use them meaningfully. In the classroom, this order may be reversed. Students are asked to utter linguistic forms that have not yet become meaningful to them, and they are often expected to express meanings for which they have not acquired a second-language representation.

The classroom differs again from an immersion environment in terms of the dynamics of interaction. The natural environment, of course, contains many times more native speakers than foreigners, and the avid language acquirer can, in general, find many occasions for one-on-one conversations with native speakers. The structure of these interactions differs greatly from normal classroom discourse both because of the ratio of learners to fluent speakers and because of the classroom's implicit hierarchy. As mentioned earlier, in a natural situation the non-fluent participant exerts considerable control over the shape of the discourse. As an equal participant in the interaction, he or she can nominate a topic, request or offer clarification, initiate or terminate an interaction, etc. In a classroom, the teacher typically controls the discourse to a much greater extent—and the student to a lesser one—than is the case with their natural-environment counterparts. The nonverbal signals that in a one-on-one conversation can indicate interest, confusion, agreement, etc. are easily lost in the behavior of a larger group; and in any case, all the constraints typically placed on students' behavior in schools continue to militate against their assuming an active role in controlling the content and the difficulty level of the ongoing discourse. This absence of feedback, in turn, makes it much more difficult for teachers to adjust their language appropriately than for fluent speakers outside of a classroom.

To illustrate some of the foregoing points—and to show some ways in which classroom discourse might be made more appropriate for language acquisition—it may be useful to look at some examples of discourse taken from introductory university-level French classes.[1] In the first example, the teacher introduces and begins an exercise on question formation through inversion in the *passé composé*. (Note: English translations of the discourse examples are provided in Appendix A.)

Example 1

(1) Teacher: Bon, dans le livre, à la page trois cent quatre-vingt treize, n'est-ce pas, il y a beaucoup de choses au sujet de l'inversion, beaucoup d'examples aussi.

(2) Faisons très rapidement exercice six, en bas de la page, pour pratiquer l'inversion.

(3) Par exemple, il y a deux personnes qui parlent, vous et votre camarade.

(4) Ton frère, a-t-il une voiture?

(5) Ici l'inversion avec le verbe "avoir."

(6) Et puis on peut répondre, "Oui, il a une voiture," "Non, il n'a pas de voiture."

(7) Okay?

(8) Brian, posez la question à John ici.

(9) Avec numero un.

(10) Student A: Ta soeur, a-t-elle une voiture?

(11) Student B: Oui, elle a, uh . . .

(12) Teacher: Une voiture?

(13) Student B: Oui, elle a une voiture.

(14) Teacher: Est-ce que vous avez une soeur, oui ou non?

(15)   Non, il n'a . . .

(16)   Mais il faut, il faut dire oui ou non, n'est-ce pas?

(17)   Oui, elle a une voiture.

(18)   Donc, ta soeur, a-t-elle, a-t-elle une voiture?

(19)   L'inversion.

One striking feature of this passage is the number of teacher utterances that are difficult to interpret. In line 1, for example, it may first appear that the teacher is simply telling the students where to look for further clarification of inversion. Only in line 2 does it become clear that she wants them to turn to the page she has mentioned and to do an exercise. In lines 3–6, it is not immediately apparent that she is reading the example sentences for the exercise she has just announced.

Much of the difficulty of interpreting the teacher's utterances seems due to a kind of constant fragmentation of focus between linguistic rules, the mechanics of accomplishing the lesson, and the "real world" of the things and people present in the classroom. In lines 15 through 19, for example, the teacher skips from the world of the student's reality (lines 14–15) to the mechanics of the exercise (line 16), then to the hypothetical frame of reference created by the exercise (line 17), and finally to a reformulation of the student's response (line 18) and a reminder of the linguistic principle being practiced (line 19)—all with no transition and with nothing to help the students identify the topic or the frame of reference within which the teacher is operating at any given moment.

It is very interesting that the students do not appear in the least confused by the constant shifts of topic or by the somewhat "telegraphic" speech style used by the teacher. Certainly none of the individual sentences presented here would be difficult to decode; on the other hand, it seems unlikely that the students are really following the chain of thought represented by the teacher's speech, given that a researcher equipped with a videotape and a written transcript finds it necessary to go over the recording more than once in order to see that chain of thought. More likely, the students are simply functioning on the basis of cues unrelated to much of the teacher's discourse. Note that at a maximum, Brian and John needed to know the page number, the exercise to be done, and the item number. If they were listening specifically for this information, they could have gotten it from the teacher's discourse without interpreting anything more; if they failed to "catch" the necessary information in the teacher's discourse, they could probably get it from other sources—e.g., finding the page on which there were examples like the one on the board, looking at another student's book, etc.

The point here is that although the lesson is conducted entirely in French, it is hard to say that there is any real possibility for linguistic intake for the students, who appear to be looking for little more than the minimal cues they need in order to respond properly. Nor do they appear to seek or to exercise any real control over the classroom interaction. In line 11, the student's hesitation appears related to the fact that the question is based on a false assumption (that he has a sister), a fact that the teacher then verifies (line 14); however, as she points out, the exercise requires a yes-or-no answer—no questioning of the truth conditions is admitted (line 16).

It is difficult to imagine a situation other than a language classroom in which a second-language acquirer would so readily accept this kind of arbitrary imposition of an untrue precondition for a conversational exchange. One might, in "real life," argue the point, abandon the topic (or, indeed, the conversational partner—by no means an insignificant alternative!), or negotiate for an imaginary frame of reference that both partners are willing to accept. The absence of such behavior in the classroom reflects the sense of priorities that structure-based curricula tend to impose on teachers and students alike. Those priorities might be stated as follows: "We are here first of all to practice language forms. If, in so doing, we can manage to exchange some information and ideas with each other, so much the better—but we must take care not to let communication carry us away from the main business of the course."

Another discourse example illustrates the difficulty of combining the aim of structured practice with that of meaningful communication. Here the class is doing an exercise designed to practice the interrogative pronoun *lequel* (which one) and its variants. The exercise calls for two students to engage in an interaction like the following:

Student A: Do you know any singers?

Student B: Yes.

Student A: Which ones do you know?

Student B: I know Anne Murray and Roberta Flack.

The difficulty this exercise presents is that while it does provide a context for practice of the linguistic rule, it violates the rules of ordinary conversation. In an everyday interaction, the first question would be interpreted as a request for the names of singers one knows, a simple yes-or-no answer could only be explained as an example either of rudeness or of conversational ineptitude. Thus, in a normal conversation the second and third lines of the interaction would not take place. The students are caught between the requirements of polite conversation and the expectation that they use a form of *lequel* in their interaction.

Example 2

    (1) Teacher: Okay, bon.

    (2)   Demandez à . . . Carol . . . si elle connaît des chanteurs et lesquels.

    (3)   Ask her if she knows any singers and which ones.

    (4) Student A: Uh . . . Connais-tu des chanteurs?

    (5) Student B: Je connais . . . Mick Jagger.
                    (Laughter)

    (6) Teacher: Okay, lesquels . . .alors lesquels est-ce qu'elle connaît?
    (7)   Which ones does she know?

    (8) Student A: xxx

    (9) Teacher: Elle connaît Mick Jagger.
                  . . . .

    (10) Teacher: Susan, est-ce que tu connais des acteurs?

    (11) Student: Oui, je connais . . .

    (12) Teacher: (Interrupting) Lesquelles?

    (13)   Oui, lesquelles?

    (14) Student: Oh, je connais . . . um . . . Shirley Maclaine, Jane Fonda . . .

The teacher's translation of her French utterances into English (lines 3 and 7) is worthy of mention. The form that the teacher is translating are virtually the same as those the students are expected to produce. If she does not expect the students to understand these cue sentences, can she really expect them to produce the longer and equally complex interaction required by the exercise? It seems more likely that the use of English has little to do with the teacher's evaluation of the students' comprehension—that it is, in fact, simply an expedient way to keep the lesson moving fairly quickly. In either case, the priority is clearly to get through the exercise, to accomplish the lesson, to "cover the material," rather than to create an atmosphere in which use of the second language is the norm.

    It is somewhat surprising to find that the students determinedly circumvent the obvious purpose of the exercise by comforming to the rules of everyday conversation—quite unlike the behavior of the student without a sister in Example 1. Perhaps learners are more willing to ignore reality conditions for discourse than to violate conversational principles; or perhaps, since the latter exercise does provide the opportunity to furnish some personal information, the students' attention is simply drawn away from the mechanics of the structural practice. In any case, in the first part of the interaction, the teacher is unsuccessful in getting the students to produce the sequence of utterances that the exercise calls for. Finally, in the second part of the example, the teacher herself takes over the first role, but nevertheless the student fails to wait for the *lequel* question before starting to provide the names of actresses she knows. The teacher therefore interrupts with *"Lesquelles? Oui, lesquelles?"* (lines 12–13). The *"oui"* appears to mean, "Yes, you are giving the right answer," but the interruption itself signals "wrong"—i.e. "Don't answer until I ask you the right question."

The awkwardness of this passage exemplifies the linguistic contortions we impose on ourselves and our students by trying to serve too many goals at once. Conversation in a second language is difficult for any learner; the attempt to manipulate it around specific linguistic structures makes it even more difficult, especially in the case of structures for which obligatory contexts are rare. However, the absence of structural requirements on classroom interaction will not in itself guarantee a solution to the problems of communication in second-language classes, as Example 3 demonstrates. Here the teacher is beginning a discussion on stereotypes about the French personality, based on a reading passage from the textbook. No specific structure is being practiced. Still, it is revealing to try imagining this conversation in any context other than a classroom.

Example 3

   (1) Teacher: Pensez-vous qu'il y a vraiment *une* personnalité française, typiquement française?

   (2)   Oui?

   (3) Students: Non.

   (4) Teacher: Non? Pourquoi?
   (Pause)

   (5)   Claudia?

   (6) Student: Um . . . Je pense qu'il y a ⎡ une

   (7) Teacher: (Interrupting)   ⎣ Qu'il y a une personnalité française?

   (8)   Bon, décrivez la personnalité française.

   (9) Student: How do you say "pride?"

   (10) Teacher: Oh . . . vous avez déjà eu deux mots.

   (11)   (Writing on blackboard) Okay, "la fierté" est comme en anglais "pride," et l'adjectif, "fier."

   (12)   Je suis fier, I'm proud.

(13)   Bon, est-ce que les Français sont très fiers?

(14)   Ils ont beaucoup de fierté?
                  (Silence)

(15)   Est-ce que les Français sont nationalistes?

By most commonly cited criteria, this interaction qualifies as an excellent example of "communicative" classroom discourse. Personal opinions are elicited, student responses need conform to no particular model, and the conversation develops around a cultural, rather than a linguistic, topic. Yet it is clear that the teacher defines her own role not as that of a conversational partner or facilitator, but as one responsible for telling her students how to speak. The motivation for interruption in line 7 is hard to explain; and it is interesting that her question in line 8 assumes her interpretation of the student's intended utterance to be correct, although she has not sought confirmation from the student that this is so. In line 9, the student asks for a vocabulary item, apparently in an attempt to prepare herself to express an opinion in French. The teacher, however, promptly and efficiently removes from the student any chance to express a genuine and personal viewpoint. In her response to the student, she first reminds her that the word requested has been introduced previously (line 10), then provides two lexical items and an example (lines 11–12); and finally, without pausing to allow the student to formulate her own thought, she questions the truth of what she now assumes the student to believe (that the French are proud), although the student has not expressed that opinion and may not have wished to.

It would be difficult to show that the student in Example 3 ceases to process the teacher's language at any point in that passage. On the other hand, a great deal of research supports the belief that language acquisition is highly sensitive to affective factors. Krashen (1980) has suggested that the acquirer's ability to receive linguistic input may be limited by an "affective filter" under stressful or threatening conditions. Scarcella and Higa (1981) suggest that acquirers' active participation in a conversational situation may "charge" the input and increase their receptivity to it. In a climate where interruption, reproval, and arbitrary interpretation of their utterances are expected, students quite possibly might minimize not only their speaking but their listening as well, and their retention of what they do hear might be reduced. All of these considerations would seem to argue the need for an instructional climate in which students' efforts to participate as equals in the communicative act are both supported and respected.

It seems clear that the issue of "manipulation" versus "communication" is not merely a matter of choosing between transformation drills and group discussion. Communication is an activity that requires two or more autonomous participants, one of whom may benefit from the other's skill in making the interaction succeed; but the more one participant's output is subject to another's control, the more the discourse becomes the sole creation of the more proficient individual—and that is not communication!

It may begin to appear that language acquisition in the classroom is being pronounced impossible or nearly so, but that is not the case. It is true that our perception of what occurs in a classroom must take into account the processes of language acquisition as we begin to discover and to understand them, and it is true that the teacher's role in the classroom must be redefined in terms of the quality of interaction furnished to students. But these changes may not be as dramatic (or as chaotic) as one might imagine. In the following example, recorded on the same day as Example 2, another teacher is working with the interrogative pronoun *lequel*. By coincidence, this lesson occurred in the same week as the "Oscar" awards, and the teacher focuses upon that event to foster conversation in class.

Example 4

(1)	Teacher:	Maintenant . . . est-ce que vous avez regardé la cérémonie lundi, à la télé, pour les prix américains du film?
(2)	Student A:	Non.
(3)	Teacher:	Personne?
(4)		Vous étudiiez, c'est ça.
(5)	Students:	(Murmurs, laughter)
(6)		Oh, oui . . .
(7)		xxx le français
(8)	Teacher:	Terri, vous avez regardé un peu, n'est-ce pas?
(9)	Student B:	J'ai vu le film de la cérémonie.
(10)	Teacher:	Uh-huh . . . bon.
(11)		Quels films étaient désignes pour le prix du meilleur film de l'année?
(12)	Student B:	*Kramer vs. Kramer*
(13)	Teacher:	Oui . . . *Kramer vs. Kramer* a gagné.
(14)		Mais quels étaient les autres films désignés pour le prix?
(15)	Student B:	Uh . . . *Apocalypse Now, Norma Rae, All That Jazz* . . .
(16)	Student C:	(Interrupting) *Breaking Away* . . .
(17)	Teacher:	*Breaking Away*, oui . . .
(18)		Lequel préférez-vous?
(19)	Student B:	Um . . . j'aime *Kramer vs. Kramer*.
(20)	Teacher:	Donc vous êtes d'accord avec le prix.

(21) Student B: Oui, mais je n'ai pas vu toutes les films.

(22) Teacher: Bon, lequel des films désignés préférez-vous, Elise?

(23) Student D: xxx je préfère *Kramer vs. Kramer.*

Compared to the earlier examples, this passage includes very active student participation, ranging from simple yes/no answers (lines 2, 6) to full sentences (lines 9, 19, 21, 23). The quality of the discussion seems perfectly natural and unforced, and there is no fragmentation of focus between content and form. It is clear from student responses that they are actively involved not only as speakers but also as listeners and that the teacher's discourse is just difficult enough to demand that they do some intelligent guessing of meanings from the context. In line 12, for example, the student interprets the teacher's question incorrectly and furnishes the name of the winning film rather than the names of those nominated. The teacher accepts the student response (line 13) but also repeats the question (line 14), thus bringing into salience the difference between her original question and the student's erroneous interpretation of it. The student then provides an appropriate response (line 15).

By adjusting her own discourse at a level that demands an active hypothesis-testing process (and therefore active attention) in order to be decoded, the teacher exerts a certain kind of control over student behavior. The choice and timing of her questions also do a great deal to shape the ongoing discussion, in terms of both the content and the structures used. At no point, however, does she impose words, forms, or content on her students; what they say is utterly their own. Her respect for student contributions is further demonstrated by her use of student responses as a basis for following moves (lines 11, 18, 20). The fact that their responses are not merely approved and then abandoned communicates to the students that what they have to say—whether they say it fluently or not—is valued and respected.

In Example 4, the students' output is, on the whole, grammatically accurate. A gender error (*toutes* for *tous*) in line 21 is disregarded, whether by design or by chance, but does not interfere with the flow of the discussion. But what if a student's error does interfere with comprehensibility? Is it not then necessary for the teacher to correct and clarify the utterance, if only in order to allow other students to follow the discourse? The situation arises in the following example, taped on the same day as Example 3 (the discussion of cultural stereotypes).

Example 5

(1) Teacher: Est-ce que vous avez une impression du caractère français typique, Donna?

(2) Student A: Ils sont très romantiques.

(3) Teacher: C'est une des idées . . . une des impressions qu'on a.

(4)   Est-ce que vous avez d'autres idées?

(5)   Paul?

(6) Student B: Le Français typique déteste les touristes américains.
                  (Laughter)

(7) Teacher: Je pense que c'est vrai, oui.

(8)   Vous avez d'autres impressions?
                  (Pause)

(9)   Roger, vous venez de faire la connaissance d'un
                  Française.

(10)   Quelles sont vos impressions?

(11) Student C: Ah . . . c'est . . . c'est ne Français typique.

(12) Teacher: Il n'était pas typique?

(13) Student C: Ne personne est typique.

(14) Teacher: Personne n'est typique?

(15)   C'est à dire qu'il n'est pas possible de généraliser,
                  c'est ça?

(16) Student C: Oui.

Once again, while the teacher does structure and facilitate the conversation, she allows students full control of their own output. It is interesting to note in passing that her acceptance of student responses takes the form of a comment on the topic (lines 3, 7) rather than that of an evaluation (e.g. *très bien*). This strategy not only communicates a nonjudgmental interest in the student's contribution, but also provides some relatively complex language for the students to attend to in a context where their interest is likely to be high. (Most of us do want to know what an authority figure has to say about our efforts.)

In lines 11–16, the teacher faces the problem of student utterances containing major grammatical errors. Although the student is somewhat slow in producing an entire utterance, and although it is clear before the end of the sentence that it contains major grammatical errors, the teacher does not intervene until the student reaches the end of his utterance. She then responds (lines 12 and 14) in a way that serves two functions: to expand the student's utterance into a correct form (a frequent strategy in parent-child discourse) and then to seek confirmation of her interpretation from the student. In this manner she invites the student to attend to the correct form, but she simultaneously recognizes him as the "meaning maker," the ultimate authority on what he really intended to say. In line 15, she paraphrases his idea, again inviting him to listen and to let her know whether or not she is accurately reflecting his idea. The teacher, then, takes on the function of a consultant, helping the students find the words and forms necessary to express their ideas, but leaving with them the final responsibility of deciding what to say.

The examples we have seen help to underscore an important point—that the quality of classroom interaction is not simply a function of the "right" method or class activity, but that it is closely linked to our most basic attitudes about the learning process, about communication itself, and about our role as teachers. These attitudes have a profound effect on the amount and degree of communication that can be achieved in our classrooms.

Traditionally, we have viewed classroom instruction as a structured, deliberately sequenced process leading to predetermined goals within given time limits; and it may be difficult to think of the classroom as an acquisition environment when language acquisition outside the classroom depends on internal structures and processes that we are only beginning to understand. Nevertheless, for whatever reasons, the success rate of non-classroom language acquisition appears to be phenomenally higher than that of classroom instruction (Asher 1981), and it would seem highly desirable for language educators to look carefully at areas in which classroom art might benefit from a closer imitation of life. The question of linguistic intake would appear to be such an area, not only because of the important role it appears to play in non-classroom language acquisition, but also, despite the many external factors that might prevent it from occurring spontaneously in the classroom, because there seems to be no *a priori* reason why it might not play a crucial role in classroom instruction to the extent that it is available.

NOTES

1. All examples used in this paper are taken from data by the author for doctoral research at the University of Illinois at Urbana-Champaign (Guthrie 1983). The data were collected in six sections of French 102 (second-semester elementary French), each videotaped on two occasions. The classes were taught by teaching assistants, most of whom were in their second semester of teaching. The texts are transcribed verbatim. Unintelligible material is represented by xxx.

REFERENCES

Asher, J. 1981. "The extinction of second-language learning in American schools: an extinction model." In Harris Winitz (ed.). *The comprehension approach to foreign-language instruction*. Rowley, Mass.: Newbury House.

Bailey, N., C. Madden, and S. Krashen. 1974. "Is there a 'natural sequence' in adult second language learning?" *Language Learning* 24: 235–243.

Bialystok, E. 1981. "Some evidence for the integrity and interaction of two knowledge sources." In Roger Andersen (ed.). *New dimensions in second language acquisition research*. Rowley, Mass.: Newbury House.

Felix, S. 1981a. "Competing cognitive structures in second-language acquisition." Paper presented at the European−North American Workshop on Cross Linguistic Second-Language Acquisition Research, Los Angeles, September 1981.

———. 1981b. "The effect of formal instruction on second-language acquisition." *Language Learning* **31:** 81−112.

———. 1982. Paper presented at the Expertenseminar of the Goethe Institute of New York, September 1982.

Freed, B. 1978. "Talking to foreigners versus talking to children: similarities and differences." In R. Scarcella and S. Krashen (eds.). *Research in second-language acquisition: selected papers of the Los Angeles second-language acquisition research forum.* Rowley, Mass.: Newbury House.

Guthrie, E. 1983. "The foreign language classroom as acquisition environment." Unpublished Ph.D. dissertation, University of Illinois at Urbana-Champaign.

Krashen, S. 1977. "The monitor model for adult second-language performance." In M. Burt, H. Dulay, and M. Finocchiaro (eds.). *Viewpoints on English as a second language.* New York: Regents.

———. 1981. *Second-language acquisition and second-language learning.* Oxford: Pergamon Press.

Long, M. 1981. "Questions in foreigner talk discourse." *Language Learning* **31**: 135−157.

Moskowitz, G. 1976. "The classroom interaction of outstanding foreign-language teachers." *Foreign Language Annals* **9:** 135−143.

Newport, E. 1975. *Motherese: the speech of mothers to young children.* LaJolla, California: Center for Human Information Processing.

Perkins, K. and D. Larsen-Freeman. 1975. "The effect of formal language instruction on the order of morpheme acquisition." *Language Learning* **25:** 237−243.

Scarcella, R. and C. Higa. 1981. "Input, negotiation, and age differences in second-language acquisition." *Language Learning* **31:** 409−438.

Snow, C. 1971. "Language acquisition and mothers' speech to children." Unpublished Ph.D. dissertation, McGill University.

Tarone, E. 1981. "Communication strategies, foreigner talk, and repair in interlanguage." *Language Learning* **30:** 417−432.

APPENDIX A

Example 1

(1) Teacher:	Good, in the book, on page 393, right, there are a lot of things about inversion, a lot of examples, too.
(2)	Let's do exercise six quickly, at the bottom of the page, to practice inversion.
(3)	For example, there are two people talking, you and your friend.
(4)	Does your brother have a car?

(5)		Here, inversion with the verb "avoir."
(6)		And then you can answer, "Yes, he has a car," "No, he doesn't have a car."
(7)		Okay?
(8)		Brian, ask John here that question.
(9)		With number one.
(10)	Student A:	Does your sister have a car?
(11)	Student B:	Yes, she has, uh . . .
(12)	Teacher:	A car?
(13)	Student A:	Yes, she has a car.
(14)	Teacher:	Do you have a sister, yes or no?
(15)		No; he doesn't . . .
(16)		But you have to, you have to say yes or no, don't you?
(17)		Yes, she has a car.
(18)		So does your sister, does your sister have a car?
(19)		Inversion.

Example 2

(1)	Teacher:	Okay, good.
(2)		Ask . . . Carol . . . if she knows any singers and which ones.
(3)		(Translates)
(4)	Student A:	Uh . . . Do you know any singers?
(5)	Student B:	I know . . . Mick Jagger. (Laughter)
(6)	Teacher:	Okay, which ones . . . so which ones does she know?
(7)		(Translates)
(8)	Student A:	xxx
(9)	Teacher:	She knows Mick Jagger.

. . . .

(10)	Teacher:	Susan, do you know any actors?
(11)	Student:	Yes, I know . . .
(12)	Teacher:	(Interrupting) Which ones?
(13)		Yes, which ones?
(14)	Student:	Oh, I know . . . um . . . Shirley MacLaine, Jane Fonda . . .

Example 3

(1)	Teacher:	Do you think there is really *one* French personality, a typically French personality?
(2)		Yes?
(3)	Students:	No.
(4)	Teacher:	No? Why? (Pause)
(5)		Claudia?
(6)	Student:	Um . . . I think that there's a
(7)	Teacher:	(Interrupting) That there's a French personality?
(8)		Good, describe the French personality.
(9)	Student:	How do you say "pride?"
(10)	Teacher:	Oh . . . You've already had two words.
(11)		(Writing on blackboard) Okay, "la fierté" is like in English "pride," and the adjective, "fier."
(12)		Je suis fier, I'm proud.
(13)		Good, are the French very proud?
(14)		Do they have a lot of pride? (Silence)
(15)		Are the French nationalistic?

Example 4

(1)	Teacher:	Now . . . Did you watch the ceremony Monday, on television, for the American film awards?
(2)	Student A:	No.
(3)	Teacher:	Nobody?
(4)		You were studying, that's it.
(5)	Students:	(Murmurs, laughter)
(6)		Oh, yes . . .
(7)		. . . French
(8)	Teacher:	Terri, you watched a little bit, didn't you?
(9)	Student B:	I saw the film of the ceremony.
(10)	Teacher:	Uh-huh . . . good.
(11)		Which films were nominated for the best film of the year award?
(12)	Student B:	*Kramer vs. Kramer.*

(13) Teacher: Yes . . . *Kramer vs. Kramer* won.

(14) But what were the other films nominated for the award?

(15) Student B: Uh . . . *Apocalypse Now, Norma Rae, All That Jazz* . . .

(16) Student C: (Interrupting) *Breaking Away.* . .

(17) Teacher: *Breaking Away*, yes . . .

(18) Which one do you like best?

(19) Student B: Um . . . I like *Kramer vs. Kramer*.

(20) Teacher: So you agree with the prize.

(21) Student B: Yes, but I didn't see all the films.

(22) Teacher: Good, which of the nominated films do you like best, Elise?

(23) Student D: xxx I like *Kramer vs. Kramer* best.

Example 5

(1) Teacher: Do you have an impression of the typical French character, Donna?

(2) Student A: They are very romantic.

(3) Teacher: That's one of the ideas . . . one of the impressions that people have.

(4) Do you have other ideas?

(5) Paul?

(6) Student B: The typical Frenchman hates American tourists. (Laughter)

(7) Teacher: I think that's true, yes.

(8) Do you have other impressions? (Pause)

(9) Roger, you've just met a French person.

(10) What are your impressions?

(11) Student C: Ah . . . he isn't a typical Frenchman.

(12) Teacher: He wasn't typical?

(13) Student C: Nobody is typical.

(14) Teacher: Nobody is typical?

(15) In other words it isn't possible to generalize, is that it?

Chapter 4

Regional Norms for English

Braj B. Kachru

Braj B. Kachru is Professor of Linguistics and coordinator of the Division of Applied Linguistics at the University of Illinois, Urbana-Champaign. He was Head of the Department of Linguistics at the same university from 1969–1979. One of his major research interests over the last two decades has been the sociolinguistic study of the spread of English, and the development of its non-native varieties across the world. His most recent publication in this area is The Alchemy of English: The Spread, Functions and Models of Non-Native Englishes.

INTRODUCTION

In discussing the norm for localized varieties of Englishes around the world, we are in a sense faced with the situation described in the entertaining Eastern fable about the elephant and the four blind men.[1] Each blind man, the story tells us, tries to describe the animal on the basis of touching one part of the large animal. One, after feeling the animal's leg, claims that an elephant resembles a gnarled tree trunk; another compares it with a thick rope, since that is how the elephant's trunk appears to him; feeling the circular belly of the animal, the third blind man exclaims, "Aha, an elephant is like a smooth round drum," and so on. Clearly, each blind man has a correct perception about an individual part of the elephant, but that part itself is not the totality termed "elephant." It is all these parts together, and various types within the species, that constitute the "elephant-ness." And this analogy applies to languages, too. When we use an identificational label for a variety (e.g., American, British, Canadian, Indian, Malaysian, Nigerian), we are actually thinking in terms of what linguists have called "common core" analysis, "over all" analysis, or a "nucleus." These terms are as abstract as the "elephant-ness," or using another example, "dog-ness," aptly suggested by Quirk et al. (1972:13):

> The properties of dog-ness can be seen in both terrier and alsation (and, we must presume, equally) yet no single variety of dog embodies all the features present in all varieties of dog. In a somewhat similar way, we need to see a common core or nucleus that we call "English" being realized only in the different actual varieties of the language that we hear or read.

The global spread of English and its various functions in the sociolinguistic context of each English-speaking country make generalizations about the language almost impossible. Because each regional variety of English has its distinct historical, acquisitional, and cultural context, the genesis of each variety must be seen within that perspective. The generalizations from one localized variety are as deceptive as the blind men's description of the elephant. At the same time, each description contributes to our understanding of the *English-ness* of world Englishes, and their specific sociolinguistic contexts.

Before further elaborating on this and related points, let us first discuss the terms "model," "standard," and "norm" as these are used with reference to English.

MODEL, STANDARD, AND NORM

These three terms are generally used as synonyms in literature related to language pedagogy or in prescriptive texts on pronunciation and usage. In language evaluation these terms refer to proficiency in language acquisition, and attitudinally they indicate acceptance in certain circles.

What Are the Norms For English?

In the case of *non-native* speakers of English, when we talk of a norm, we imply conformity with a model based on the language used by a segment of the native speakers. The language use of this segment attains the status of a preferred norm for mainly extralinguistic characteristics (for example, education, class, and status).

In English the prescribed norm does not refer to the use by a majority. The motivations for such a preferred norm stem from pedagogical, attitudinal, and societal reasons, and are not due to any authoritative or organized move for codification, as is the case with some other European and non-European languages.

The imposed norms for English lack any overt sanction or authority; whatever norms there are have acquired preference for social reasons. These are indirectly, or sometimes directly, suggested in dictionaries of English, in pedagogical manuals, in preferred models on television and radio, and in job preferences when a particular variety of language is attitudinally considered desirable by an employer, whether it is a government agency, private employer, or a teaching institution. Through such imagined or real societal advantages of a norm, parents develop their preferences for the type of instruction their children should get in the school system. The case in point is Black English in the United States. On linguistic (or logical) grounds one cannot consider it a *deficient* variety (see, for example, Burling 1973 and Labov 1970), but for current attitudinal reasons it certainly restricts access to the cherished spheres of activities that all enlightened parents want their children to enter and succeed in. The same is true of various local varieties of British English. Thus members of a speech community share the belief that adherence to a certain preferred norm provides advantages for mobility, advancement, and status. In Britain, what are called "public" schools became the centers fostering adherence to such norms, and conscious efforts were made there to cultivate and preserve them.

The lack of an organized agency for language codification did not dampen the enthusiasm of the proponents of such norms for English. It is a fact—and a well-documented one (see, for example, Heath 1977; Kachru 1981b; Kahane and Kahane 1977; Laird 1970)—that the "guardians of language" failed to provide such codification as has been provided by the Academies for French, Spanish, Italian, or, more recently, Hebrew. It was, however, not for want of such effort. Attempts to establish an academy for the standardization of English were made on both sides of the Atlantic in the eighteenth century, just sixty years apart. In 1712, Jonathan Swift wrote an often-quoted letter to "the Most Honourable Robert, Earl of Oxford and Mortimer, Lord High Treasurer of Great Britain," outlining "A Proposal for Correcting, Improving and Ascertaining the English Tongue." The proposal was both a complaint and a plea:

My Lord; I do here, in the Name of all the Learned and Polite Persons of the Nation, complain to your Lordship, as *First Minister*, that our Language is extremely imperfect; that its daily Improvements are by no means in proportion to its daily Corruptions; that the Pretenders to polish and refine it have chiefly multiplied Abuses and Absurdities; and, that in many Instances, it offends against every part of Grammar.

What did Swift have "most at Heart?" He wanted codification with the aim "that some Method should be thought on for *ascertaining* and *fixing* our Language for ever, after such Alterations are made in it as shall be thought requisite." The persons undertaking this task "will have the example of the French before them, to imitate where they have proceeded right, and to avoid their mistakes." The proposed goal then would be to provide linguistic watchdogs:

Besides the grammar part, wherein we are allowed to be very defective, they will observe many gross improprieties, which, however authorized by practice, and grown familiar, ought to be discarded. They will find many words that deserve to be utterly thrown out of our language, many more to be corrected, and perhaps not a few long since antiquated, which ought to be restored on account of their energy and sound. (Swift, reprinted 1907:14−15)

The second such proposal, submitted by John Adams, came before the Continental Congress of another major English-speaking country, the United States, in 1780. This proposal, somewhat more precise than its predecessor, asked for a "public institution" for "refining, correcting, improving, and ascertaining the English language" (1856:VII:249−50). This proposal is almost an echo of Swift's. Swift's proposal did not go too far because of Queen Anne's death, and Adam's proposal was disapproved, as Heath states (1977:10), since "the founding fathers believed the individual's freedoms to make language choices and changes represented a far more valuable political asset to the new nation than did a state decision to remove these freedoms from the individual." It was therefore "a policy not to have a policy."

In retrospect, the failure to establish such an academy for English had its advantages. Since there was no authorized establishment for linguistic codification, no organized resistance to a norm could develop. It is not so easy to fight against the subtle and psychologically effective means of codification that were used for establishing a norm for English.

One might, therefore, say that each identifiable native variety of English can provide a norm for English. The identification may be in terms of some characteristic formal features that are realized in pronunciation, lexicon, or grammar. These features may then be associated with the localized variety of English. In linguistic terms, one may identify the *Americanness* in American English; and in a geographical (political) sense, one might use terms such as

"Canadian English" or "Australian English." One is, of course, aware of further subvarieties within these broad categories. The natively spoken varieties are: American (182 million); Australian (13 million); British (55 million); Canadian (13 million); and New Zealand (3 million).

But in reality the question is not that simple. The native varieties of English also have a long history of debate concerning the desirability of having an exo-normative (external) or an endo-normative (local) model. This controversy developed into a fascinating debate in, for example, America (see Kahane and Kahane 1977; Mencken 1919), and is of specific interest to a student of language loyalty and language attitudes. Once that controversy was settled, two main models (norms) remained: Received Pronunciation (RP), and General American (GA) English.

These models gained currency for two reasons. Attitudinally, the prestige of the speakers of such varieties resulted in their emulation by others. Pedagogically, they served as two well-documented models of pronunciation. For example, in the works of Jones for RP and Kenyon for GA (see also Krapp 1919), we have earlier valuable manuals and descriptions of pronunciation and dictionaries.

Received Pronunciation has alternately been termed "BBC English" (standing for the British Broadcasting Corporation), "educated English," and "public school English." (The term "public" school, when used in the British sense, traditionally means a "private" school.) "Public schools" refers to the old typically British institutions which, as Abercrombie says (1951:12), "are themselves unique." Received Pronunciation is by and large acquired unconsciously; therefore, as Abercrombie observes, "there is no question of deliberately teaching it." (See also Gimson 1962 and Ward 1929). It has, however, been treated as the main pedagogical norm for the *export* variety of British English, especially for tapes and records and pronunciation manuals used in classrooms.

But the status of this accent, and the term used for it, has been controversial. The "social judgment" that gave it a predominant position and prestige is now being challenged—after all, it had no official status. However, RP was considered a proper and desirable "accent" for government assignments and diplomatic services, and it was widely used by the ubiquitous BBC. But within the changed British context Abercrombie (1951) has provided three valid arguments against RP. First, recognition of such a standard variety is "an anachronism in present-day democratic society" (p. 14); second, it provides an "accent bar" reminiscent of the color bar, and "to many people, on the right side of the bar, it appears eminently reasonable" (p. 15); lastly, it is also debatable whether RP represents "educated English," since RP speakers are "outnumbered these days by the undoubtedly educated people who do not talk RP" (p. 15).

On the other side of the Atlantic, the use of "General American" is misleading, since the term covers parts of the United States and most of

Canada. GA is spoken by 90 million people in the central and western United States and Canada. Kenyon's motivations for describing GA were almost opposite to those of his British predecessor Jones. As I have stated elsewhere (Kachru 1982a:34), Kenyon is "conscious of the harm done by the elitist, prescriptivist manuals for pronunciation," and his concern is that "we accept rules of pronunciation as authoritative without inquiry into either the validity of the rules or the fitness of their authors to promulgate them" (1924:3). He is, therefore, attacking the shibboleth of correctness, the validity of prescriptive "judgments" and "advice" concerning pronunciation. He rightly believes that the underlying cause for such judgments is that people tend to be influenced by "certain types of teaching in the schools, by the undiscriminating use of textbooks on grammar and rhetoric, by unintelligent use of the dictionary, by manuals of 'correct English,' each with its favorite (and different) shibboleth" (1924:3).

Kenyon clearly expresses the evident disparity between linguistic norm and behavior and rightly asserts that "probably no intelligent person actually expects cultivated people in the South, the East, and the West to pronounce alike. Yet much criticism, or politely silent contempt, of the pronunciations of cultivated people in other localities than our own is common" (1924:5). In his perhaps too simplistic view, the remedy for such an attitude is the study of phonetics, since a student of phonetics "soon learns not only to refrain from criticizing pronunciations that differ from his own, but to expect them and listen for them with respectful, intelligent interest."

What, then, is the generally accepted norm for English? There are several ways of answering this multifaceted and attitudinally loaded question. Ward (1929:1) has taken one extreme position concerning a standard when she says, "No one can adequately define it, because such a thing does not exist." It is clear that Daniel Jones would not necessarily agree. Strevens (1981:8) answers this question very differently. In his view, in the case of English, "standard" does not mean "imposed," or a language "of the majority"; he believes that an interesting aspect of Standard English is "that in every English-using community those who habitually use *only* Standard English are in a minority: over the global population of English-users mono-dialectal Standard English users are in a very small minority" (1981:8). The situation seems to be that "the phenomenon of Standard English exists and maintains itself without any conscious or coordinated programme of standardization" (p. 8).

Despite these positions, the dictionaries and manuals do indicate preferred pronunciation as well as the use of certain grammatical forms and lexical items. The "minority" use in such cases does not necessarily refer to the numerical use, but may refer to preference in attitudinal terms, too. A frequent usage is not always the usage that is attitudinally or socially accepted.

Teaching materials and teacher training programs do not generally present a "linguistically tolerant" attitude toward non-native localized varieties, or toward the speakers of varieties considered different from the "standard" ones. As mentioned earlier, in the United States one notices this attitude toward Black English (or other ethnic Englishes). In Britain such an attitude has traditionally been present toward the speakers of regional varieties. Therefore, it is not only the non-native users of English who suffer from this attitude.

Norm for Non-Native Englishes

The historical development of non-native varieties of English is closely related to colonization. Attitudinally, the colonizers' English became the preferred norm once English was introduced in the linguistic network of a country. But actually, the "norm" provided by the representatives of the Raj was not always the "standard" variety of English. In a number of cases, English teachers were not even native speakers of the language, especially in convent schools, or in other missionary establishments using Belgian, French, or Irish teachers. (The native speakers were very rarely RP speakers; for instance, a significant number of them came from Scotland, Wales, or Ireland.)

We thus have, broadly speaking, two models for non-native Englishes. The largest population of non-native English speakers considered British English as their model in large parts of Asia, Africa, and the Caribbean. On the other hand, American English served as a model where American influence reached because of colonization (the Philippines, see Llamzon 1969, Samonte 1981; Puerto Rico, see Zentella 1981), trade and commerce (Japan, see Stanlaw 1982), or geographical proximity and other impact (Mexico, Cuba, or other parts of Latin America).

There was, however, a mythical quality about the native models. In reality, it is doubtful that one homogeneous model was ever introduced in the colonies. Colonial administrators, teachers, and military personnel provided a confusing spectrum of varieties of English. Thus the native speakers of English never formed more than a fraction of English instructors in a majority of the colonies; certainly in South Asia their numbers were insignificant, and their impact on the teaching of English was negligible.

Types of Non-Native Englishes

The varieties of non-native Englishes cannot be presented in terms of a misleading and unrealistic native–versus–non-native dichotomy. An earlier study (Kachru 1982d:37) has suggested that one must consider these varieties in the following four contexts: *acquisitional, sociocultural, motivational,* and *functional.*

A further division is possible; for example,

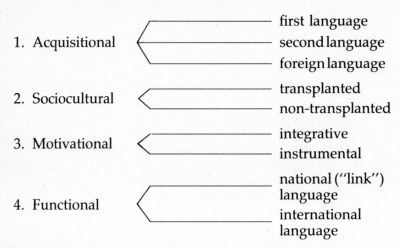

1. Acquisitional ⟨ first language / second language / foreign language

2. Sociocultural ⟨ transplanted / non-transplanted

3. Motivational ⟨ integrative / instrumental

4. Functional ⟨ national ("link") language / international language

In literature another well-motivated distinction has already been introduced (see Catford 1959; Halliday et al. 1964) between the *first-*, *second-*, and *foreign*-language varieties of English (see also Kachru 1982a). Alternately, the second- and foreign-language varieties have been termed the *institutionalized* and *performance* varieties (see particularly Kachru and Quirk 1981; Kachru 1981 and 1982d). This is an important distinction, because it brings us to the question of exo-normative (external) and endo-normative (local) standards for the non-native Englishes.

A non-native variety generally acquires an identity in terms of either political boundaries (e.g., *Indian* English, *Lankan* English, *Kenyan* English) or a larger geographical area (e.g., African English, South Asian English, or Southeast Asian English).[2] The identificational labels of the first type (Indian, Lankan), which provide clues to the political boundaries, are not necessarily instructive. The impression of divisiveness in world Englishes that such labels present is actually not present in real-life contexts. The variety-marking clues are determined, by and large, by the underlying linguistically and culturally shared characteristics of an area. In this sense, then, terms such as "African English" or Africanization (see Bokamba 1982) or South Asianization (see Kachru 1969 [1978] and 1982b) are more appropriate. But these terms, too, are useful only to the extent that they provide insights about the shared characteristics at various levels within various regional varieties. They are only as reflective of the true situation as are the terms "American English" or "British English." They mask the linguistic heterogeneity within a region, and to some extent serve to reassure those who are alarmed by what is considered divisiveness within the English-speech community.

We then have, on the one hand, a "standard" or "educated" variety for a larger region, and within it several subvarieties. There is thus a cline in bilingualism in English (Kachru 1965). Subvarieties are identifiable on the basis of region, ethnic identity, education, function, etc. In each region we have studies that identify such subvarieties—e.g., in Nigeria (Bamgbose 1982); Kenya (Zuengler 1982); India (Schuchardt 1891 [1980]; Kachru 1969 [1978] and 1983); Singapore and Malaysia (Platt and Weber 1980; Wong 1981; Tay and Gupta 1981); and the Philippines (Llamzon 1969 and 1981).

A speaker of a non-native variety may engage in a variety-shift, depending on the participants in a situation. An educated Indian English speaker may attempt to approximate a native-English model while speaking to an Englishman or an American, but switch to the localized educated variety when talking to a fellow Indian colleague, and further Indianize his English when communicating with a shopkeeper, a bus conductor, or an office clerk. These are thus degrees of approximation to a norm, depending on the context, participants, and the desired end result of a speech act.

The concept of cline in non-native varieties of English has been recognized for almost a century now (see Schuchardt 1891 [1980]), and has been illustrated in various studies (for example, for South Asian English see Kachru 1965 and later; for a general bibliography see Kachru 1983 and 1982d). Strevens (1977: 140–141) sums up the situation well with references to Indian English:

> The Indian (Pakistani) doctor who communicates easily in English with professional colleagues at an international medical conference is using a type of "Indian English" . . . in which Standard English dialect is spoken with a regional accent. The Indian clerk who uses English constantly in his daily life for communicating with other Indians, by correspondence or telephone, may employ an "Indian English" in which the dialect is not Standard English and the accent is regional or local. The lorry-driver who uses English occasionally, as a *lingua franca*, may be using an "Indian English" which is for all practical purposes a pidgin. It is the second of these three examples which constitutes the typical "Indian English" and which frequently attracts the criticism of the teaching profession. But is criticism justified? The ultimate test of effectiveness of a variety of language is whether it meets the communication needs of those who use it. Clearly, "Indian English" of this second type would not be adequate for the professional man to communicate with an international audience, but it probably does serve local needs well enough, just as all local dialects and accents do. (See also Kachru 1981a.)

It is difficult to say how many people use various types of Englishes (say, as standard localized varieties or pidgins) as non-native varieties across cultures and languages. One has no reliable way of knowing it since English is learned around the world in unimaginable situations. On the one hand, people learn it in "English teaching shops" in bazaars from people who can hardly use the language. On the other hand, those who have resources learn English from highly accomplished teachers in ideal language learning situations. Whatever the actual statistics, the number of bilinguals who know English is fast increasing, and English has already acquired the status of a universal language (see

Kachru 1981b). This status is essentially due to the use of English in non-native contexts. The spread of English continues, and is now controlled by its non-native users; it is their initiative that is planning and coordinating the role of English in the developing world. The figures in Table 4.1 give some idea about the demographic distribution of English around the world, but they exclude a large number of users who are not enrolled in traditional educational establishments.

TABLE 4.1. ENROLLMENT IN ENGLISH AS A
SECOND LANGUAGE

Area	Students (millions)
India	17.6
Philippines	9.8
USSR	9.7
Japan	7.9
Nigeria	3.9
Bangladesh	3.8
Republic of South Africa	3.5
West Germany	2.5
Malaysia	2.4
France	2.4
Indonesia	1.9
Mexico	1.9
South Korea	1.8
Pakistan	1.8
Kenya	1.7
Ghana	1.6
Brazil	1.6
Egypt	1.5
Quebec	1.5
Thailand	1.3
Taiwan	1.2
Sri Lanka	1.2
Netherlands	1.1
Iran	1.0
Tanzania	1.0

Source: Gage and Ohannessian 1974

Development of Localized Norms

The various historical phases involved in the development of localized models for English cannot be traced precisely. Instead, one must trace the changing attitudes toward such varieties. It is like recognizing the presence of a linguistic behavior that was there all along but that attitudinally lacked status. The Indians, the Africans, the Malays, or the Filipinos have struggled with this myth and reality since English first became part of their educational system and linguistic repertoire. University teachers generally defended the exo-normative standard, often not realizing that they themselves used and taught to their students a transparent local accent. More important, the ever-present localized innovations in lexis and grammar (e.g., Africanisms, Indianisms) gradually gained currency.

But then the conflict in attitudes toward local varieties was also always present. Therefore, when we discuss the development of a model, we are not focusing on the distinct stages through which a norm passes before it gains some kind of ontological status. These attitudinal stages have been presented in Kachru 1982a, and we shall briefly summarize them here with a note of warning. These stages are not clear-cut and mutually exclusive; they are primarily related to the extent of the diffusion of bilingualism and to the institutionalization of a variety. The first stage seems to be non-recognition of a localized variety and clear indifference to it. This is followed by a stage in which the localized variety is recognized (e.g., Indian, Lankan, Kenyan); but it is always the *other* person who uses it. Again, there is clear disparity between the norm and behavior. The third stage shows a reduction in such an attitude. A controversy develops between the defenders of the localized variety and those who prefer a exo-normative standard (see Kachru 1982a: 39–40). This is clearly evident in the following study of Indian English users.[3] The study is based on a questionnaire given to 700 undergraduates and 196 faculty members at major universities in India. In Table 4.2 and 4.3 percentages do not sum to 100 percent because the numbers are based on the total sample, whether or not respondents answered these questions. In the final stage, teaching materials for English are prepared with nativized contexts; English is not used just with an integrative motivation involving another culture, but essentially as an instrument for exposing students to their own culture. It is like turning an "external"

TABLE 4.2. INDIAN GRADUATE STUDENTS'
ATTITUDE TOWARD VARIOUS MODELS OF
ENGLISH AND RANKING OF MODELS ACCORDING
TO PREFERENCE

Model	Preference		
	I	II	III
American English	5.17	13.19	21.08
British English	67.60	9.65	1.08
Indian English	22.72	17.82	10.74
I don't care		5.03	
"Good" English		1.08	

TABLE 4.3. FACULTY PREFERENCE FOR MODELS OF
ENGLISH FOR INSTRUCTION

Model	Preference		
	I	II	III
American English	3.07	14.35	25.64
British English	66.66	13.33	1.53
Indian English	26.66	25.64	11.79
I don't know		5.12	

TABLE 4.4. GRADUATE STUDENTS'
SELF-LABELING OF THE VARIETY
OF THEIR ENGLISH

Identity Marker	%
American English	2.58
British English	29.11
Indian English	55.64
"Mixture" of all three	2.99
I don't know	8.97
"Good" English	.27

Source: Kachru 1976:230–232.

language around for an "inward" look. The "window on the world," or "library language," becomes a window on one's own culture, history, and traditions. Furthermore, the variety develops its own nativized registers and is used in imaginative or creative contexts (see Kachru 1981a, 1982c, and 1983), albeit by a small group of people. In this sense, English becomes part of the local literary and cultural traditions (see, for example, Sridhar 1982).

Norm at Various Levels

The term "norm," as is generally discussed in literature, does not apply only to the phonetic/phonological levels. A language user may reveal his or her variety of lexical, grammatical, or discoursal features. However, the largest number of attitudinal comments—or displays of intolerance—concern pronunciation (generally discussed in terms of a person's "accent.") This is the aspect of use discussed in various manuals. The variety's lexical, collocational, grammatical, and discoursal features are often looked upon as "mistakes." This aspect has been discussed in several studies, and I shall not reiterate it here (see Kachru 1982b).

In linguistic literature, it was in the 1960s that attention was first drawn to the distinction between a "mistake" and a "deviation" in the context of non-native Englishes. (For references and discussion, see particularly Kachru 1982a.) The deviation at various levels is directly related to the degree of nativization (see Kachru 1981a and Kachru and Quirk 1981). The attitude toward nativization is determined by the extent of a variety's institutionalization; the institutionalization, in turn, depends on the *range* and *depth* of a variety in a particular context. The range of a variety refers to its extension into various cultural, social, educational, and commercial contexts. The greater the range of functions, the more subvarieties a variety develops. The term *depth* relates to the penetration of bilingualism into various strata of society.

The attitude toward variety-specific characteristics (for example, lexical and grammatical; see Smith 1981; Kachru 1982d, Bailey and Görlach 1982) is largely determined by whether a variety is used as a first or a second language. Labelling a word or a formation an Americanism, Australianism, or Canadianism is one way of characterizing it as deviant from "mother English." The history of attitudinal conflict even toward the native transplanted varieties is fascinating and has been discussed in a variety of popular and scholarly works.[4] The case of institutionalized non-native varieties has been much more difficult. Any deviation in such varieties has been termed a "mistake" or an "error." The "native speaker" has traditionally determined the extent of acceptable deviation, both linguistic and contextual (see Kachru 1965).

It is clear that, for English, the concept of "native speaker" has doubtful validity.[5] Since English is used across cultures and languages in a multitude of international and intranational contexts, the "deviations" must be seen in those functional contexts. This, then, leads us to another question that is crucial for understanding the relationship of the localized (or regional) varieties and the norm: What are the motivations for deviations?

The deviations in localized non-native varieties cannot in every case be characterized as linguistic aberrations because of acquisitional inadequacies. That rash generalization would miss serious underlying reasons for such innovations and would thus imply negating the context in which a language functions. The acculturation of a variety occurs over a period of time in a distinctly "un-English" context.[6] (A number of such case studies have been presented in Kachru, ed., 1982d.) The English language has now ceased to be a vehicle of Western culture; it only marginally carries the British and American way of life. In 1956, the British linguist J. R. Firth correctly observed (Firth 1956 in Palmer 1968:97):

> . . . "The study of English" is so vast that it must be further circumscribed to make it at all manageable. To begin with, English is an international language in the Commonwealth, the Colonies and in America. International in the sense that English serves the American way of life and might be called American, it serves the Indian way of life and has recently been declared an Indian language within the framework of the federal constitution. In another sense, it is internatonal not only in Europe but in Asia and Africa, and serves various African ways of life and is increasingly the all-Asian language of politics. Secondly, and I say "secondly" advisedly, English is the key to what is described in a common cliché as "the British way of life."

English is thus a medium that in its various manifestations, East and West, results in cultural adaptations. In South Asia it connotes the Indian, Lankan, or Pakistani ways of life and patterns of education and administration. The nativized formal characteristics acquire a new pragmatic context, a new defining context, culturally very remote from that of Britain or America. I have provided a number of illustrations in various studies (see Kachru 1965 and later, particularly 1982b) in which deviations have been related to the "social meaning" of the text peculiar to the culture in which English is used as a non-native language. I am taking the liberty of quoting the relevant parts below (1982b:329–330).

In terms of acculturation, two processes seem to be at work. One results in the deculturation of English, and another in its acculturation in the new context. The latter gives it an appropriate identity in its newly acquired functions. The Indians have captured the two-faceted process by using the typical Sanskrit compound *dvija* ("twice-born") for Indian English. (The term was originally used for the Brahmins who, after their natural birth, are considered reborn at the time of caste initiation.) Firth (1956: in Palmer 1968:96) therefore is correct in saying that "an Englishman must de-Anglicize himself"; as must, one could add, an American "de-Americanize" himself, in their attitudes toward such varieties, and for a proper appreciation of such acculturation of Englishes (see Kachru 1983).

This initiation of English into new culturally and linguistically dependent communicative norms forces a redefinition of our linguistic and contextual parameters for understanding the new language types and discourse types. Those who are outside these cultures must go through a variety shift in order to understand both the written and the spoken modes of such varieties. One cannot, realistically speaking, apply the norms of one variety to another variety. I am not using the term "norm" to refer only to formal deviations (see Kachru 1982a); rather, I intend to refer to the underlying universe of discourse which makes linguistic interaction a pleasure and provides it with "meaning." It is the whole process of, as Halliday says, learning "how to mean" (1974). It is a very culture-bound concept. To understand a bilingual's mind and use of language, one would have, ideally, to be ambilingual and ambicultural. One would have to share responses to events, and cultural norms, and interpret the use of L2 within that context. One would have to see how the context of culture is manifest in linguistic form, in the new style range, and in the assumptions one makes about the speech acts in which L2 is used. A tall order, indeed!

This redefined cultural identity of the non-native varieties has not usually been taken into consideration. There have been primarily three types of studies in this area. The first type forms the main body—understandably so, since these are devoted to pedagogical concerns. In such studies, any deviation has been interpreted as violating a prescriptive norm, and thus resulting in a "mistake." The urge for prescriptivism has been so strong that any innovation which is not according to the native speaker's linguistic code is considered a linguistic aberration. If one makes too many such "mistakes," it is treated as an indication of a language user's linguistic deprivation or deficiency. Second, some linguistic studies focus on formal characteristics without attempting to relate them to function, or to delve into the contextual needs for such innovations. This separation between use and usage has masked several sociolinguistically important factors about these varieties. The third group of studies deals with the "contact literature" in English, perhaps used on the analogy of "contact languages." Such literature is a product of multicultural and multilingual speech communities, and it extends the scope of English literature to "literatures in English." Most such studies are concerned with the themes, rather than with style. (For further discussion, see, e.g., Sridhar 1982.)

Norm vs. Intelligibility

One major motivation for having a norm is that it maintains intelligibility (see Nelson 1982, Smith 1979)[7] among speakers of distinct localized varieties of English. According to this view, a prescriptive norm is vital for communication. At least three problems exist in using the concept of intelligibility with any rigor. First, although one always encounters this term in pedagogical literature and in studies on second-language acquisition, it is unfortunately the least researched and least understood concept in cross-cultural and cross-linguistic contexts. Second, whatever research is available on the second-language varieties of English primarily focuses on phonetics, specifically on the segmental phonemes. (The limitations of such research have been discussed by Nelson 1982.) The interference in intelligibility at other levels, especially in communicative units (see, for example, Kachru 1982b) has hardly been understood. Third, in the case of English, we must be clear about whom we have in mind when we talk of participants in a linguistic interaction. What role does a native speaker's judgment play in determining the intelligibility of non-native speech acts that have intranational functions in, for example, Asia or Africa? The variety-specific speech acts are vital for communication, as has been shown in Chishimba (1981) and various studies in Kachru (1982d). In international contexts certainly one might say that an idealized native speaker could serve as a model. But in the cases of institutionalized varieties, a *native* speaker is not a participant in the actual speech situation. Localized uses are determined by the context of each English-using country, and the phonetic approximation is only part of the language act. The nativized lexical spread and the rhetorical and stylistic features are distinctly different from those of the native speaker.

How many users of the institutionalized varieties use English to interact with *native* speakers of English? I have shown in another pilot study (Kachru 1976:233) that, out of all users of Indian English, only a fraction have an interaction with native speakers of English. For example, among the graduate faculty of English in the universities and colleges I surveyed, 65.64 percent had only occasional interaction with native speakers, and 11.79 percent had no interaction with them. Only 5.12 percent claimed to have daily interaction with native speakers. I should, however, warn the reader that this survey was restricted to a highly specialized segment of the English-using population of India—professionals involved in teaching English at the graduate level (see Kachru 1975a and 1976). The results for those not involved in the teaching of English, especially at the graduate level, will be different. What, then, is the issue? The issue is more complex than has been presented in literature.

There can be no one "mononorm" approach to this concern. As is true with native varieties, the intelligibility of the (non-native) institutionalized varieties of English forms a cline. The intelligibility within the extended group depends on various sociolinguistic parameters of region, age, education, and social role. Ward (1929:5) gives some indication of the situation in Britain:

> It is obvious that in a country the size of the British Isles, any one speaker should be capable of understanding any other when he is talking English. At the present moment, such is not the case: a Cockney speaker would not be understood by a dialect speaker of Edinburgh or Leeds or Truro, and dialect speakers of much nearer districts than these would have difficulty in understanding each other.

This observation, made over half a century ago, is still valid. One might add that, given the ethnic, cultural, and linguistic pluralism of the United States, the situation has become even more complex there (see Ferguson and Heath 1981). Once we move to the second-language contexts of English in Africa, Asia, or the Pacific, the situation appears to be perplexing.

But there is a pragmatically refreshing side to all these situations. What appears to be a complex linguistic situation at the surface, in Britain, in America, in Africa, or in South Asia, is less complex if one attempts to understand it from another perspective. In his cone-shaped diagram (reproduced in Ward 1929:5; see Figure 4.1), Daniel Jones has graphically shown that "as we near the apex, the divergences which still exist have become so small as to be noticed only by a finely trained ear" (Ward 1929:6). Ward rightly provides the argument of "convenience or expediency" (p. 7), suggesting that "the regional dialect may suffice for those people who have no need to move from their own districts."

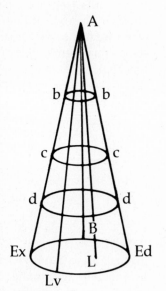

Figure 4.1.

In this I find a clear case of parallelism between the native and institutionalized non-native varieties of English. The intelligibility is functionally determined with reference to the sub-region, the nation, political areas within the region (e.g., South Asia, Southeast Asia), and internationally. True, educated (standard) Indian English, Singapore English, Nigerian English, or Kenyan English is not identical to RP or GA. It is different; it *should* be different. Do such educated varieties of non-native Englishes create more problems of intelligibility than does, for example, a New Zealander when he or she talks to a midwestern American?

In some situations, the markers of *difference* may establish a desirable identity. Such formal markers provide a regional and national identity and help in establishing an immediate bond with another person from the same region or country. The desire for retaining such markers has been well presented in the following observation by T. T. Koh, Singapore's Representative to the United Nations:

> . . . when one is abroad, in a bus or train or aeroplane and when one overhears someone speaking, one can immediately say this is someone from Malaysia or Singapore. And I should hope that when I'm speaking abroad my countrymen will have no problem recognizing that I am a Singaporean (cited in Tongue 1974:iv).

Almost half a century ago, the British linguist J. R. Firth (1930:196) presented the same idea in a wider context and in stronger words. He rejected "a shameful negative English" that "effectually masks social and local origin." He went a step further and considered such attempts "a suppression of all that is vital in speech."

ATTITUDES TOWARD LOCALIZED NORMS

Let us consider the attitudes of two distinct groups toward the localized norms of English. One group consists of the *native* English speakers who traditionally have been considered crucial for such judgment. This group's attitude is reflected in three ways—first, in the teaching materials produced for non-native users. Until recently, such texts attempted primarily to introduce the reader to Western (British or American) culture; this is, however, slowly changing now. Second, one notices the native speaker's attitude in the books specifically written to train teachers of English as a second language. Such books make no attempt to show the institutionalization of English in other cultures, or to portray the non-Western contexts in which English is nativized. Third, practically no mention is made of the development of non-native English literatures, and of the uses one can make of this body of literature. In this discussion of English across cultures we find on the one hand the extreme position of, for example, Prator (1968), versus the position typified in Smith 1981 (see especially the Introduction by Kachru and Quirk). The position presented in Smith (1981) or in Kachru (1982d) is still held by only a small group of people and does not represent the view of the profession.

The fact that non-native users of English have demonstrated no unified identity and no loyalty toward localized norms, does not, however, imply that there has been no serious thinking in this direction. One does notice a shift from earlier conflict between the actual linguistic behavior and the norm; attitudinally now there is a realization about the pragmatics of language use. The discussion is either directly related to the question or indirectly related to this issue. This debate, however, is not recent; rather, it started when the institutionalization of English was recognized, and the English language—in spite of the attitude toward the British raj—was being considered an important member of the local linguistic repertoire. In India, for example, the educator and a distinguished English scholar Amar Nath Jha said, in 1940, almost with tongue in cheek:

> May I . . . venture to plead for the use, retention, and encouragement of Indian English? . . . Is there any reason why we need be ashamed of Indian English? Who is there in the United Provinces [Uttar Pradesh] who will not understand a young man who had enjoyed a *freeship* at college, and who says he is going to join the *teachery* profession and who after a few years says, he is engaged in *headmastery*? Similarly, why should we accept the English phrase *mare's nest*, and object to *horse's egg*, so familiar in the columns of *Amrita Bazar Patrika*? Why should we adhere to *all this* when *this all* is the natural order suggested by the usage of our language? Why insist on *yet* following *though* when in Hindustani we use the equivalent of *but*? Must we condemn the following sentence because it does not conform to English idiom even though it is literal translation of our own idiom? *I shall not pay a pice what to say of a rupee.* Is there any rational ground for objecting to *family members* and adhering to *members of the family*? . . . A little courage, some determination, a wholesome respect for our own idioms and we shall before long have a virile, vigorous *Indian English* (quoted in Kachru 1965).

Dustoor (reproduced in Dustoor 1968:126; see also Kachru 1982c) makes a firmer claim by saying that "there will be a more or less indigenous flavor about our English. In our imagery, in our choice of words, in the nuances of meaning we put into our words, we must be expected to be different from Englishmen and Americans alike."

We lack in-depth empirical studies concerning the opinions of teachers, students, and educators about an exo-normative standard. But educators in those areas where English has been institutionalized (e.g., Africa, Asia, the Pacific) have commented on this question in asides, or in discussion of other issues related to the localized varieties. In Nigeria, Bamgbose (1971:41) clearly indicates that "the aim is not to produce speakers of British Received Pronunciation (even if this were feasible). . . . Many Nigerians will consider as affected or even snobbish any Nigerians who speak like a native speaker of English." In Ghana, an *educated* Ghanaian is expected to speak, as Sey says (1973:1), the localized *educated* variety of English, and it does not mean, warns Sey, "the type that strives too obviously to approximate to RP. . . ." An imitation of RP "is frowned upon as distasteful and pedantic."

In South Asia, one notices the same reaction to the imitation of exo-normative standards such as RP or GA. In the case of Sri Lanka (Ceylon) Passé comments (1947:33), "It is worth noting, too, that Ceylonese [Sri Lankans] who speak 'standard English' are generally unpopular. There are several reasons for this: those who now speak standard English either belong to a favored social class, with long purses which can take them to English public schools and universities, and so are disliked too much to be imitated, or have rather painfully acquired this kind of speech for social reasons and so are regarded as the apes of their betters; they are singular in speaking English as the majority of their countrymen cannot or will not speak it. . . . Standard English has thus rather unpleasant associations when it is spoken by Ceylonese [Sri Lankans]." During the last half-century the tendency in Sri Lanka is more toward favoring the localized norm (see Kandiah 1981). In the Philippines, "Standard Filipino English" is *"the type of English which educated Filipinos speak and which is acceptable in educated Filipino circles"* (Llamzon 1969:15).

In such observations one notices that an unrealistic adherence to an exonormative standard is clearly not attitudinally desirable. In most cases such discussions are specifically addressed to the spoken norm for English. Localized lexical innovations have always been recognized as legitimate and as a manifestation of nativization. (I have discussed this aspect in detail in Kachru 1973, 1975b, and 1980.) But the nativization is not restricted to phonology and lexis. As stated in an earlier study (see Kachru 1982d:7), it also shows in "collocational innovation, in syntactic simplification or overgeneralization, and in the use of native rhetorical and stylistic devices. In short, nativization creates a new ecology for non-native language. Who is to judge the appropriateness (or acceptance) of formations such as *swadeshi cloth*, *military hotel* (nonvegetarian hotel), or *lathi charge* in the Indian context; *dunno drums*, *bodim bead*, *chewing-sponge*, or *knocking-fee* in the African context; and *minor-wife* in the Thai context?"

CONCLUSION

The question of norms for localized Englishes continues to be debated, though the tone is becoming more one of realism and less one of codification. Furthermore, the *educated* non-native varieties are now being increasingly recognized and defended, both on attitudinal and on pedagogical grounds. The national uses of English are being separated from the international uses, and the nativized innovations are now being considered as essential stylistic devices for non-native English literatures. One notices a shift of opinion toward considering such localized varieties *different*, not necessarily *deficient*.

One has to realize that there are several tendencies in the current spread of English. First, as stated earlier, perhaps English will soon have more nonnative users than native users. The non-native users show a wide range of proficiency, almost ranging from ambilingualism to broken English. But functionally, each variety within a variety serves its functional purpose. Second, the planning for the spread of English is steadily passing into the hands of its non-native users. These users have developed their own norms that are not identical to the norms labelled RP and GA. In some cases the deviation from the native norm is the result of economic and other reasons, for example, a lack of good teachers, non-availability of teaching equipment and materials. Thus the British or American norm actually is never presented to students learning English. In other situations, the recognition of a localized norm is used as a defense mechanism to reduce the "colonial" and "Western" connotations associated with English. Such an attitude is one way of expressing what may be termed "linguistic emancipation." But that is only part of the story. There are other more significant reasons, too. First, this is how human languages seem to work. After all, the example of Latin is before us which eventually evolved into Romance languages. And, in spite of strict codification, Sanskrit has developed into numerous regional varieties in South Asia. Second, there is no doubt that the development of non-native literatures in English (contact literatures) have contributed to the "norm-breaking" trend in English around the world. The most interesting nativized innovations are the result of such contact literature.

The complex functions of English across cultures and languages make it very clear that whatever is said about it internationally will present only part of the picture. Therefore, the moral of the Eastern story of the elephant and the four blind men should serve as a warning; it should encourage us to undertake more empirical work across cultures to comprehend the totality. That type of research has yet to be initiated in a serious sense.

NOTES

An earlier French version of this paper has appeared in *La Norme Linguistique*, edited by Edith Bédard and Jacques Maurais, Conseil de la Langue Française, Gouvernement du Québec, 1983. I am grateful to the Direction Générale des Publications Gouvernementales for their permission to publish this English version.

1. A selected bibliography on this topic is given in Kachru 1976, 1982a, and in Smith 1981.

2. For further discussion, see Kachru 1982c and "Introduction: The Other Side of English" in 1982d.

3. For further details about the sample and method used for this pilot study, see Kachru 1975a, 1976.

4. See, for discussion and references, among others, Finegan 1980; Heath 1977; Kahane and Kahane 1977, Kachru 1982d; Mencken 1919.

5. Note, for example, C. A. Ferguson's observation (in Kachru 1982d:vii): "Linguists, perhaps especially American linguists, have long given a special place to the native speaker as the only truly valid and reliable source of language data, whether those data are the elicited texts of the descriptivist or the intuitions the theorist works with. Yet much of the world's verbal communication takes place by means of languages which are not the users' mother tongue, but their second, third, or nth

language. . . . In fact, the whole mystique of native speaker and mother tongue should probably be quietly dropped from the linguists' set of professional myths about language."

6. See Kachru 1965 and later for discussion of this phenomenon in the case of South Asian English; for African English, see Bokamba 1982 and Chishimba 1981; 1983.

7. A comprehensive list of references on this topic is given in Nelson 1982.

REFERENCES

Abercrombie, D. 1951. "R. P. and local accent." *The Listener* **6**, September 1951. [Reprinted in D. Abercrombie, *Studies in phonetics and linguistics*. London: Oxford University Press, 1965.]

Bailey, R. W. and Görlach, M. (eds). 1982. *English as a world language*. Ann Arbor: University of Michigan Press.

Bamgbose, A. 1971. "The English language in Nigeria." In John Spencer (ed.) *The English language in West Africa*. London: Longmans.

———. 1982. "Standard Nigerian English: issues of identification." In Kachru (ed.) 1982d.

Bokamba, E. 1982. "The Africanization of English." In Kachru (ed.) 1982d.

Burling, R. 1973. *English in black and white*. New York: Holt, Rinehart, and Winston.

Catford, J. C. 1959. "The teaching of English as a foreign language." In R. Quirk and A. H. Smith (eds.). *The teaching of English*. London: Martin, Secker and Warburg. [Reprinted London: Oxford University Press, 1964.]

Chishimba, M. M. 1981. "Bilingual and bicultural aspects of African creative writing." Manuscript.

———. 1983. "African varieties of English: text in context." Ph.D. dissertation, Department of Linguistics, University of Illinois.

Dustoor, P. E. 1968. *The world of words*. Bombay: Asia Publishing House.

Ferguson, C. A. and S. B. Heath, eds. 1981. *Language in the USA*. New York: Cambridge University Press.

Finegan, E. 1980. *Attitude toward English usage: the history of a war of words*. New York: Teachers College Press.

Firth, J. R. 1930. *Speech*. London: Ernest Benn. (Reprinted London and New York: Oxford University Press. 1966.)
———. 1956. "Descriptive linguistics and the study of English." In F. R. Palmer (ed.) *Selected papers of J. R. Firth, 1952–1959*. Bloomington, IN: Indiana University Press.

Gage, W. W. and S. Ohannessian. 1974. "ESOL enrollments throughout the world." *Linguistic Reporter* **16.9**: 13–16.

Gimson, A. C. 1962. *An introduction to the pronunciation of English*. London: Edward Arnold.

Halliday, M. A. K. 1974. *Learning how to mean: explorations in the development of language*. London: Edward Arnold.

Halliday, M. A. K., A. McIntosh, P. Strevens. 1964. *The linguistic sciences and language teaching.* London: Longmans.

Heath, S. B. 1977. "A national language academy? Debate in the nation." *Linguistics: An International Review,* **189:** 9–43.

Jones, D. 1918. *An outline of English phonetics.* [Rev. ed., 1956.] Cambridge: Heffer.

———. 1956. *Everyman's English pronouncing dictionary.* London: Dent.

Kachru, B. B. 1965. "The *Indianness* in Indian English." *Word* **21:** 391–410.

———. 1966. "Indian English: a study in contextualization." In C. E. Bazell, J. C. Catford, M. A. K. Halliday, R. H. Robins (eds.). *In memory of J. R. Firth.* London: Longmans.

———. 1969. English in South Asia. In T. Sebeok (ed.). *Current trends in linguistics.* The Hague: Mouton. [A revised version in J. A. Fishman (ed.). *Advances in the study of societal multilingualism.* The Hague: Mouton. 1978.]

———. 1973. "Toward a lexicon of Indian English." In B. B. Kachru, R. B. Lees, Y. Malkiel, A. Pietrangeli, S. Saporta (eds.). *Issues in linguistics: papers in honor of Henry and Renée Kahane.* Urbana: University of Illinois Press.

———. 1975a. "A retrospective study of the Central Institute of English and Foreign Languages and its relation to Indian universities." In Melvin J. Fox. *Language and development: a retrospective survey of Ford Foundation language projects 1952–1974.* New York: The Ford Foundation.

———. 1975b. "Lexical innovations in South Asian English." *International Journal of the Sociology of Language* **4:** 55–94.

———. 1976. "Models of English for the third world: white man's linguistic burden or language pragmatics? *TESOL Quarterly* **10(2):** 221–239.

———. 1977. "The new Englishes and old models." *English Language Forum.* **3:** 29–35.

———. 1980. "The new Englishes and old dictionaries: directions in lexicographical research on non-native varieties of English." In L. Zgusta (ed.). *Theory and method in lexicography: western and non-Western perspectives.* Columbia, SC: Hornbeam Press.

———. 1981a. "The pragmatics of non-native varieties of English." In Smith 1981.

———. 1981b. "American English and other Englishes." In C. A. Ferguson and S. B. Heath (eds.) 1981.

———. 1982a. "Models for non-native Englishes." In Kachru (ed.) 1982d.

———. 1982b. "Meaning in deviation: toward understanding non-native English texts." In Kachru (ed.) 1982d.

———. 1982c. "South Asian English." In Bailey and Görlach (eds.) 1982.

———. ed. 1982d. *The other tongue: English across cultures.* Urbana IL: University of Illinois Press.

———. 1983. *The Indianization of English: the English language in India.* New Delhi and New York: Oxford University Press.

Kahane, H. and Kahane, R. 1977. "Virtues and vices in the American language: a history of attitudes." *TESOL Quarterly* **11(2):** 185–202.

Kandiah, T. 1981. "Lankan English schizoglossia." *English Worldwide: A Journal of Varieties of English* **2(1):** 63–81.

Kenyon, J. S. 1924. *American pronunciation.* Ann Arbor: George Wahr.

Kenyon, J. S. and Knott, T. A. 1953. *A pronouncing dictionary of American English.* Springfield, Mass.: Merriam.

Krapp, G. P. 1919. *Pronunciation of standard English in America.* New York: Oxford University Press.

Labov, W. 1970. "The logic of non-standard English." In J. E. Alatis (ed.). *Report of the 20th annual roundtable meeting on linguistics and language studies.* Monograph series on languages and linguistics. Washington: Georgetown University Press. pp. 1–43. Also in Labov, *Language in the inner city: studies in the black English vernacular.* Philadelphia: University of Pennsylvania Press.

Laird, C. 1970. *Language in America.* Englewood Cliffs, N.J.: Prentice-Hall, Inc.

Llamzon, T. A. 1969. *Standard Filipino English.* Manila: Ateno University Press.

———. 1981. "Essential features of new varieties of English." Paper presented at the seminar on varieties of English, SEAMEO Regional Language Center, Singapore, April 20–24, 1981.

Mencken, H. L. 1919. *The American language.* New York: Alfred A. Knopf.

Nelson, C. 1982. "Intelligibility and non-native varieties of English." In Kachru (ed.) 1982d.

Passé, H. A. 1947. "The English language in Ceylon." Unpublished Ph.D. dissertation, University of London.

Platt, J. T. and Weber, Heidi. 1980. *English in Singapore and Malaysia: status, features, functions.* Kuala Lumpur: Oxford University Press.

Prator, C. H. 1968. "The British heresy in TESL." In J. A. Fishman, C. A. Ferguson, and J. Das Gupta (eds.). *Language problems of developing nations.* New York: Wiley.

Quirk, R., S. Greenbaum, and J. Svartvik. 1972. *A grammar of contemporary English.* London: Longmans.

Samonte, A. L. 1981. "Teaching English for international and intranational purposes: the Philippine context." In Smith (ed.) 1981.

Schuchardt, H. 1891. "Das Indo-Englische." *Englische Studien* **15:** 286–305. [English translation in *Pidgin and creole languages: selected essays by Hugo Schuchardt,* ed. and trans. Glenn G. Gilbert. London and New York: Cambridge University Press.]

Sey, K. A. 1973. *Ghanian English: an exploratory survey.* London: Macmillan.

Smith, L. E., ed. 1981. *English for cross-cultural communication.* London: Macmillan.

Smith, L. E. and Rafiqzad, Khalilullah. 1979. "English for cross-cultural communication: the question of intelligibility." *TESOL Quarterly* **13(3):** 371–380.

Sridhar, S. N. 1982. "Non-native English literatures: context and relevance." In Kachru (ed.) 1982d.

Stanlaw, J. 1981. "English in Japanese communicative strategies." In Kachru (ed.) 1982d.

Strevens, P. 1977. *New orientations in the teaching of English.* London and New York: Oxford University Press.

―――. 1981. *Teaching English as an international language.* Oxford and New York: Pergamon.

Swift, J. 1907. "A proposal for correcting, improving and ascertaining the English tongue (1712)." In T. Scott (ed.). *The prose works of Jonathan Swift, vol. XI. Literary Essays.* London: Bell.

Tay, M. W. J., and Anthea F. Gupta. 1981. "Toward a description of standard Singapore English." Paper presented at the Sixteenth Regional Seminar, SEAMEO Regional Language Center, Singapore, April 20–24, 1981.

Tongue, R. K. 1974. *The English of Singapore and Malaysia.* Singapore: Eastern Universities Press.

Ward, I. C. 1929. *The phonetics of English.* Cambridge: Heffer.

Wong, I. F. H. 1981. "English in Malaysia." In Smith (ed.) 1981.

Zentella, A. C. 1981. "Language variety among Puerto Ricans." In Ferguson and Heath (eds.) 1981.

Zuengler, J. E. 1982. "Kenyan English." In Kachru (ed.) 1982d.

Chapter 5

"I Got Religion!"— Evangelism in Language Teaching

Alan Maley

Alan Maley has spent the past 20 years in the TEFL field, mainly in teacher education: primary school teacher training in Ghana, secondary/high school in Yugoslavia, Italy and France, and tertiary work in China. He is presently First Secretary with the British Council Cultural Section of the British Embassy in Peking. His many publications include TEFL textbooks and books for teachers.

INTRODUCTION

To avoid misunderstanding, I wish to clarify my standpoint from the outset.

This is not a criticism of any approach or method *per se*. For the purposes of this paper, I am less interested in the way a given approach functions methodologically than in the fact that it exists at all, or in the way in which certain, if not all, approaches develop along a roughly similar path of evolution, and share certain characteristics. In other words this paper is more concerned with the sociology of methodology than with its pedagogy.

I have drawn an analogy between the process and practices of religion and those of some methodological approaches. This is purely for convenience and should not be taken literally. No one is suggesting that teachers literally seek salvation in this way—though some I have known have come perilously close to it.

This leads to my third point—namely, that although analogies can be drawn between the nature and complexity of life/existence and the nature and complexity of learning and teaching, they are emphatically *not the same*. Put in its crudest form, I am saying that there are more important things in life than language teaching and that anyone who becomes too closely bound up with it risks adding an emotive supercharge to what is only one part of the life experience.

I quote from a recent letter sent to me by a friend who is into psycho-something-or-other approaches. "I had a fantastic success: out of a dozen participants, I had one woman burst into tears, one throwing up, and at least one virtually falling head over heels in love with me—raving mad—you see the type. Well, I declare, teachers are an odd lot, and I'd rather deal with 100 students than 10 teachers."

Learning and teaching involve stressful situations. But so do getting a mortgage, looking for work, crossing the road, sharing a flat, having a baby, going to the hospital, and so on. We are perhaps in danger of overemphasizing the threat inherent in learning situations, and forgetting that, for most learners, such situations are embedded in a matrix of other equally, or more, important concerns.

The degree of importance accorded to the threat of learning in the States perhaps reflects an important cultural difference between Europe and America. It would seem to most Europeans an exaggeration to speak of "laying one's life on the line" whenever engaging in a foreign-language interaction. Perhaps we in Europe are inured to the hostility of the other. Our ways of dealing with other people are perhaps more clinical, less personalized. This is not to make a value judgment on the more participatory interpersonal type of event, but simply to draw attention to the fact that people everywhere do not attribute equal importance to such events.

THE PROBLEM

Let us now look briefly at the mind-blowing complexity of learning a foreign language. I feel particularly well equipped to do this just now as I have been locked in unequal combat (this surely reflects an "incorrect" attitude) with Mandarin Chinese for over a year.

It is sobering sometimes to think of just how many interlocking and simultaneous psychological and physiological processes are involved: the need to recognize and reproduce comprehensibly the phonemic, stress, and formal features of another system; to hold incomplete sequences in short-term memory for long enough to make sense of them, or to formulate chains of sound rapidly enough to interact before the discourse has moved on; to coordinate phonetic, syntactic, and lexical systems simultaneously in what may be quite stressful circumstances; and to commit to long-term operational memory a multiplicity of rules and meanings. Leaving aside the problem of an alien script, all of this is a Herculean task for the learner—but perhaps even more so for the teacher, who is aware of just how complex and mammoth a job it is, and who has, additionally, to cope with the problems of dealing simultaneously with these factors in a number of learners who are all different.

Faced with this complexity, teachers quite naturally look for convenient solutions. These may take the form:

1. of avoidance behaviour (simply refusing to recognize that there is a problem)—"I give them the basics" "Pronunciation is what I concentrate on"; "If they have the grammar rules, then they can make up their own sentences"; "What they need is the grammatical framework"; etc.

2. of abdication of responsibility to a published text book. "I use *Kernel*. It seems to be very systematic"; "I swear by *Communicate*. It's the best there is."

3. of making eclectic decisions based on the range of choices available to solve a given set of learning problems. "None of these materials seem wholly satisfactory, but I use X for the listening part, supplemented by some of my own material. Then I use Y as a self-study unit."

4. of seeking salvation from someone who seems to offer a way to the Promised Land. The fascination that such figures or movements exert is phenomenal. To cite a trivial example, my co-author Alan Duff several years ago wrote an article titled "The Use of the Telephone Directory in Language Leaning." It was written up deadpan in an acceptable style and published in a journal in France. It was, of course, a complete send up. He nevertheless received a largish number of letters from enthusiasts wanting to know more about this new approach. We are all, I suppose, infinitely suggestible. (For those interested in more recent developments in the art of

spoof, I recommend the article by Michael Swan and Catherine Walter (1982) titled "The Use of Sensory Deprivation in Foreign-Language Learning.")

It is then this third process, the flight to the enchanter (to misquote Iris Murdoch), that we shall be looking at.

THE BIRTH OF A METHOD

The effect of naming is magical. Once a thing has been named, a wall has been built around it which sets it apart and distinguishes it from other things with other names. (This may seem a truism, but the act of naming does change one's viewpoint; as Monsieur Jourdan discovered in *Le Bourgeois Gentilhomme: "Vous faites de la prose sans le savoir."*)

So it is, too, with methodological approaches. Once named, they seem to take on an independent existence, which to some extent at any rate, removes them from the control of their creators and dispenses those who use the name from any but the simplest of referential relationships (for example, Einstein *is* Relativity, Freud *is* Psychoanalysis, Newton *is* Gravity, Gattegno *is* Silent Way, Curran *is* Community Language Learning, Lozanov *is* Suggestopaedia, Wilkins *is* Functions, Krashen *is* the Monitor Model). The approach gathers about it a ritual set of procedures, a priesthood (complete with the initiatory courses necessary to license practice), and a body of holy writ and commentary. As crystallization progresses, the number of those who have invested their belief in it increases, and room for manoeuvre is narrowed.

To survive, it is necessary to claim that the approach offers comprehensive answers to the problems, yet given the complexity of the variables involved, it is clear that such answers do not exist. Seen from outside, the problem is that the process of dialogue is inhibited. If discussion can only take place on the terms bounded by a given set of beliefs, then true dialogue cannot occur. Cross-fertilizing dialogue is precluded, as in the religion of Marxism, since the system is internally self-defining and not susceptible to arguments from without.

With naming, then, comes a hardening of the intellectual arteries, a creation of a sort of orthodoxy that it becomes necessary to defend or justify. In this respect these approaches partake somewhat of the characteristics of religious movements.

1. They present a reductionist view, in which salvation is made available only when critical judgment is suspended. Such views reduce a problem's true complexity by offering a set of procedures for the practitioner to follow. While it is true that things are often simpler than they are made out to be, it is true that they are also, and simultaneously, a great deal more complex than we often allow. This is one of the great paradoxes of life. Approaches

that focus on a reduced view of the problems are invidious because they divert attention away from more complex and subtle factors that might interfere with the neatness of their own solutions.

2. This goes along with a fairly authoritarian streak. As I have already pointed out, the act of naming isolates and makes it necessary to defend the fortress of faith against others. If others are right, we must be wrong— and we are *not* wrong. (I have seen very little propensity to engage in constructive dialogue between the kinds of approaches I have in mind. A glance at the bibliographies of their seminal works is sufficient. They contain only confirming instances.)

3. One also notes a tendency to exclusivity. Just as one cannot become a Roman Catholic priest without undergoing the period of indoctrination called for by the orthodoxy, so it is not possible to do Community Language Learning (CLL) (or Silent Way or Suggestopaedia) without the imprimatur of those who decide what CLL is. The *reductio ab absurden* of this is that an approach is what those licensed to exercise it say it is. We should not be surprised at this (it is, after all, the basis, however open to question, upon which the legal and other professions rest), but we should not neglect to note it.

4. They are not open to refutation because they define and operate within their own terms. They can assert, but they cannot prove (a point I shall refer to later in connection with the definition of science). In just the same way, religious movements, at least those of the West, are able to assert with conviction that they offer a pathway to heaven—but no one has yet returned to prove the validity of their assertions.

5. The fact that demonstrable proof cannot be arranged often leads to a degree of obscurantism. As Gattegno states in the Acknowledgements to his *The Common Sense of Teaching Foreign Languages* (1976): "A suggestion which I could not incorporate in the text was to make the text easy to read. My style is found by many to be demanding. Perhaps this is because I write concisely and I avoid developments that readers feel they need but which do not suggest themselves to me." I have to admit that the result of such an attitude is a peculiarly rebarbative style (and one which in places does not fit the rules of English particularly happily).

Curran's works (1972, 1976) are virtually unreadable without exegesis. One can accept that new ideas are sometimes difficult to express freshly in existing resources of the language, but there comes a point when the style becomes an obstacle rather than an aid to understanding.

Much of Lozanov's prose too is masked by the terminology of pseudo science (see, for example, Lozanov, 1979). One is reminded of Lord Rutherford's remark that it should be possible to explain one's ideas in language that even the barmaid in the local pub would understand.

6. In one way or another these approaches are driven to make strong claims for their methods. (What justification for separate existence would they have otherwise?) Hence "Once I understand what students have to do, I am able to invent techniques and materials that help them be as good as the natives in what they are facing" (Gattegno 1976:vi–vii). Suggestopaedia makes similarly strong claims for items remembered after its courses and CLL for the depth of acquisition in its sessions. None of these claims can be substantiated in any way that would be acceptable to a researcher in the hard sciences.

The interesting thing about such movements/approaches is their concern for scientific respectability. But like any teaching/learning theory, they are not open to the principle of verification because the number of variables is too large to be held constant. Likewise they are not open to the Popperian criterion of falsifiability since they are not framed in a way that can be tested. Scientifically they are neither true nor false, since no adequate tests can be performed upon them. They have the status of *myth* rather than theory.

This does not mean that they should be ruled out as useless since, as we shall see, they have provided considerable insights into the language-learning process. It does mean, however, that they entail an act of faith that is more closely related to religion than to science.

POSITIVE INSIGHTS

In case I may seem to be indulging in negative criticism, I would wish now to emphasize some of the positive insights which such approaches have provided.

1. **Change in the roles of teacher and learner.** It is now inconceivable to regard the teacher as sole arbiter and controller of what goes on in language classrooms. The independent and individual role and status of the learner is fully accepted (if not always applied) by most theorists and practitioners.

2. **The importance of group supportiveness.** There are now few approaches that do not harness the group dynamic. The group is recognized to be more than its separate components. It also offers a security system for learning.

3. **The importance of relaxation and the reduction of threat.** Nowadays few would contest the fact that we learn better when relaxed, and when not made to feel inadequate.

4. **The realization of the hidden capacity of the human brain.** Until fairly recently we were content to think that learning was an arduous and slow process. More recent approaches have shown just how much brain capacity is left unused in normal circumstances and how important the role of peripheral and subconscious learning is.

5. **The role of play in learning has been enhanced.** Indeed the value of the

ludic function of language has been rediscovered and reapplied. Learning is no longer synonymous with solemnly serious activity.

6. **The view of error and its correction have been greatly altered.** Errors are no longer regarded as sinful but are recognized as a necessary and systematic part of the learning process. And the resources for correction (and self-correction) are much expanded.

7. **The importance of building inner criteria.** Fuller realization has come about that it is the *learner* who is responsible for his own learning, and the teacher's job is to help him find his own way to do it best.

8. **Creative silence is not now looked upon as a waste of time.** We recognize the need for a period of incubation between input and output, and the need for learners to work over material internally.

The list is not complete, and not all the approaches mentioned embody all these points. However, in themselves these points constitute a revolution in our ways of thinking about teaching and learning, and even if we do not subscribe to all the tenets or practices of all these approaches, we owe them collectively an enormous debt.

CONTRADICTIONS

As I have already suggested, however, there are a number of contradictions or inconsistencies between these various approaches. One has only to think of the carefully phased, step-by-step approach advocated in the Silent Way and the massive initial input of Suggestopaedia to see just how divergent these approaches can be. Likewise the emphasis on the learner as an isolated and independent striver in the Silent Way contrasts strongly with the comfort of the group afforded by CLL. The Suggestopaedia teacher would be uncomfortable with the alienation of the Silent Way, and the Silent Way teacher should be dismayed by the waste of energy involved in the group process of CLL. One could go on drawing contrasts.

While I think it worthwhile to point up these incompatibilities, I do not think it detracts from their value as language-learning paradigms (or myths!)—so long, that is, as no *one* of them lays claim to total truth. While it is possible for there to be different paths to the mountain of enlightenment, it is not possible to accommodate such widely divergent approaches within a scientific framework.

RECAPITULATION
AND CONCLUSION

My main concerns in this paper have been the description of a sociological process in methodology somewhat akin to religion, which I find fascinating, *and* the articulation, perhaps rather obliquely so far, of a worry.

Let me first recapitulate the process. A new prophet appears with a message. This is articulated in writ (books/articles) and ritual procedures (techniques); converts are gained; temples (research centers) are set up and initiation ceremonies (courses) evolved to license others in the practice of the new sect (approach). Proselytisation goes on, and differentiation from other sects is strengthened.

Now to a slightly clearer articulation of my worry. This concerns teachers, especially young teachers. (I do not think one need worry about the effect of any method on learners—they are pretty resilient anyhow and have a multitude of concerns outside the classroom which effectively insulate them from harm.) Teachers by contrast tend to be constantly exposed to the stresses of their profession in a way very few others are. The temptation for them to trade in their critical faculty for the security of the system of beliefs that offers the comforting certainty that one is doing the right thing, is therefore correspondingly greater.

Over the past twenty years I have dealt with large numbers of teachers of English as a foreign language, and the grail-seekers among them have always been in the majority. It will not be difficult to persuade someone who is consciously or unconsciously looking for the magic method that will turn his stuttering students into golden-tongued prodigies, that he has found it. But there is no such certainty. We know only that we do not know. "As for certain truth, no man has known it, Nor shall he know it . . . . For even if by chance he were to utter the final truth, he would himself not know it" (Xenophanes). And this is as true now as it was over 2000 years ago.

This does not of course mean that we should not continue to search for better solutions—provided we always realize that they are bound to be provisional, and open to criticism. But this has to be conditional upon the exercise of independent judgment in rapidly changing circumstances. And it is this which I fear is undermined by a too ready adherence to this or that system or approach.

REFERENCES

Curran, C. 1972. *Counseling-learning.* New York: Grune & Stratton.

————. 1976. *Counseling-learning in second languages.* Apple River, Ill.: Apple River Press.

Gattegno, C. 1976. *The common sense of teaching foreign languages.* New York: Educational Solutions, Inc.

Lozanov, G. 1979. *Suggestology and outlines of suggestopedy.* New York: Gordon and Breach.

Swan, M. and C. Walter. 1982. "The use of sensory deprivation in foreign language learning." *ELT Journal* **36**: 183–185.

Section II

Methods and Materials

Chapter 6

Beyond Notions and Functions: Language Teaching or the Art of Letting Go

Günter Gerngroß
Herbert Puchta

Günter Gerngroß is Professor of English at the Pädagogische Akademie Graz and is a member of the faculty at the University of Graz, Austria. He has had extensive experience teaching both 10–18 year olds and adults and in his research has focused on levels of interaction within the classroom. He has contributed to several EFL textbooks published in Austria.

Herbert Puchta teaches English as a foreign language to 10–14 year olds and is a member of the Faculty at the Pädagogische Akademie-Graz where he teaches foreign language teaching methodology. He has published several articles in the area of foreign language teaching.

TEACHING ENGLISH AS A
FOREIGN LANGUAGE IN AUSTRIA

Currently the majority of Austrian schoolchildren learn English. Starting in 1983 all pupils, however, will be exposed to an introductory language program in the primary schools (almost exclusively in English, with a few classes in French) which will be based on a modern functionally-notionally oriented syllabus. The primary purpose of this program (60 hours spread over two years) is to sensitize 8- and 9-year-old pupils to a foreign language. By 1985 all students in the secondary schools will receive approximately 500 hours of English within four years and about 25% of them will continue studying the language for another four years.

All language teaching in Austrian schools has to fit into the framework of a syllabus issued by the Ministry of Education. Research, however, has shown that the textbook is the crucial factor influencing what goes on in the classroom. The textbooks must, of course, be compatible with the official syllabus. At the moment experts are beginning to revise the present syllabus, with its heavy emphasis on grammatical progression, to create one that will reflect the view that language ought to be taught as communication.

Our research findings (Gerngroß 1982, Puchta 1982) reveal that meaning is sadly neglected in many classrooms, while a truly communicative atmosphere prevails in a modest number of classes with enthusiastic teachers. Experiences in in-service training sometimes remind us very much of a photo in *Newsweek* (November 15, 1982) showing a Chinese teacher holding a flashcard with a bus on it and pointing at the blackboard on which the learners can read the sentences

"What's this? Is this a bus?

It's a bus. Yes, it is."

The underlying concept of a great many lessons seems to be based on the belief that the addition of grammar and vocabulary produces language and that the structures must be mastered before communication can take place. The learners are looked upon as receptacles to be filled with grammar and words according to the textbook's pace, neglecting essentials such as the message of texts and the emotions, attitudes, and needs of the pupils.

DEVELOPING NEW LANGUAGE
TEACHING MATERIALS

We consider the term "communicative language teaching" a broad one. This has the disadvantage, however, that it is easy to put the label "communicative" on materials that amount to nothing more than a compilation of texts and exercises arranged according to the current staple diet of language-teaching techniques. However, here it should be emphasized that we certainly do not hold the technical side in low esteem. A host of new ideas in language teaching, such as the information gap (a situation in which one participant in an exchange has information the others do not know and need to find out) and problem-solving activities, have proved extremely valuable. Yet we do not think that techniques alone are a sufficiently broad basis for teaching materials that claim to foster communication among the pupils in a classroom situation.

Because the majority of teachers seem to be closely guided by their textbook, a quantum leap forward presupposes two things:

1. The creation of teaching materials that enable teachers to put the ideas of communicative teaching into practice.

2. A significant change in teachers' attitudes, a process to which we will refer to later as "letting go."

Judging from our in-service training experience in Austria, a great number of teachers are willing to change their approach and teaching methods provided the necessary teaching materials are readily accessible. Otherwise the hoped-for revolution will stop short in front of the classroom door.

What should the materials on which communicative language teaching can be based look like? We highly value the work on syllabus construction by D. A. Wilkins (1976) and J. van Ek (1977), but we do not think that the functional-notional approach can be the core concept of a new curriculum (although a functional-notional and a grammatical progression is necessary for any course material). If we really want our pupils "to do things with words" in a foreign language, the key concept must be a pedagogical one linking the pupils' selves with the topics relevant to them.

Making them act out the role of somebody who complains or apologizes in a certain situation is important, but it is certainly not enough because a teaching course following a litany of functions (formerly: structures) might help to activate the children's minds but certainly not win their hearts. We rather envisage material that not only enables them to buy a ticket or to make suggestions, but that also fosters classroom processes that revolve round the here and now—thus blending objectives for a distant future with the pupil's immediate needs.

For a long time our approach has been eclectic, and we have integrated every useful technique. We readily admit that our ideas are based on a concept that we ourselves do not see as complete, but still open for discusson. We do believe, however, that the focus of language teaching must be on the learners' self, integrated in a "learning-by-doing process" that allows both second-language acquisition and learning. It is not possible to go into detail here, but we should like to mention that a theoretical concept with practical examples has already been developed and is to be found in Puchta and Schratz 1983.

As far as our ideas about teaching materials are concerned, there are some requirements that we consider absolutely necessary but that teachers woefully miss in materials currently used. It must be made clear what sort of text is being presented. Materials abound in "non-texts" whose characteristic feature is that they occur only in schoolbooks and nowhere else. We have found that materials containing roles that reflect the pupils' own world stimulate processes of greater depth (Stevick 1976) because the learners say or write what they want to get across. The role of the one who receives messages or produces utterances must be clear.

One of the textbooks widely used in Austria contains a scene in which English children are shown having a pet show. Even when learners act out this scene creatively and enthusiastically, they do not reach the depth of involvement that is almost tangible when they act out a short text that presents a family conflict revolving round the question of whether the children should be allowed to have a pet or not. Here the observer feels that a great many of the pupils seem to throw themselves into the situation, thus *acquiring* language rather than *learning* it (Dulay, Burt, and Krashen 1982).

This corresponds to the response given when we asked a class we have watched closely for about two years what kind of lesson they liked best. Many referred to a situation in which they had writen poems stimulated by simple drawings and were given written feedback on their classmates' poems. Their evaluation reminded us very much of Stevick (1976) quoting Curran, who claimed that a student may even develop a new language self. Quite a lot of these pupils, who were then 13 years old, seemed to be more at ease in expressing feelings in English than in their native German.

One final example may suffice. Many of the newly-labelled textbooks and materials provide a host of such boring texts as how to repair a puncture on your bike, the underlying idea being that kids like to ride bikes. (They do, but they learn to repair them by watching someone patch a tire, not by reading instructions.) Literary texts, fables, fairy tales are often neglected. One of the most appreciated texts we used was a story in which an elephant and a flower quarrel about their identity (Patten 1974). The pupils cherished its literary value and they spontaneously wanted to act out several role-plays in which they, in the roles of imaginary animals and plants, strongly defended themselves against threats to their identity. Materials must be such that it is a rewarding task for the pupils to talk about them and about how they felt when they read or listened to them or acted parts of them out. The teaching situation itself becomes an important topic in its own right and the pupils "grow" by exposure to different perceptions, ideas, and emotions to the same situation and by gradually learning to share them.

CLASSROOM ENCOUNTERS

Since we began developing our own ideas about communicative language teaching, we have often been struck by a phenomenon that can be observed in any teaching/learning situation: A number of teachers seem able to elicit processes of language learning that encourage the learners to express themselves in the foreign language; many with at least the same theoretical background and perhaps even better training seem unable to do this at all. Their lessons are boring and if you watch them, you become aware that the students, although taking part in various activities, do not get involved with their real interests and intentions. What else is it then that in addition to suitable and motivating materials triggers off in the pupils a crossing of the borderline between compliance with the teaching situation (which becomes obvious in the question "What does the teacher want me to do?") and the emergence of their real selves?

As said above, there is obviously little or no connection between the strikingly different results and the teachers' levels of methodological knowledge. Apart from aspects of the "outer world" affecting the teaching/learning situation—such as situational and social factors, level of the students' foreign language, etc.—it will be suggested in the following that the teaching/learning process is crucially influenced by the "inner world" of the teacher (and of the learners, of course). In traditional methodology courses this aspect is totally neglected; this does not mean, however, that it cannot become part of a teacher-training that attempts to integrate both the outer and the inner conditions. No doubt the teachers must have a wide set of techniques at their disposal. But recent studies have shown that effects of personality on the learners have a vital influence on their second-language development. "All the things being equal, the self-confident, secure person is a more successful language learner," Dulay, Burt, and Krashen (1982:75) suggest.

If this is true, and our experience confirms it, teaching techniques are useful but are by no means sufficient to allow for growth of the learners' personality. If teachers want to establish an atmosphere that allows personal as well as linguistic development, they must be aware that their own personalities play a decisive role.

Most of the time it is our anxieties that hinder us from being aware of what is really going on in the lesson; that is why many teachers find it difficult to discuss topics going beyond the mere technical side of the problem. Quite frequently, these aspects of the inner world are suppressed and consequently denied in discussions about language teaching.

In the last few years we have frequently demonstrated practical examples of communicative language teaching in the classroom situation before going into the theoretical concepts. The two following lessons were given individually by the authors as teaching demonstrations in the course of an in-service training seminar in December 1982 with 50 teachers as critical observers. By trying to describe parts of the teaching/learning process as seen from the teachers' point of view (our own, in this particular case), and by presenting lesson plans and texts written by the learners, we hope to give an overall idea of our concepts. In doing so, we are aware that a great number of spectators adds elements of the unusual and the normal routine may be distorted. We nevertheless chose to describe these two lessons, as the pressure and the wish to succeed inherent in such a situation enhanced our awareness of the difficulty in letting go.

The two lessons presented here are intended to show a certain progression from one to the other—the first one, given in a sixth-grade class (average age 12 years) after approximately 200 lessons of English (45 minutes each), can be characterized as one of the first of many steps to establish an atmosphere of self-concept and self-oriented language learning. The second class is already a couple of steps further on in this process. Accordingly the first lesson follows a more teacher-centered curriculum that implies that the methodological sequences are less open than in the second. This second lesson cannot be regarded as typical for the teaching/learning situation in that class (eighth grade, after approx. 400 lessons). We regard it as an experiment that we believe, however, is worth talking about.

A characteristic feature of the type of school at which the lessons were given is that the pupils are of widely varied proficiency, since most of the clearly academically able students attend another type of school.

Lesson 1

The objective of this lesson was to introduce the topic "Where I live." The pupils were expected to read and understand the dialogue and to write their own text based on "Mini Memory" models. (T stands for teacher, P for pupil; the pupils' quotations are from tape transcripts.)

Step one: T writes the following words on the blackboard:

Steve—Philip—clouds—poster—real butterflies—sister—nosey—kite—
birthday—Africa

T: Let's talk about the words. (A minute of silence ensues.)

I'm beginning to feel scared. What will I do if they don't say anything? What if the method doesn't work? How will I be able to compensate? Chris Brumfit's advice pops into my head: "Kids should be given time to think about what they are going to say." But are they really thinking? Or are they just waiting for me to do something? I realize that my anxiety stems from the fact that I am doing something in order to achieve something else. I badly want to convince my colleagues that our approach works. And it occurs to me that I must forget my plans and throw myself into the silence, making it the topic—but now the kids start pouring out sentences.

P 1: I think it's a story.

P 2: What does the word nosey mean?

P 3: I think Steve and Philip have a poster with real butterflies.

P 4: Steve and Philip buy a poster with clouds and butterflies as a birthday present for their sister.

The concept applied here is known as "advance organisers" which tie the topic to already existing associations in pupils' minds thus getting them involved from the very beginning.

Step two:

T: Can you use the words and make something out of them?

This may sound more open than it actually is. The children usually either make a story together or prepare a role-play. This time they all opt for a role-play. At this stage the teacher withdraws, available to answer questions, but does not interfere with the group process. It has not yet become fully transparent to us how the children manage to come up with a role-play in about 5−7 minutes, but they do. They seem to have ready-made parts of scenes for almost every situation stored in their minds once they have learned to tap and trust their resources and feel free and secure to make use of them. Since they have formed groups of their own liking, the process of negotiating the roles, lines, and content is given the greatest attention.

Everybody's position and rank in the group seems clear. English is spoken most of the time, although students sometimes fall back into German when strong emotions seem to make an immediate reply imperative. As teachers it has taken us quite a while to learn to live with self-imposed passivity at this stage. We have experienced that when the children are trusted, they will sense it and work hard without being supervised. They know that the teacher respects their ideas and that linguistic mistakes do not matter while planning the role-play.

I realize, however, that I'm getting impatient. Why can't they work faster? I already know the next step and the one after that. It's a feeling I have much too often. It's the attitude of teachers who think "they must get their students through the textbook by the end of the course" (Stevick 1982:8).

Step three: Role-play

All the groups want to perform their role-play but for the sake of showing all of the steps, only the first group to finish is picked to perform. The children introduce themselves first as Steve, Philip, the mother, the shop assistant, and the sister.

Mother:	Steve and Philip.
Steve and Philip:	Yes?
Mother:	Go in the shop and buy for Elke a present.
Steve and Philip:	Yes. (To Elke) Elke, what do you want for your birthday?
Elke:	I would like a poster with a butterfly or a kite.
Steve and Philip:	Yes, okay.

In the shop.

Shop Assistant:	Hello.
Steve and Philip:	Hello.
Steve:	We are buy a . . . (Philip interrupts)
Philip:	want . . .
Steve:	We want to buy a real butterfly.
Shop Assistant:	I have not a real butterfly.
Philip:	Have you got a poster with a butterfly?
Shop Assistant:	Yes, here.
Steve:	How much is it?
Shop Assistant:	One pound.
Steve and Philip:	Here you are.
Shop Assistant:	Thanks. Good-bye.

At home.

Steve and Philip:	Here is the poster.
Mother:	It's very good.
Steve and Philip:	Here, Elke, here your present for your birthday.
Elke:	Thank you.

The teacher's reaction is very important for the pupils. We have learned that fixed expectations prevent the teacher from appreciating unusually imaginative versions that often provide interesting insights into the pupils' minds and often stimulate lively talk about the text. Inconsistencies (Elke wants a poster but first Steve tries to buy a real butterfly) are only dealt with if the pupils themselves point them out.

A note concerning error correction: For us it is a question of when and how. When the focus of interest is on meaning, we hardly ever correct unless an unobtrusive correction is possible. When the focus is on form, we always correct, helping to develop a monitor in the pupil's mind to prevent fossilization of incorrect utterances even though they cause no problems for understanding. We believe that it takes most teachers a lot of time to learn to correct in a constructive way. Many tend to become angry since the pupils are not doing what they want them to do—namely, to speak correctly—or they may see the pupils' mistakes as evidence that their methods have failed.

Step Four: The text (Gerngroß, Puchta, and Schratz 1982) is handed out.

Scene 1. Two children are looking at a poster in a shop window.

Steve:	Look at that poster! Isn't it beautiful?
Philip:	Which one do you mean?
Steve:	The one with the cornfield.
Philip:	Yes, it's great. The clouds and all the butterflies.
Steve:	Do you like butterflies?
Philip:	Yes, very much.
Steve:	I've got some really big ones from Africa at home.
Philip:	Have you?
Steve:	Would you like to see them?
Philip:	Yes, very much.
Steve:	Can you come with me?
Philip:	Sure.

Scene 2. In Steve's flat.

Steve:	Hi, mum. This is Philip. He is in my class.
Mrs. Perkins:	Hello Philip.
Philip:	Good afternoon, Mrs. Perkins.

Scene 3. In Steve's room.

Philip:	Shall I shut the door?
Steve:	Please do. Then my sister can't hear us.
Philip:	Is she a problem?
Steve:	Yes, she is so nosey.
Philip:	I see.
Steve:	Come on, the butterflies are in my desk.
Philip:	Ah! They are wonderful. Such beautiful colours. This one looks like a Chinese kite.

Scene 4. Philip at home.

Philip: Hello mum.

Mother: Philip, where have you been? It's five o'clock.

Philip: Mum, my birthday is on the eleventh, isn't it?

Mother: Yes, I know. Why?

Philip: I'd like five really big butterflies from Africa.

The pupils read silently. They ask questions:

> P 1: What is sky?

or comment on the text:

> P 2: I have . . . oh that's an Admiral.
> We have at home three books of butterflies, yes.
> They belong to my brother.

Step five:

Since reading and interpreting texts are highly idiosyncratic skills, this next step takes this into account by its openness. The teacher initiates discussion about the text with the question: *"Can we talk about the text?"* This step requires a lot of self-discipline since the process of negotiating meaning is slow and requires patience. As we understand it, communicative language teaching puts great emphasis on listening in a Rogerian sense, which implies an active will to try to understand others. We find this one of the hardest tasks to achieve since the children are used to listening to the teacher but not to their peers. There are no quick, set recipes. That the teacher be a patient listener is the basic requirement.

> P 3: Scenes one and four are very long, scene two and three is not very long.
>
> T: Do you like long or short scenes?
>
> P 3: Yes.
>
> T: What do you mean 'Yes?'
>
> P 3: Pardon?
>
> T: Which do you like better, long or short scenes?
>
> P 3: Long scenes.
>
> . . . .
>
> P 4: My mother is also very nosey. (Laughter)
>
> T: Do you mean she checks your homework and everything?

P 5: She must check the homework.

T: Why?

P 5: What's *Fehler* in English?

T: Mistake.

P 5: Because . . . the mistakes.

Step six:

The teacher tells the pupils to underline the important words. (They know how to handle this technique, the function of which is to make sure that everybody has actually understood the text.) When they have finished, the underlined words of one or two pupils are written on the chalkboard and the class tries to restore the text orally. Those who failed to understand parts of the text when they read it silently will hopefully grasp the meaning with the help of this "safety net." The teacher helps along, correcting if necessary.

P 6: There are miss some words.

T: You mean some words are missing.

P 6: Yes.

Step seven: Two Mini Memory Texts are handed out.

Text 1
Nice things in my room
I have got three beautiful posters of animals. A tiger, a dog, and a cat. There is a map of England over my desk and some photos from our holiday in Italy. On cold days I like my warm bed best.

Text 2
A room I'd like to have
I'd like to have a nice room. With a big bed, a big desk and lots of photos on the wall. I like pets very much. I'd like to have a budgie or a hamster. I'd like blue curtains with white butterflies on them.

The idea, originating with H. E. Piepho (1982), is that as far as structure and content are concerned, the texts are to resemble the level of the writing skill of the pupils who can and do identify with them as their own. These texts form the basis for dictation exercises and tests and for homework in which variations are produced. The pupils are to study them carefully. The idea is that they store such texts in their long-term memory in order to create a pool from which they can randomly take bits of information whenever they are faced with the task of text production.

My room

I have got five posters on the wall in my room.
The first poster is a racing car, the second a house
and the three posters are dogs. I like dogs, we
have got one, it's a Schäfer. It's name is Senta.
On my desk is my foto. I like my room very
much.

Lesson 2

*Well, here I am, waiting for pupils to come and aware of the hundred threatening
eyes of my colleagues. How could I have been so foolish as to believe that I could try
out something experimental in the presence of so many who are "ready-to-see-me-
fall"? Try to calm down again, relax, look at them. How do you know they are so
negatively inclined? I am glad we agreed to ask them all to take part actively in the
fantasy trip. Anyway, it* must not *go wrong. The steps are clear: I hand out the
photocopies to the pupils, wait for reactions (what if there aren't any?), guide them
over to the fantasy trip, ask them to close their eyes (what if they don't?) and. . . .*

When the class is ready (sitting at groups of desks), they are given photocopies of photographs with scenes from beaches, seashores, pictures of sea-
gulls, etc. (The picture in Bach's book *Jonathan Livingston Seagull* may give an
idea of what they were like.) Each of these photocopies has one of the following
texts:

I am sitting on a rock The waves are playing with my toes Time to think	Flying high and fast— Together

The sun is going down
I can feel the warm sand under my feet
It was a good day

I must take my time To look Where I am going	The sky and ocean Wide. . . I am free to go wherever I like

It feels good
To try
What you have never done before
I am strong

I wonder how the kids will react. Will they react at all? (Silence.) Perhaps there are too many spectators? Am I expecting too much of this class? I know I have to wait. But so long? . . . They seem to be getting involved and interested. They are swapping sheets, they seem to be thinking about the texts. Eva is nodding her head. Peter is about to say something. Thank God! He is going to break the ice. . . .

P 1: I don't know what we should do with these.

I would have hoped for a better start. But wait—let's see what we can make out of this. I find myself thoughtfully looking at Peter.

T: I see, the pictures and the texts don't tell you anything. . . .

P 1: Not that. I mean the pictures . . . they are nice. They look nice. But I can't see a meaning in the texts.

P 2: That's not right. For example, the text on this picture says, 'Flying high and fast—together.' That's a good meaning.

T: What do you understand by that?

P 2: I think this means . . . er . . . when you have a friend when you do something not alone . . . I mean you work together . . . you can make it better . . .

P 1: I see what you mean.

P 3: The pictures . . . when I look at them I thinking of the holidays . . . in Italy last year . . . of situations on the . . . what's *Strand* in English? Beach.

P 3: Yes. On the beach with my friends. . . .

After a couple of other pupils have verbalized their associations, they are all confronted with the idea of making a fantasy trip together. They (as well as the spectators) are asked to close their eyes and try to find a position in which they feel comfortable.

I switch on the cassette recorder and feel how the tension lets up when the music begins to fill the room. We have chosen an instrumental version of Neil Diamond's music to Jonathan Livingston Seagull. *I regain a certain confidence, but my voice is still trembling slightly when I suggest some relaxing exercises. Relaxing myself by looking directly at the children and colleagues in front of me, I begin to feel safer and I notice how I sound soft and calm now.*

T: When you have closed your eyes, just stay in your position and re-lax . . . take a deep breath and be conscious of it . . . let yourself breathe slowly and deeply . . . notice any part of your body that needs to relax. . . .

For those interested in trying out similar exercises in their classrooms, it might be helpful to look at what Moskowitz (1978:178) says about them and their introduction. There are also a number of carefully described fantasies which can easily be tried out in classes.[1]

Now I begin to conduct the fantasy journey. My voice comes out firmly and calmly. After every sentence I pause, sometimes turning the volume of the music up again, then lowering it while I am speaking so it recedes into the background. (The whole fantasy lasts for about 15 minutes.)

I want you to imagine that you are at the seashore/Can you hear the water coming in and going out again?/Can you feel the sand?/Look around you./ What can you see?/Are there any mountains?/What is the sky like?/Is it cloudy?/ Can you feel the sun?/Can you feel the wind on your body now?/Imagine you are slowly flying away with the wind./What does it feel like?/Are you looking down or up in the sky?/Can you feel the wind?/Now imagine you see the land below you./You are going down a bit. You can see something far away, but you don't know what it is./What is it?/You are going nearer and nearer. . . .
Longer break: music louder

What does it look like?/Is it something you have seen before?/Touch it./ What does it feel like?/Is it warm? Is it soft?/What does it mean for you?/What do you feel when you look at it?
Longer break: music louder

Now that you have seen what it is, slowly say goodbye to it. Touch it once more before you slowly move away from it. Go back to the seashore now./Can you feel the sand under your body again?/Take some time until you want to be back with me in class again./Don't hurry./Don't come back before you want to./When you feel ready, open your eyes again. . . .

In foreign-language teaching, there are various ways to take advantage of the insights into ourselves that become possible by working with fantasies. We have, for example, created another one ("I'm a kite") which makes it perfectly possible for pupils (even at any early stage in their language learning) to experience the notion of the progressive tense within themselves by being conducted in the fantasy, e.g.: Now you are flying over a big park. The people underneath you are . . . etc.

At first I saw a peacefull country, with rocky's, red sand, the sea and a clean air, the sun shone brightly and warm. I felt the warm sand under my feets and the hot sun, the wind. Then I saw a bird. It was flying, not fast and I thought it was flying to the sun.
Then I saw a horse at the back of a rock. I went to him and touch it slowly. I felt the warm coat under my fingers, then I rode with the horse on the beach.
I felt free and cheerful. And the fiery horse ran with me into the sky. It was a wonderful feeling.

I have been on the beach. I felt the sun and the wind. I flew away. I saw a land with near and dead people. I flew over it. Then I saw something huge. I flew nearer and nearer. It was a big palace made of glas. I touched the glass and I felt that it was cold. Very cold. I looked into the palace and I saw the prince. He was not free, he had to stay in the glass place. He couldn't go out. He was arrested. I would like to help him, but the wind blew me away. I fell asleep. When I woke up I was on the beach and the sun was shining into my face.

In the case at hand there are no specific linguistic aims. What we have in mind is to stimulate the pupils' imagination and to make them share their images and experiences afterwards. Talking about these might have been constructive as well, but we chose to have them write texts since we were afraid that they would have inhibitions and therefore not be ready to talk about their experiences as freely as usual in this new situation. Their texts show a wide spectrum of different experiences, dreams, hopes, worries, and images. Two of them are presented here.

In the follow-up lesson the texts are discussed in class. The learners seem to be enthusiastic about their own and their classmates' experiences. Undoubtedly, their thoughts show a remarkable dimension of depth, which obviously involves them completely. This is an excerpt from the discussion in class after the above text has been read aloud:

P 1:   I think the idea in this text is just like mine. You want away . . . er . . . want to have peace . . . away from here.

P 2:   Yes, but it's different because you write about a ski-jumper and I have seen the war in my fantasy trip.

P 1:   Yes, but you also go away from this world to another world and you also want to find peace.

T: While you were having the images of war and of the land with the dead . . . were you afraid?

P: Not, really, perhaps a little, but I flew away.

P 3:   I like what you write from the glass palace. It's a good picture.

P 4:   Yes, the glass palace . . . I think part of this we are ourselves. We don't want the peace to go out . . . if we would we had to do much more for it.

P 5:   Yes, I think some people they say they want peace but they don't do it. If you want peace you must do peace.

P 6:   I meet . . . I sometimes meet . . . when I speak to somebody I feel that they are not themselves . . . that they do not say what they really mean.

THE INNER TEACHER

We hope that the descriptions of the two lessons have given a feeling of what we understand by "inner world" of the teacher. It is primarily the teachers' anxieties that prevent them from letting go in the actual teaching situation and from becoming a facilitator for the pupils' language development instead of acting as a control mechanism. Take the following situation:

A teacher might react to the utterances "I has five poster" with "I *have* five posters, don't forget it is *I have* and posters must be in the plural." Or he might simply ask: "You have got five posters? Have you also got one with butterflies?" We could provide lots of pro and con arguments for both reactions. It does, however, rarely depend on rational reasons as to whether a teachers' reaction is one way or the other in the actual situation, but rather on strong unconscious, internal patterns. Stevick (1980:29) quotes Galway's "Inner Game" and suggests that the best learning can take place when the Conscious, Critical Self and the Performing Self are in agreement with one another. Very often it is this Critical Self that interferes with a process's possible growth by passing judgment on the teacher's or the pupil's contribution. Such patterns are, of course, sometimes influenced by the way teachers themselves experience language learning. We suggest the concept of an "Inner Teacher" (by which we mean the strict, demanding, intolerant ego that often influences the teacher's reaction). The anxieties caused by the "Inner Teacher" are easily transferred into the learning situation and onto the pupils.

From conversations with teachers we have found that one of the principal anxieties to surface stems from the problem of how to handle errors. "Why can't they discuss the problem lucidly? I think I should interfere and stop this boring gibberish, full of errors. If I allow them to go on making so many mistakes, others will pick them up. Wouldn't it be better to correct every mistake immediately? At least it would soothe my conscience."

Brumfit (1980:126) writes that pupils should be given plenty of opportunity to make mistakes. Many teachers, however, are strongly influenced by a rigid negative attitude toward errors. An error is looked upon as something for which there is no place in the classroom, which is to be avoided at all costs since it might spread like a contagious disease. We suspect that the strong feeling aroused by pupils' mistakes are a result of the teachers' own feeling of inadequacy since they suspect that the number of pupils' mistakes has indirect correlation to teaching ability.

The solution we suggest is to get teachers involved in an intensive L2 discussion (in the foreign language) and then interrupt whenever an error occurs. This procedure enables teachers to identify with the learners' negative feelings when they are interrupted by the teacher's comments on accuracy.

During a teaching training seminar, once an atmosphere of mutual trust had carefully been established, teachers talked about their anxieties. Here are some examples of what they wrote down afterwards:

"It is difficult for me to endure silence. What does the pupils' silence mean? Are they thinking? Have they sunk into apathy? Have I presented something which they don't understand or which they can't manage? Why don't they say so? Are they afraid?"

"Why does it take them so long to make a statement, to talk? I know it's important that they should be given the chance to grope for words but sometimes it seems to be more than I can stand. We should have mastered lesson X long ago and here we are, right in the middle of it. It's like being caught in a swamp."

"When I look at the book and the curriculum I feel this pressure. There are so many things in the books my pupils don't know anything about. How can I make them learn faster and more intensively?"

"Are my pupils good enough? I've no idea how good the English of other groups is. Maybe they would be better if I knew more of the language and about how to teach it more effectively."

"I know I should convey a feeling of security, but how can I do it when I'm in doubt about what I'm doing? I wish to be told how to do everything—in detail. First they sold us the audio-lingual approach, and now we are warned not to do so many pattern drills. What should I think of it all, when even the experts do not seem to know for sure?"

We suspect that many teachers share the contents of these inner monologues, as their reactions in the classroom seem to indicate. The pressure caused by being unable to throw themselves into the situation, to take advantage of the here and now, is often transferred to the pupils.

It is an indisputable fact that most of us go into the lesson with a given set of expectations; if we realize that these expectations might not be fulfilled, we begin to look for reasons and excuses, mostly either blaming ourselves or shifting the blame onto the students. This attitude can have fatal results. If the teachers use up all available energy in trying to judge whether the outcome of a specific situation is good enough to withstand the severe evaluation of the eyes (or ears) of the Inner Teacher, they run great risks—it might become impossible for them to hear what the pupils really say and to react effectively, and they might have problems establishing an atmosphere that allows the pupils to experiment with the new language. Brown says that ". . . . the inhibitions, the defenses, which we place between ourselves and others can prevent us from communicating in a foreign language" (1980: 106).

We readily admit that the nonjudgmental attitude we have advocated here may conflict with the task of evaluating the pupils' results. Although we have not found the ultimate solution to this problem, we consider it helpful in establishing an understanding between the teacher and the pupils in regulating these problems.

We began by saying that progress demands new materials and a change in teachers' attitudes. Obviously it is much easier to produce textbooks, tapes, etc. that meet the requirements of the communicative approach than it is to embark on the task of changing patterns of behavior. There is no short-cut but only the prospect of a long march. Our experience in in-service training shows that supplying information is important, but not enough. The rigidity of the Inner Teacher is not softened by brainwork alone. We do not let go when we know we can but only when we feel it.

It's confidence, not mere knowledge of the possibility, that enables us to let go.

NOTES

1. As far as the fantasy trip presented here is concerned, we are grateful to Gerlinde Puchta, who has helped us to make our vague ideas concrete and practicable.

REFERENCES

Brown, H. 1980. *Principles of language learning and teaching*. Englewood Cliffs, N.J.: Prentice-Hall.

Brumfit, C. 1980. *Problems and principles in English teaching,* Oxford: Pergamon Press.

Dulay, H., M. Burt, and S. Krashen. 1982. *Language two.* New York: Oxford University Press.

Gerngroß, G. 1982. *Der lehrplan als steuerungsinstrument des englischunterrichts in den schulen der zehn- bis vierzehnjährigen.* Dissertation. University of Graz, Austria.

Gerngroß, G., H. Puchta, and M. Schratz. 1982. "The butterfly and other stories." Unpublished teaching materials.

Moskowitz, G. 1978. *Caring and sharing in the foreign-language class.* Rowley, Mass.: Newbury House.

Patten, B. 1974. "The elephant's petals." In: B. Maybury (ed.). Bandstand. Oxford: Oxford University Press.

Piepho, H. E. 1982. *Contacts 5.* Bochum, West Germany: Ferdinand Kamp.

Puchta, H. 1982. *"Dialogfähigkeit" als teillernziel des englischunterrichts aus der sicht traditioneller und alternativer unterrichts-konzeption.* Dissertation. University of Graz, Austria.

Puchta, H., and M. Schratz. 1983. *Handelndes lernen im englischunterricht.* Limburg, West Germany: Frankonius.

Stevick, E. 1976. *Memory, meaning and method: some psychological perspectives of language learning.* Rowley, Mass.: Newbury House.

Stevick, E. 1980. *Teaching languages: a way and ways.* Rowley, Mass.: Newbury House.

Stevick, E. 1982. *Teaching and learning languages.* Cambridge: Cambridge University Press.

Van Ek, J. 1977. *The threshold level for modern language learning in schools.* London: Longman.

Wilkins, D. 1976. *Notional syllabuses.* Oxford: Oxford University Press.

Chapter 7

Preparing ESL Teachers for a Communicative Curriculum— American Style

Pearl Goodman

Pearl Goodman has taught the ESL teacher training practicum and been Director of the ESL Instructional Materials Center at the University of Illinois at Urbana-Champaign since the early 1960s. Her special professional interests are teacher training and the adaptation, development, and evaluation of teaching materials for ESL.

INTRODUCTION

Fortunately, I was long ago converted to the Hegelian dialectic. How else could I have survived the last twelve years as a practicum supervisor for ESL teachers! After all, the practicum is the place where one must deal with day-to-day teaching techniques, no matter what theoretical storms swirl about. Since the truth or falsehood of any current theory is not always immediately apparent, and since it is pernicious to permit oneself to be buffeted about the ebb and flow of theoretical brandishments, the task at hand is to take the long view. Hence, I feel that my belief in Hegel's concept of the contradictions of opposites (thesis and antithesis) and their continual resolution (synthesis) has kept me from some of the worst pedagogical follies and pitfalls.

Rightly or wrongly, my approach has been one of incorporation, and over the last twelve years this has resulted in considerable mental and emotional gymnastics. Having barely incorporated the generative revolution in linguistics and the cognitive revolution in psychology, the sociolinguistic revolution was upon us with its communicative competence imperatives: culture, paralinguistics, social functions, semantico-grammatical notions, discourse, etc. It was soon apparent that my single-lesson approach to training teachers could incorporate only so many of these elements, but not all. To synthesize everything it was necessary to think in terms of larger segments of teaching units, syllabuses, curricula.

The British have, of course, been approaching the problem on a syllabus/curriculum (often using the two words interchangeably) level for some time now. In fact, in the summers of 1980 and 1981 while working with a group of visiting African English teachers, my colleague Rebecca Finney and I tried to apply the Breen and Candlin communicative curriculum model (1980). We were able to achieve a workable demonstration of the model over a six-week period, but we could not come up with what might be considered a useful assignment in syllabus design for the African teachers. In the course of that six-week period in the summer of 1981, Sandra Savignon came to speak to the African teachers on the subject of communicative competence and communication activities. I do not recall any specific point that stood out from the others on that occasion, but six months later, when I was again grappling with the problem of creating a good practical assignment that would come to grips with all the elements in a communicative syllabus/curriculum, I decided to discuss the Breen and Candlin model with her. I explained that this model was proving too contingent on circumstances and too *ad hoc* in implementation to constitute a coherent and manageable assignment for a practicum.

I could hardly have come to a better place to discuss these concerns. The communicative curriculum was precisely Professor Savignon's concern, and in fact she had a book in manuscript dealing with that very subject. When I read "Shaping the Curriculum," Chapter 5 of the now published *Communicative*

Competence: Theory and Classroom Practice, I knew my quest was ended. Here was a way to achieve the kind of synthesis I believed in and a way to incorporate all that had proved valuable. The components of the curriculum were firm but moveable, and the proportions of the components were left flexible according to the needs of the class and talents of the teacher. Most important, however, was the fact that the components were of a kind that could be adapted to language learners at all levels and could be used to create a multi-dimensional syllabus. Chapter 5 of Savignon 1983 became the basis for a culminating assignment for the teachers in the practicum.

The assignment that grew out of this exchange has been very successful. Not only have results often been surprisingly inventive and fruitful, but student teachers have offered that they found the assignment extremely worthwhile. This is the third semester I have given the assignment, and it is fair to say it has been field-tested and enthusiastically integrated into my course.

The assignment and some of its results follow, but first a few words about the conditions that prevail at the University of Illinois at Urbana-Champaign, in both the Division of English as a Second Language and the course I teach.

Initially the practicum was set up to provide a micro-teaching experience for MA candidates in Teaching English as a Second Language. Selected writing and teaching assignments in grammar and pronunciation were made after appropriate demonstrations with a class of twelve to fifteen beginning-level (not 0 level) English-language learners, participants in a Special English Program (SEP), organized for this purpose each semester. However, the teaching assignments are no longer limited to micro-teaching. Now, using two textbooks, one grammar-based and one function-based, the student teachers actually conduct the class. They also write some of their teaching materials for dictation, listening, grammar, and pronunciation. In addition, they write the course tests. Aside from teaching and participating in interaction activities with the SEP classes, they observe the class being taught in fifteen different demonstration lessons, ranging from reading and writing to communication activities. They also attend a two-hour-a-week seminar consisting of lectures and workshops.

I have summarized all this activity to impress on the reader that by the time the student teachers receive this culminating syllabus/curriculum assignment, they have acquired considerable discipline and have been exposed to a wide variety of techniques. Thus they have acquired many resources to bring to bear on the assignment and are also in a position to exercise their own creativity. In short, they have been prepared on a continuing basis with people whom they have come to know. Their syllabus units are based on real-world knowledge as well as on their imagination, which makes them all the more valuable and interesting.

Before looking at examples of proposals that some of the student teachers made, a copy of the assignment is given, together with some explanatory notes.[1] Five examples of unit plans that give a rounded picture of the results follow. They have been freely labeled "Do You Hear What I Hear?" "A Critical Incident," "What's the Story?" "A TV Guide to Commercials," and "Sing Out!"

THE ASSIGNMENT AND SAMPLE UNIT OF A COMMUNICATIVE CURRICULUM

ASSIGNMENT: Design a unit of a communicative syllabus/curriculum for the SEP class.

1. Your unit will cover three 50-minute periods.
2. Each 50-minute period will have a different component as the dominant focus. The five components proposed as essential to a communicative curriculum are:
   a. Language Arts
   b. Language for a Purpose
   c. My Language is Me: Personal L2 Use
   d. You Be, I'll Be: Theater Arts
   e. Beyond the Classroom
3. The three components chosen for the three periods should be interrelated, and yet independent. *Interrelated* in the sense that the first should help prepare the students for what they will do in the second, and the second for the third. *Independent* in that you could potentially move from one into different directions. In other words, a period should not ONLY be seen as 'prep work' for the next period.
4. Each 50-minute class period should be outlined and the purpose and goals listed.

SAMPLE UNIT

   I. *Component: Language Arts*
      A. Lesson Plan
         1. Listen to descriptions read by the teacher and guess the place. (Ask for repetition before writing down answer, if necessary.)
         2. "Twenty Questions" (three stages) about:
            a. Commonplace objects that were concealed.
            b. Unusual objects that were shown by the teacher.
            c. Cultural objects from SEP students' countries, shown by SEP students.
      B. Purpose: to provide students with an instrument for negotiation of meaning.
         1. To make guesses about unfamiliar objects.

    2. To seek further information by requesting confirmation of guesses.

    3. To make decisions about what further information is needed.

    4. To increase tolerance of ambiguity.

II. *Component: Beyond the Classroom*
(A visit to the World Heritage Museum of the University of Illinois)

  A. Lesson Plan

    1. A guided tour
      a. Listen and make guesses.
      b. Ask questions of the guide and each other (SEP students and teachers).
      c. Homework: Name some likes and dislikes (writing).

  B. Purpose: to expose the students to a community facility.

    1. To interpret what is seen and heard by making guesses.

    2. To express oneself in a 'real-life' L2 situation by asking questions.

    3. To negotiate meaning with a native L2 speaker outside of the classroom by requesting further confirmation.

III. *Component: My Language is Me: Personal L2 Use*
(Expressing likes and dislikes)

  A. Lesson Plan

    1. Recall of experience (What did you see?).

    2. Vocabulary.

    3. Likes and dislikes (oral discussion).

    4. Example of a completed letter to the museum director.

    5. Letter with appropriate blanks for students to fill in with opinions and comments.

  B. Purpose: to let students express their own feelings and opinions

    1. To express and interpret what was seen.

    2. To establish a common lexis to refer to a shared experience.

    3. To express and interpret personal preferences and opinions orally to each other.

    4. To express interest and feelings of appreciation in writing in the appropriate register.

    5. To express personal opinions in writing in the appropriate register.

Note that the assignment requests that the three components be related, but independent. This was done to encourage a new way of looking at the component parts of a unit and their relationship to each other. For example, a conventional approach to a field trip would prepare the students by describing the place the students were going to visit and by exposing the students to the vocabulary they might need. This would probably be done with the aid of pictures and brochures. In order to forestall the obvious, the sample unit deliberately reverses the order of dealing with vocabulary and postpones it until after the field trip. The students are prepared for their visit to a museum by a series of guessing games about known and unknown objects. The guessing games could stand as an independent activity. A unit that begins with vocabulary would require and be tied to a follow-up activity. Each component is to be thought of as having both intrinsic merit as well as a relationship to another component.

Note also that the sample unit puts a very heavy emphasis on the purpose of each component. This was done to compel the student teachers to consider in some depth why they were going to do something, regardless of the nature of the activity (e.g., a game, a role-play, or simulation). ESL teachers usually know why they teach grammar or pronunciation and they usually have some rationale for activities that follow lessons of that kind. However, in the case of communicative activities that are not pegged to conventional goals, I believe teachers need guidance in considering other kinds of goals and how they might accomplish them.

THE UNITS

Do You Hear What I Hear?—*Angela Moore*

The following unit plan comes to grips with the goals of expression and interpretation in an extremely interesting way.

>   I.   *Component: Language Arts*—What does that sound mean?
>   A. Lesson Plan
>   1. Listen to sound effects from various sources (horns, laughter, water, animals, etc.)
>   a. What is the sound?
>   b. Where might you hear it?
>   c. What does it make you think of? feel? (Briefly describe a place, scene, feeling—one word or phrase.)
>   2. Listen to tape of conversations, either gibberish or muffled words, so that only *intonation* and *stress* will clue meaning.
>   a. What do you think is being said?
>   b. Are the speakers angry? happy? etc. (vocabulary of emotions)
>   c. How do you know?
>   3. Discuss the effects of *sounds* (paralinguistics) on what you understand. (Teacher asks questions that lead students to *discover* influence of sound on meaning/understanding.)

B. Purpose: to provide students with awareness of paralinguistic cues to meaning and means of expressing (describing) images and feelings associated with sounds. (Vocabulary, phrases such as "I picture," "I imagine," "I feel," "It reminds me of . . .")

1. To make guesses about the nature of sounds.
2. To make further inferences about those sounds.
3. To make guesses about the meaning of utterances based on stress and intonation.
4. To express emotions, thoughts, images (describing).

II. *Component: Beyond the Classroom* (a symphony concert at local performing arts center, or on videotape, PBS, or record)

A. Lesson Plan

1. Give students handout of instruments (pictures and names—classification).
2. Attend a concert.
   a. Listen for conductor's introductions.
   b. Listen for different sounds produced by instruments, rhythm, and melody.
   c. Think of possible "interpretations" (images).
   d. Homework: Write some thoughts—likes, dislikes, favorite part (movement), instrument. (Vocabulary: superlatives, phrases such as "I liked," "I didn't like," "My favorite . . ."

B. Purpose: to expose students to a real community asset; further appreciation of Western arts.
1. To listen to another English speaker (conductor) if in English-speaking community.
2. To experience another stimulus for L2 use.
3. To express likes and dislikes in writing.

III. *Component: My Language is Me—Personal L2 Use* (Expressing feelings, interpretations; describing images)

A. Lesson Plan

1. Recall of experience: What did you hear?
2. Vocabulary: Listen to record or tape "Modern Symphony Orchestra" (a Golden Book record) describing instruments of orchestra: their sounds, classifications, etc.
3. Oral discussion: images, thoughts, associated with sounds produced by various instruments on tape.
4. Example of composition describing imaginary scene (use overhead projector or handout) associated with music.
5. Students write a one-paragraph composition *as a class* with teacher guidance on board or OHP describing a picture or painting (possibly a landscape or seascape).

6. Homework: Students write a paragraph describing images associated with a favorite song or one from the concert they attended.

B. Purpose: to allow students to express ideas, images; to describe; to use analogy, simile, metaphor. To use sounds to interpret meaning.
   1. To interpret sounds and express interpretations.
   2. To encourage use of imagination.
   3. To encourage use of sounds to interpret meaning.
   4. To describe mental pictures and emotions in writing.

A Critical Incident—*Yukiko Abe*

This unit was created by a Japanese student teacher; it makes use of a variation of the culture assimilator technique developed at the University of Illinois by Professor Harry Triandis, Department of Psychology, and materials developed specifically for Japanese English learners by one of his graduate students. The technique offers a whole reservoir of opportunities for language teachers in both L1 and L2 environments. It is highly exportable to any country and applicable to every language. I am pleased that this assignment elicited an adaptation of it.

Introduction:
For this lesson plan, I would like to use a "critical incident" approach. This approach was originally used to help second-language learners and immigrants understand the target culture and to be well-prepared for adapting themselves to it. Various critical incidents are presented, and the students are to solve the problem of why these conflicting results happened. Thus, the students are enabled to develop deeper insight into the customs and the culture of the target country.

> *Example:* Yukiko goes to a restaurant with her host family. When the soup is served, she drinks it with a loud noise. The host family seems upset about her behavior.
> *Question:* Why do you think the host family seems upset?

I. *Component: Theater Arts*
   A. Lesson Plan
      1. Two or three teachers act out a critical incident between an American and a foreigner. The students are to watch and interpret the story.
      2. Question and discussion: The teacher asks the following questions, focusing on an American's way of thinking and having the students guess it.

    a. What is the problem?

    b. How do the students know the problem—by linguistic cues or by paralinguistic cues?

    c. Why does it happen?

  3. Have the students read another incident and discuss it in the way mentioned above.

  4. Have the students form pairs; give each pair a different critical situation and have the students act it out. In this case, one of them plays the role of an American and guesses what an American would do in the given situation. The other plays the role of a foreigner.

B. Purpose: To develop insights into American culture.

  1. To develop the students' skills in using paralinguistic cues.

  2. To have the students become aware of the difference between American culture and their own culture and to understand American culture better.

  3. To have the students make guesses about the characteristics of Americans.

  4. To encourage student interaction and to increase motivation.

II. *Component: Beyond the Classroom*

A. Lesson Plan

  1. Go to a movie theater together and see a move that describes some interesting aspects of American life (example: *Kramer vs. Kramer*).

    a. Watch, listen, and interpret the story by making guesses.

    b. Homework: Write a short summary based on the following questions:

      i) Is Mr. Kramer a successful businessman?

      ii) Is Mrs. Kramer happy being at home all the time?

      iii) Does Mrs. Kramer leave home with her child?

      iv) What does Mr. Kramer do after Mrs. Kramer has left home?

      v) Why do Mr. and Mrs. Kramer fight in court?

      vi) Which of them wins in court?

      vii) Where does the child stay after the court decision has been made?

B. Purpose: To expose the students to a part of the target culture.

  1. To develop active listening skill by using whichever clues are available to the students.

  2. To develop deeper insights into the target culture.

III. *Component:* My Language is Me

A. Lesson Plan

1. Recall the story by presenting the summaries to each other and by collecting information.
2. Extract some points of American culture that the students think differ from their own culture. In this process, the teacher should guide the students toward the specific point (in this case, ideas about marriage).
3. Have the students discuss their ideas about marriage in America. Like or dislike? How are they different from those of their own culture?
   (Small group discussion—larger group discussion)
4. Have the students complete the following passages by filling in the blanks.

   Passage 1:
   If I were Mrs. Kramer, I would ＿＿＿＿＿＿ home. I

   think that personal desire is ＿＿＿＿＿ important than

   family. So Mrs. Kramer ＿＿＿＿＿ selfish.
   Passage 2:
   I think that Mr. and Mrs. Kramer ＿＿＿＿＿ divorce

   because they ＿＿＿＿＿＿＿＿ . A child

   ＿＿＿＿＿ be happy if s/he has only one parent.

Note: The students are encouraged to extend the passages.

B. Purpose: To let the students express their own feelings and opinions, and share information about different cultures.

1. To express and interpret what they have seen.
2. To express personal preference and opinions.
3. To encourage understanding and appreciation toward other culture and people.

What's the Story?—*Brad Reed*

Since this unit was actually taught in the SEP class, references are provided to the teaching materials used or samples of the teaching materials themselves. The project was carried out quite successfully in all its phases. The idea of preparing ESL students for a visit to an American nursery school, where they would be watching the children from a one-way observation booth, by having them sequence, interpret, and complete picture stories was particularly interesting. Picture composition is widely used, but its purpose here had a very original twist.

I. *Component: Language Arts*

A. Lesson Plan

Objective—Create a description of an event based on clues from which a number of conclusions may be drawn.

1. Single picture description/sequence (Heaton 1966).
   a. Present tense description of pictures uncovered one at a time.
   b. Link the four pictures together to form a coherent story line.
   c. Change the story to past tense.
2. Sequence ordering (Markstein and Grunbaum 1981).
   a. Students discuss sequence possibilities (no teacher input).
   b. Individual students give order and story.
   c. When nominal consensus is reached, a group story is created.
   d. Assignment: Create a "fifth picture" for the story by making up a possible ending to the group story.

B. Purpose:
1. To interpret ambiguous information.
2. To change present to past tense.
3. To relate an event to others.

II. *Component: Beyond the Classroom*

A. Lesson Plan

Objective—Visit the Child Care and Development Center

1. Observe the children and answer questions provided as a guide.
2. Ask questions of other SEP students and the teachers.
3. Draw conclusions as to what was seen.

B. Purpose: Expose students to a real-life situation, the type of which should elicit an opinion, with a minimal amount of explanation as to what will be seen. Provide students with an opportunity to see an ongoing University project.

1. To interpret ambiguous information.
2. To formulate ideas and opinions.
3. To prepare to describe the experience and express an opinion on it.

III. *Component: Language for a Purpose*

A. Lesson Plan

Objective—Recall the experience and relate it to another who is soliciting information.

1. Review question formation and vocabulary.
2. Students formulate questions based on provided answers.
3. Students interview each other using the questions obtained in #2.

       4. Homework: Students write a summary of interview in paragraph form.

    B. Purpose: Use of language both to solicit and to give information concerning a past event.

       1. Practice in question creation based on specific objectives.

       2. Communication between knower and questioner.

       3. Description of past event and expression of opinion.

       4. Summary of event as described by another.

Questions for observation of the child development lab

You will observe three groups of children today. For each group, answer the questions below. Your answers will help you in our discussion of what was seen.

1. How many children are in the room?
2. How old do you think they are? Are they all the same age?
3. Are most of them boys or girls?
4. What are the children doing?
5. Are they all doing the same thing?
6. Are the children working independently or in groups?
7. What kinds of materials are the children using in their activities? (For example, are they using certain toys, or some everyday items like pencils, paper, scissors, etc.?)
8. Is there an adult in the room with the children? What does the adult seem to be doing? Is s/he just watching the children or is s/he guiding the activity?
9. Do you think the children are enjoying themselves?
10. Why do you think they are doing what they are doing?

IMPORTANT—Remember to bring these questions and your answers to class on Tuesday so we can talk about what we did today.

Questions and Answers

Read the answers written below and then make up a question that would suit the answer. For example, if the answer is "It's two o'clock," the question might be "What time is it?"

    1. Q: _____

       A: I went to the Child Development Lab last Tuesday.

2. **Q:** _____
   A: Two o'clock in the afternoon.

3. **Q:** _____
   A: I saw two groups of children there.

4. **Q:** _____
   A: I think the children were about four or five years old.

5. **Q:** _____
   A: They were listening to a story in a dark room.

6. **Q:** _____
   A: They were playing different games.

7. **Q:** _____
   A: Some of them were building things. Some of them were playing house, and others were playing games on a table.

8. **Q:** _____
   A: Yes. There were adults in both rooms with the children.

9. **Q:** _____
   A: Yes. I think the children were happy.

10. **Q:** _____
    A: Yes, I would because I think it is a good school. The children were happy and they were learning useful things.

When you have written the questions, find someone and ask them your questions. Be sure to write down the answers they give you because we will use them in a little while.

A TV Guide to Commercials—*Laura Koertge*

Increasingly television is becoming a way to achieve a "Beyond the Classroom" experience for language students. Wherever TV equipment is available, it is possible to build on its "global village" character. Therefore, I decided to include a lively unit using the medium.

   I.   *Component: Beyond the Classroom* (students watch TV commercials)

      A. Lesson Plan

         1. Students bring in descriptions of two TV commercials they have seen. One commercial they liked; one they didn't.

           a. Descriptions are guided by a handout asking:

              i) What is the name of the product?

              ii) Is there a song? What is it like?

          iii) Who are the people in the commercial?

          iv) What are they saying?

          v) Why is the commercial good/bad?

       b. Students fill out the handouts as they view the commercials.

    2. Students and teacher tally in class the "good" commercials and the "bad" commercials.

    3. Students discuss "good" and "bad" points about American commericals.

    4. Students view a videotape of an American commericial and discuss:

       a. What is happening in the commercial?

       b. Are commercials like this in your country?

       c. Would you buy this product?

       d. Do commercials change your mind about a product?

       e. What are some words you often hear in commercials?

       f. What are some words to describe American commercials?

B. Purpose: To expose the student to American media.

    1. To provide a listening exercise.

    2. To interpret and express the content of commercials seen.

    3. To clarify attitudes toward American commercials.

    4. To express opinions in writing and speaking.

    5. To establish common vocabulary to refer to a shared experience.

II. *Component: My Language is Me* (students give own advertisement)

A. Lesson Plan

    1. Teacher gives demo advertisement (perhaps the day before).

       a. The teacher's own personality (not "advertising techniques" *per se*) is dominant in the presentation.

       b. Students use the demo as a model.

    2. Students give prepared, five-minute advertisements for an item from their culture.

B. Purpose: To allow students to creatively explain something from their own cultures.

    1. To negotiate meaning with other students by explaining their "product."

    2. To express an interesting part of one's culture.

    3. To use a certain context to describe something.

III. *Component: You'll Be/I'll Be* (group commercials for videotape)

A. Lesson Plan

    1. Students are divided into groups of three to four.

    2. Each group receives an object to advertise.

       a. The object is "brandless" and may be related to American culture.

    b.　i) Ideas: a can of soda, make-up, frozen pizza, shampoo, etc.

      ii) Students name the product.

  3. Each group presents an advertistement, which is videotaped for later viewing.

B.　Purpose: To allow students to work as a team towards a goal of a product.

  1. To elicit creative ideas for the presentation of and the uses of various products.

  2. To elicit attitudes toward various products and perceptions of TV commercials.

  3. To encourage natural dialog as students work in groups.

  4. To encourage speech in a certain register and context.

Sing Out!—*Kristin Lems*

A unit on language teaching through the arts completes the picture. There is nothing new about teaching songs in a language class, but the author of this unit, a professional singer, has some especially pertinent things to say about which songs are best to teach and what songs can accomplish in terms of bonding and connectedness. She also provides a procedure for teaching a song, which is all too often left up to the individual teacher with very disappointing results.

  I.　*Component: Language Arts/(Musical) Theatre Arts*

    A. Lesson Plan

      1. Listen to a tape of Peter, Paul, and Mary singing "Blowin' in the Wind" after short introduction of artists, song title, and author.

      2. Pass out handout with song lyrics; teach unknown vocabulary on board; have students explain/interpret song line by line, allowing and encouraging several interpretations (song is simple but rich in meanings).

      3. Teacher plays song on guitar while students follow handout.

      4. Students mark stress timing as teacher sings with exaggerated stress markers.

      5. Students sing along on chorus, while teacher sings verses solo.

      6. Students sing verses and chorus, at slower tempo, with teacher.

      7. Teacher works on discrete point pronunciation difficulties, goes over problem lines separately from whole song, "drills" the line a couple of times.

      8. Students, finally, sing whole song at tempo, with teacher dropping out and allowing them to sing solo when sufficient confidence is attained.

B. Purposes
1. To teach students a well-known artifact of recent American culture.
2. To promote discussion of universal questions of justice and human rights (and show that Americans, too, think about these things!).
3. To give a participatory preliminary lesson in locating stress and ear training practice.
4. To build classroom spirit.

II. *Component: Beyond the Classroom*
A. Lesson Plan
1. Either bring in a folksinger or take classes to a coffeehouse where folksingers are performing.
2. After performance, have singer chat with them, answering any questions they have (if this is a coffeehouse, plan ahead so that singer has set aside time to chat afterwards).

B. Purpose
1. To introduce students to an area musician and the format of a live folk performance.
2. To encourage self-expression by having a dialog with an American artist.
3. To train and tune their ears to spoken English.
4. To give further examples of American music (folk music was chosen because it is portable, accessible, not expensive, and has a heavy focus on language, rather than music).

III. *Component: My Language is Me*
A. Lesson Plan
1. Students discuss their experience listening and talking to the folksinger (recall of experience, vocabulary words, personal preferences).
2. Students present a song in their native language, prepared in advance as homework, on cassette tape, record, or live, and give a brief summary of it.
3. Other students ask questions about the song, the singer, the topic, etc.
4. Each student explains why s/he likes the song s/he chose.
5. At the end, students sing "Blowin' in the Wind" together again for reinforcement.

B. Purpose
1. To build communicative competence in expressing one's feelings, opinions, and preferences.

2. To expose class to cross-cultural music, and to the feelings of other class members.
3. To bring an important part of students' life in their native country into the L2 classroom, therefore bringing more of the person's personality into the developing "L2 ego."
4. To move toward memorization of "Blowin' in the Wind" so it can be shared with others in their culture upon returning, and be used to build sense of connectedness to American culture (also, perhaps, to encourage children to learn L2, and have something to offer their own kids).

Remarks: This lesson plan presupposes friendly contacts between the teacher and some local singers. I started this three-week series with the most structurally-oriented, rather than the least, because I feel that lays the foundation for the other two weeks better than the other way around. This way, after they have actually sung an American song together, they can feel a sense of self-interest in hearing the folksinger in concert, since they have performed a song of their own (so much the better if the folksinger is willing to sing "Blowin' in the Wind" in concert). I know that in a sense the first lesson is the "hardest," but it is also a group activity rather than an individual one, and the most participatory for the whole class. Also, it should be noted that the third lesson would be unlikely to be completed in one classroom hour; it should probably be stretched out into two, or even three, class sessions.

I have tried to present a cross section of the results of the communicative syllabus/curriculum assignment thus far. The variety and creativity of the responses is indicative of the assignment's liberating effect. The extent to which the student teachers explored their own interests and exploited their own talents is a measure of the need to design assignments that not only invite them to do so but also provide them with a framework that will guide them to do so intelligently and coherently.

Our British colleagues have pointed us in an important direction, but because they work in a cultural (and traditional) context different from ours, their teaching precepts do not always fit our style and milieu. Obviously we need some indigenous guidelines to function at our best. Toward that end, the Savignon model provides a set of parameters that both student teachers and I feel comfortable with and, in our attempts to realize communicative goals, helps us on our way.

NOTES

1. This assignment was developed with the cooperation of Lu Doyle, my practicum colleague at the time, and Katherine Varchetto, who was then a student.

REFERENCES

Breen, M. and C. Candlin. 1980. "The essentials of a communicative curriculum in language teaching." *Applied Linguistics* **1** 89–112.

Heaton, J. 1966. *Composition through pictures.* London: Longman.

Markstein, L. and D. Grunbaum. 1981. *What's the story?* London: Longman.

Savignon, S. 1983. *Communicative competence: theory and classroom practice.* Reading, Mass.: Addison-Wesley.

Chapter 8

Teaching Strategic Competence in the Foreign-Language Classroom

Elaine Tarone

Elaine Tarone received her Ph.D. at the University of Washington in 1972. Since that time, she has taught ESL classes and directed ESL programs at the University of Washington, and trained ESL teachers at the University of Washington, University of Minnesota and North-western University. Her research on second-language acquisition has been published in such journals as Language Learning, TESOL Quarterly *and* Applied Linguistics.

Many foreign-language textbooks that aim to teach "communicative competence" in the language seem to equate this term with "sociolinguistic competence," that is, the knowledge of what is socially acceptable in a language. However, the concept of communicative competence is in fact much broader than this; Canale and Swain (1980) have shown that it incorporates at least three components:

1. grammatical competence—the knowledge of what is grammatically correct in a language;

2. sociolinguistic competence—the knowledge of what is socially acceptable in a language; and

3. strategic competence—the knowledge of how to *use* one's language to communicate intended meaning.[1]

It seems clear that a student learning a foreign language may develop competence in each of these areas at different rates. While none of these components can be developed in total isolation from the others, learners in different settings do seem to develop different patterns of proficiency.

For example, one may imagine a student who has acquired grammatical competence in a foreign language, and who manages to get a basic message across using that language, but who fails to do so in a sociolinguistically appropriate manner. Imagine such a student, intent upon disagreeing with a teacher's point in class, shouting, "No! You're wrong!" Certainly there is nothing grammatically wrong here, and the message that the student disagrees is clear enough; the problem has to do with the appropriateness of such an utterance in a classroom lecture situation. Or, to give another example, we may imagine a student with some grammatical competence and a general awareness of sociolinguistic register, who is nonetheless unable to get intended meaning across. Some of our best classroom students complain, for example, that when they arrive in Germany (or Spain, or France) they are unable to go from the train station to the hotel using the language they have learned. Similarly, we may observe that our ESL students, when they become teaching assistants for a course in astronomy, are unable to explain the subject matter to their American students. This is not necessarily because their vocabulary or grammar is inadequate, but because they have not learned how to convey information effectively by using the linguistic resources they have. "Street learners," on the other hand, often excel in strategic competence. Those who have had the opportunity to develop their second-language skills *outside* the classroom are typically able to get their message across long before they have developed native-like grammatical competence. Similarly, immersion students have been observed to excel in strategic competence (Swain and Lapkin 1981).

The three components of communicative competence we are considering here may be defined in somewhat more detail. Grammatical competence is the knowledge of the grammatical, morphological, and phonological rules of the

What sorts of resources are needed for this purpose? We may obtain a clue by looking at the strategies used by native speakers who are confronted by similar communication problems. Native speakers typically use the strategies of circumlocution and approximation (Tarone and Yule 1983), strategies that require certain basic or "primitive" vocabulary and sentence structures useful for describing, for example, shape, size, color, texture, function, analogy, hyponymy, and so on. We would expect foreign-language learners who are given practice in dealing with communication problems to develop the resources needed to use circumlocution and approximation as well.

What can the teacher do to encourage students' use of such communication strategies? The foreign-language classroom can provide (a) opportunities for *practice*, and (b) actual *instruction* in the use of strategies. Actual *teaching* of communication strategy use can occur in a variety of ways. Strategies can be isolated, named, and discussed. Exercises like the ones described below can be interrupted in order to evaluate and analyze problems that arise. Teachers can take notes on such problems, and discuss them after the activity. Or students may be asked to consciously attend to strategies, "discover" and evaluate them on their own.[2]

Exercises designed to give the student *practice* in using communication strategies to solve communication problems should require that the speaker alone have information that the listener or listeners require in order to complete some task. One type of activity that provides *practice* in strategy use involves asking a speaker to describe an object for which the target language vocabulary is unknown—describe it so clearly that a listener, who cannot see the object being described, can (a) pick out the correct photograph of the object from a group of photos of similar objects, or (b) draw the object. For example, a student asked to describe a kitchen colander might find a need for basic vocabulary and phrases such as the following:

made of metal (or plastic)

silver (or orange, or white)

half-spherical in shape (or bowl-shaped)

eighteen inches in diameter

handles located on the rim

perforated with small holes

used to drain liquid from food

This task relies on the fact that the speaker is unfamiliar with the correct target language word for the object to be described; ignorance of the vocabulary item is the communicative problem that must be overcome.

In fact, this sort of situation occurs frequently when one is using one's native language and finds oneself unable to recall the name of an object or person. The communication strategies of circumlocution and approximation

---

language, and the ability to use these rules in producing correct utterances in a language. Sociolinguistic competence is knowledge of pragmatic and speech act conventions in a language, of norms of stylistic appropriateness, and of the uses of the language in establishing and maintaining social relations. Strategic competence is the ability to convey information to a listener and correctly interpret information received. It includes the use of communication strategies to solve problems that arise in the process of conveying this information.

Each of these components of communicative competence is extremely important as a goal in the foreign-language classroom—a student who has failed to develop competence in any one of these components cannot truly be said to be proficient in the foreign language. Yet it is only recently that foreign-language and ESL curricula have included more than instruction in the grammatical, morphological, and phonological properties of the target language. The goal has been quite simply the development of grammatical competence. Only recently have foreign-language and ESL curricula begun to include the second and third components of communicative competence (sociolinguistic and strategic competence) as goals of instruction in the classroom.

Although we now see an increasing number of pedagogical books and articles, as well as textbooks for learners, advocating a "communicative approach" to the teaching of a second language, many such materials fail to establish clearly the nature of the "communication" skills being taught. Are the new materials designed to teach sociolinguistic skills? Formal and informal register? Stylistic norms? Or are they designed to give students practice in getting information across to a listener, regardless of grammatical form or sociolinguistic appropriateness? Often, the new materials seem to be trying to achieve both goals at once, or they may be unclear as to what is, in fact, the goal of a particular exercise. Many of the newer "notional-functional" syllabuses seem to aim for the goal of strategic competence in that they attempt to provide the learner with the resources needed to transmit information (notions) or messages (functions, like apologies or commands). Yet proponents of many notional-functional approaches to syllabus design do not always seem to clarify the important distinction between sociolinguistic and strategic competence.

Given that a teacher has decided that one goal of the language classroom should be improved strategic competence, what sorts of input and exercises should be provided for the students to enable them to achieve this goal? Two aspects of strategic competence should be considered:

1. the overall skill of the foreign-language learner in successfully conveying information to a listener; and

2. the learner's ability to use communication strategies when problems are encountered in the process of conveying information.

These two aspects of strategic competence should, I believe, be considered separately.

Many of the exercises included in "communicative syllabuses," such as exercises involving group problem solving, are designed to give the learner practice in transmitting real information using the target language. Such practice, it is believed, will result in an increase in the learners' overall skill in conveying information. And in fact, anecdotal evidence suggests that such practice is helpful. Certainly students whose foreign-language background has *not* included such practice seem to be very unwilling to even *try* to communicate real information in the foreign language outside the class, unless they have rehearsed their utterances many times to ensure grammatical correctness. Such materials as do exist focus on improving overall skill in conveying information by (a) *teaching* students phrases and sentences useful for conveying particular notions and functions (as in many notional-functional syllabuses, where students may be taught different expressions of quantity, or of spatial relations); or by (b) providing students with *practice* in conveying information (as by setting up group exercises in which students must give instructions, or share information in order to accomplish some task).

However, few, if any, materials presently available teach students how to use *communication strategies* when problems are encountered in such group exercises. Students not only need instruction and practice in the overall skill of conveying information using the target language; they also need instruction and practice in the use of communication strategies to solve problems encountered in the process of conveying information. That is, if the expressions learned in, for example, a notional-functional syllabus *fail* the learners in their attempt to convey information, they have been given no instruction to help them to find alternative means of expressing that same informational content. How might such instruction and practice be provided?

Students' skills in communication strategies may benefit from the sort of exercise that asks them to transmit information to a listener in a situation in which the speaker faces some problem, such as unfamiliarity with a target language vocabulary item or grammatical structure, or inability to pronounce a word or phrase clearly enough for the listener to identify it. Faerch and Kasper (1983) define communication strategies as "potentially conscious plans for solving what to an individual presents itself as a problem in reaching a particular communicative goal." Tarone (1981a) sets out the following criteria as characteristic of a communication strategy:

1. A speaker desires to communicate a meaning *x* to a listener.

2. The speaker believes the linguistic or sociolinguistic structure desired to communicate meaning *x* is unavailable, or is not shared with the listener.

3. The speaker chooses to do one of the following:
   a. avoid—that is, not attempt to communicate meaning *x*; or
   b. attempt alternate means to communicate meaning *x*. The speaker stops trying alternatives when it seems clear to the speaker that there is shared meaning.

Some examples of communication strategies used by second-language learners in research studies (Tarone 1977; Tarone and Yule 1983) are provided below. This list of strategies is not intended to be a final categorization of all communication strategies; it is simply provided to help clarify the notion of communication strategy.

1. *Avoidance*
   a. Topic avoidance. The learner simply tries not to talk about concepts for which the target language item or structure is not known.
   b. Message abandonment. The learner begins to talk about a concept but cannot continue and stops in mid-utterance.

2. *Paraphrase*
   a. Approximation. The learner uses a single target language vocabulary item or structure, which the learner knows is not correct, but which shares enough semantic features in common with the desired item to satisfy the speaker (e.g., use of superordinate term: *pipe* for *waterpipe;* use of analogy: *like an octopus*).
   b. Word coinage. The learner makes up a new word or phrase in order t communicate a desired concept (e.g., *airball* for *balloon*).
   c. Circumlocution. The learner describes the properties of the object action instead of using the appropriate target language item or struct (e.g., "It's oval and shiny," "She is, uh, smoking something . . . th Persian.").

3. *Borrowing*
   a. Literal translation. The learner translates word-for-word from t tive language (e.g., "He invites him to drink" for "They toas other.").
   b. Language mix. The learner uses the native language term bothering to translate (e.g., Turkish *tirtil* for *caterpillar*).

4. *Appeal for assistance*. The learner asks for the correct term (e.g., this? What called?").

5. *Mime*. The learner uses nonverbal tactics in place of a lexical iter (e.g., clapping one's hands to illustrate applause), or to acco other communication strategy (e.g., "It's about this long.").

A more detailed typology of communication strategies, providin ple, a breakdown of types of circumlocution, is available in Parik

Obviously, some of these communication strategies will be ful in transmitting information than others. The initial reaction of little practice in dealing with communication problems is a avoidance does not lead either to communication of intended m development of the resources needed to deal with future problems.

are most useful for solving this sort of communication problem. *Circumlocution*, involving a description of the properties of the object (material, color, size, shape, texture, and component parts and their location relative to the whole object) and the function of the object, is most useful. *Approximation*—involving, for example, the use of a superordinate term ("It's a type of _____"), an analogy ("It's like an octopus, but it's not an octopus"), or a related term ("It's a cigarette" for "It's a cigar")—may also be of use.

In our research (Tarone and Yule 1983) we have found that even advanced ESL students may fail to use such basic terms as "end," "top side," "strap," all useful in circumlocution. Clearly, direct instruction, either before or after the use of such an activity as that described above, will be helpful in providing students with a basic set of vocabulary items useful for describing properties and functions. Certain vocabulary items and grammatical patterns will be useful again and again as these exercises are repeated: for example, shapes (*circular, oval, square, disc-shaped, bowl-shaped, triangular*) or locative phrases (*on each end, in the middle, on the rim, two inches from the top*).

A variation on this exercise involves showing a speaker how to carry out a procedure (such as assembling an object). Yule *et al.* (1982) ask subjects to give instructions on how to assemble a meat grinder. The speaker can be shown a videotape of the procedure, or a series of pictures depicting the procedure, and then be asked to give instructions to a listener, who has the task of (a) carrying out the procedure, or (b) selecting the correct series of pictures to depict the procedure. Obviously the speaking task is much more difficult if the speaker cannot see what the listener is doing. This task involves *both* description of the parts of the object, *and* mastery of a set of instructional verbs (both basic verbs like *put* and *take*, and more technical instructional verbs like *insert, stir, screw, clamp*). Again, the teacher may find it helpful to teach the students some of these verbs explicitly.

Another variation on this activity involves practice in narration on the part of the speaker. The speaker is shown a series of pictures or a videotape depicting several individuals in a story sequence. A story sequence used in Tarone and Yule (1983) involves a teacher who draws geometric figures on the chalkboard and then leaves the classroom. Two students then take turns converting the teacher's geometric figures into a drawing of the teacher. The teacher returns and scolds the students, who blame each other. The listener who hears the speaker's narrative must pick the correct series of pictures out of three or four possible picture series. It should be pointed out that in research (Tarone and Yule 1983) using all three variations of this exercise (description, instruction, narration), the narration task seemed to be the easiest part for the learners—*not* in the sense that learners made fewer grammatical errors or fewer errors in transmitting information, but in the sense that the speakers did not seem to be aware of many communication problems necessitating communication strategy use. Occasionally an object crucial to the narration would be hard to describe, but on the whole the linguistic resources necessary for story

narration generally seemed much more accessible to learners than those required for description and instruction. The problems that did arise—problems
of which the learners did not always appear to be aware—related to maintaining clarity of reference to the actors in the stories. This activity can provide
more practice in maintaining clarity of reference if it involves stories in which
all the protagonists are of the same sex and same general appearance, so that
speakers are forced to make some effort at keeping reference straight by means
of relative clauses or other nominal modifications (e.g., *the girl who came in first*,
or *the second girl*).

Another sort of activity that encourages the development of communication strategies was developed by Eric Nelson at the University of Minnesota to
help students become more effective in communicating when *pronunciation* got
in the way. This activity differs from the description of the colander, where the
goal was to improve students' communicative effectiveness when *limited vocabulary* got in the way. This exercise requires students to produce words and
phrases that cause pronunciation problems, and encourages speakers who
find they cannot get their message across because of pronunciation problems to
use communication strategies to transmit the same information by other
means. To ensure that this activity provides practice for cases where pronunciation is a problem, other possible variables (e.g., words and content of the
sentences) are controlled. Thus, the content of every sentence is old information taken from earlier lessons, and all the vocabulary items have already been
encountered in the class. The entire class is given a handout with twenty to
thirty incomplete sentences such as the following:

1. Pollution is a problem _____ .

2. Many American _____ .

3. _____ is important in the U.S.

4. _____ in Minneapolis is very

   _____ .

5. Advertising is sometimes _____ .

Each student also receives complete versions of two to three of the sentences,
which must be said out loud so that the rest of the class can fill in the incomplete
sentences on the handout:

1. Pollution is a problem <u>all over the world</u>.

2. Many American <u>surnames end in -son</u>.

3. <u>Punctuality</u> is important in the U.S.

language, and the ability to use these rules in producing correct utterances in a language. Sociolinguistic competence is knowledge of pragmatic and speech act conventions in a language, of norms of stylistic appropriateness, and of the uses of the language in establishing and maintaining social relations. Strategic competence is the ability to convey information to a listener and correctly interpret information received. It includes the use of communication strategies to solve problems that arise in the process of conveying this information.

Each of these components of communicative competence is extremely important as a goal in the foreign-language classroom—a student who has failed to develop competence in any one of these components cannot truly be said to be proficient in the foreign language. Yet it is only recently that foreign-language and ESL curricula have included more than instruction in the grammatical, morphological, and phonological properties of the target language. The goal has been quite simply the development of grammatical competence. Only recently have foreign-language and ESL curricula begun to include the second and third components of communicative competence (sociolinguistic and strategic competence) as goals of instruction in the classroom.

Although we now see an increasing number of pedagogical books and articles, as well as textbooks for learners, advocating a "communicative approach" to the teaching of a second language, many such materials fail to establish clearly the nature of the "communication" skills being taught. Are the new materials designed to teach sociolinguistic skills? Formal and informal register? Stylistic norms? Or are they designed to give students practice in getting information across to a listener, regardless of grammatical form or sociolinguistic appropriateness? Often, the new materials seem to be trying to achieve both goals at once, or they may be unclear as to what is, in fact, the goal of a particular exercise. Many of the newer "notional-functional" syllabuses seem to aim for the goal of strategic competence in that they attempt to provide the learner with the resources needed to transmit information (notions) or messages (functions, like apologies or commands). Yet proponents of many notional-functional approaches to syllabus design do not always seem to clarify the important distinction between sociolinguistic and strategic competence.

Given that a teacher has decided that one goal of the language classroom should be improved strategic competence, what sorts of input and exercises should be provided for the students to enable them to achieve this goal? Two aspects of strategic competence should be considered:

1. the overall skill of the foreign-language learner in successfully conveying information to a listener; and

2. the learner's ability to use communication strategies when problems are encountered in the process of conveying information.

These two aspects of strategic competence should, I believe, be considered separately.

Many of the exercises included in "communicative syllabuses," such as exercises involving group problem solving, are designed to give the learner practice in transmitting real information using the target language. Such practice, it is believed, will result in an increase in the learners' overall skill in conveying information. And in fact, anecdotal evidence suggests that such practice is helpful. Certainly students whose foreign-language background has *not* included such practice seem to be very unwilling to even *try* to communicate real information in the foreign language outside the class, unless they have rehearsed their utterances many times to ensure grammatical correctness. Such materials as do exist focus on improving overall skill in conveying information by (a) *teaching* students phrases and sentences useful for conveying particular notions and functions (as in many notional-functional syllabuses, where students may be taught different expressions of quantity, or of spatial relations); or by (b) providing students with *practice* in conveying information (as by setting up group exercises in which students must give instructions, or share information in order to accomplish some task).

However, few, if any, materials presently available teach students how to use *communication strategies* when problems are encountered in such group exercises. Students not only need instruction and practice in the overall skill of conveying information using the target language; they also need instruction and practice in the use of communication strategies to solve problems encountered in the process of conveying information. That is, if the expressions learned in, for example, a notional-functional syllabus *fail* the learners in their attempt to convey information, they have been given no instruction to help them to find alternative means of expressing that same informational content. How might such instruction and practice be provided?

Students' skills in communication strategies may benefit from the sort of exercise that asks them to transmit information to a listener in a situation in which the speaker faces some problem, such as unfamiliarity with a target language vocabulary item or grammatical structure, or inability to pronounce a word or phrase clearly enough for the listener to identify it. Faerch and Kasper (1983) define communication strategies as "potentially conscious plans for solving what to an individual presents itself as a problem in reaching a particular communicative goal." Tarone (1981a) sets out the following criteria as characteristic of a communication strategy:

1. A speaker desires to communicate a meaning x to a listener.
2. The speaker believes the linguistic or sociolinguistic structure desired to communicate meaning x is unavailable, or is not shared with the listener.
3. The speaker chooses to do one of the following:
   a. avoid—that is, not attempt to communicate meaning x; or
   b. attempt alternate means to communicate meaning x. The speaker stops trying alternatives when it seems clear to the speaker that there is shared meaning.

Some examples of communication strategies used by second-language learners in research studies (Tarone 1977; Tarone and Yule 1983) are provided below. This list of strategies is not intended to be a final categorization of all communication strategies; it is simply provided to help clarify the notion of communication strategy.

1. *Avoidance*
   a. Topic avoidance. The learner simply tries not to talk about concepts for which the target language item or structure is not known.
   b. Message abandonment. The learner begins to talk about a concept but cannot continue and stops in mid-utterance.

2. *Paraphrase*
   a. Approximation. The learner uses a single target language vocabulary item or structure, which the learner knows is not correct, but which shares enough semantic features in common with the desired item to satisfy the speaker (e.g., use of superordinate term: *pipe* for *waterpipe*; use of analogy: *like an octopus*).
   b. Word coinage. The learner makes up a new word or phrase in order to communicate a desired concept (e.g., *airball* for *balloon*).
   c. Circumlocution. The learner describes the properties of the object or action instead of using the appropriate target language item or structure (e.g., "It's oval and shiny," "She is, uh, smoking something . . . that's Persian.").

3. *Borrowing*
   a. Literal translation. The learner translates word-for-word from the native language (e.g., "He invites him to drink" for "They toast each other.").
   b. Language mix. The learner uses the native language term without bothering to translate (e.g., Turkish *tirtil* for *caterpillar*).

4. *Appeal for assistance.* The learner asks for the correct term (e.g., "What is this? What called?").

5. *Mime.* The learner uses nonverbal tactics in place of a lexical item or action (e.g., clapping one's hands to illustrate applause), or to accompany another communication strategy (e.g., "It's about this long.").

A more detailed typology of communication strategies, providing, for example, a breakdown of types of circumlocution, is available in Paribakht (1982).

Obviously, some of these communication strategies will be more successful in transmitting information than others. The initial reaction of students with little practice in dealing with communication problems is avoidance, and avoidance does not lead either to communication of intended meaning or to the development of the resources needed to deal with future communication problems.

What sorts of resources are needed for this purpose? We may obtain a clue by looking at the strategies used by native speakers who are confronted by similar communication problems. Native speakers typically use the strategies of circumlocution and approximation (Tarone and Yule 1983), strategies that require certain basic or "primitive" vocabulary and sentence structures useful for describing, for example, shape, size, color, texture, function, analogy, hyponymy, and so on. We would expect foreign-language learners who are given practice in dealing with communication problems to develop the resources needed to use circumlocution and approximation as well.

What can the teacher do to encourage students' use of such communication strategies? The foreign-language classroom can provide (a) opportunities for *practice*, and (b) actual *instruction* in the use of strategies. Actual *teaching* of communication strategy use can occur in a variety of ways. Strategies can be isolated, named, and discussed. Exercises like the ones described below can be interrupted in order to evaluate and analyze problems that arise. Teachers can take notes on such problems, and discuss them after the activity. Or students may be asked to consciously attend to strategies, "discover" and evaluate them on their own.[2]

Exercises designed to give the student *practice* in using communication strategies to solve communication problems should require that the speaker alone have information that the listener or listeners require in order to complete some task. One type of activity that provides *practice* in strategy use involves asking a speaker to describe an object for which the target language vocabulary is unknown—describe it so clearly that a listener, who cannot see the object being described, can (a) pick out the correct photograph of the object from a group of photos of similar objects, or (b) draw the object. For example, a student asked to describe a kitchen colander might find a need for basic vocabulary and phrases such as the following:

made of metal (or plastic)

silver (or orange, or white)

half-spherical in shape (or bowl-shaped)

eighteen inches in diameter

handles located on the rim

perforated with small holes

used to drain liquid from food

This task relies on the fact that the speaker is unfamiliar with the correct target language word for the object to be described; ignorance of the vocabulary item is the communicative problem that must be overcome.

In fact, this sort of situation occurs frequently when one is using one's native language and finds oneself unable to recall the name of an object or person. The communication strategies of circumlocution and approximation are most useful for solving this sort of communication problem. *Circumlocution*, involving a description of the properties of the object (material, color, size, shape, texture, and component parts and their location relative to the whole object) and the function of the object, is most useful. *Approximation*—involving, for example, the use of a superordinate term ("It's a type of _____"), an analogy ("It's like an octopus, but it's not an octopus"), or a related term ("It's a cigarette" for "It's a cigar")—may also be of use.

In our research (Tarone and Yule 1983) we have found that even advanced ESL students may fail to use such basic terms as "end," "top side," "strap," all useful in circumlocution. Clearly, direct instruction, either before or after the use of such an activity as that described above, will be helpful in providing students with a basic set of vocabulary items useful for describing properties and functions. Certain vocabulary items and grammatical patterns will be useful again and again as these exercises are repeated: for example, shapes (*circular, oval, square, disc-shaped, bowl-shaped, triangular*) or locative phrases (*on each end, in the middle, on the rim, two inches from the top*).

A variation on this exercise involves showing a speaker how to carry out a procedure (such as assembling an object). Yule *et al.* (1982) ask subjects to give instructions on how to assemble a meat grinder. The speaker can be shown a videotape of the procedure, or a series of pictures depicting the procedure, and then be asked to give instructions to a listener, who has the task of (a) carrying out the procedure, or (b) selecting the correct series of pictures to depict the procedure. Obviously the speaking task is much more difficult if the speaker cannot see what the listener is doing. This task involves *both* description of the parts of the object, *and* mastery of a set of instructional verbs (both basic verbs like *put* and *take*, and more technical instructional verbs like *insert, stir, screw, clamp*). Again, the teacher may find it helpful to teach the students some of these verbs explicitly.

Another variation on this activity involves practice in narration on the part of the speaker. The speaker is shown a series of pictures or a videotape depicting several individuals in a story sequence. A story sequence used in Tarone and Yule (1983) involves a teacher who draws geometric figures on the chalkboard and then leaves the classroom. Two students then take turns converting the teacher's geometric figures into a drawing of the teacher. The teacher returns and scolds the students, who blame each other. The listener who hears the speaker's narrative must pick the correct series of pictures out of three or four possible picture series. It should be pointed out that in research (Tarone and Yule 1983) using all three variations of this exercise (description, instruction, narration), the narration task seemed to be the easiest part for the learners—*not* in the sense that learners made fewer grammatical errors or fewer errors in transmitting information, but in the sense that the speakers did not seem to be aware of many communication problems necessitating communication strategy use. Occasionally an object crucial to the narration would be hard to describe, but on the whole the linguistic resources necessary for story

narration generally seemed much more accessible to learners than those required for description and instruction. The problems that did arise—problems
of which the learners did not always appear to be aware—related to maintaining clarity of reference to the actors in the stories. This activity can provide
more practice in maintaining clarity of reference if it involves stories in which
all the protagonists are of the same sex and same general appearance, so that
speakers are forced to make some effort at keeping reference straight by means
of relative clauses or other nominal modifications (e.g., *the girl who came in first*,
or *the second girl*).

Another sort of activity that encourages the development of communication strategies was developed by Eric Nelson at the University of Minnesota to
help students become more effective in communicating when *pronunciation* got
in the way. This activity differs from the description of the colander, where the
goal was to improve students' communicative effectiveness when *limited vocabulary* got in the way. This exercise requires students to produce words and
phrases that cause pronunciation problems, and encourages speakers who
find they cannot get their message across because of pronunciation problems to
use communication strategies to transmit the same information by other
means. To ensure that this activity provides practice for cases where pronunciation is a problem, other possible variables (e.g., words and content of the
sentences) are controlled. Thus, the content of every sentence is old information taken from earlier lessons, and all the vocabulary items have already been
encountered in the class. The entire class is given a handout with twenty to
thirty incomplete sentences such as the following:

1. Pollution is a problem _____ .

2. Many American _____ .

3. _____ is important in the U.S.

4. _____ in Minneapolis is very

   _____ .

5. Advertising is sometimes _____ .

Each student also receives complete versions of two to three of the sentences,
which must be said out loud so that the rest of the class can fill in the incomplete
sentences on the handout:

1. Pollution is a problem <u>all over the world</u>.

2. Many American <u>surnames end in -son</u>.

3. <u>Punctuality</u> is important in the U.S.

4. The weather in Minneapolis is very unpredictable.

5. Advertising is sometimes misleading.

The complete sentences can be assigned deliberately so the teacher *knows* the speaker will have difficulty pronouncing the missing words and phrases. So, for example, number 4 might go to a student who the teacher knows (through previous experience) will say "za wezzah." If the speaker's pronunciation is clear enough for the class to understand, the speaker may go on to the next sentence; if it is not clear enough, the speaker must use communication strategies to begin negotiations with the rest of the class in order to get the meaning across in other words. This exercise thus provides practice in using communication strategies for overcoming pronunciation problems in reaching a communicative goal.

All these activities are, of course, both *speaking* tasks and *listening* tasks. They can be structured so as to place the burden primarily on the speaker (for example, by requiring that listeners maintain silence and not ask questions of clarification). But in most real-life situations, a complex negotiation occurs between speaker and listener, who work together to clarify the intended message. To provide practice in negotiation, the teacher can provide instruction for the listener in these activities as well as for the speaker. Such instruction might involve the isolation, naming and discussion of behavioral interpretive strategies (cf. Tarone 1981b) such as appeals for repetition (e.g., "What?"), mime (e.g., puzzled facial expressions of various types), questioning repeats (e.g., A: The water table. *B: The water . . . ?* A: Water table.), and approximation or paraphrases (e.g., A: The jugworm. B: . . . *Junkworm*? C: Jugworm.). A behavioral interpretive strategy often taught to counselors involves the use of extended paraphrase of the speaker's message, as in "I hear you saying that . . . Is that correct?" Such instruction may take place either before or after the class has participated in the activities, and may be either inductive or deductive in nature.

Exercises like these provide practice in the use of communication strategies and should be effective in building up resources that will enable students to be more flexible in finding ways to transmit information in real-world interactions. It is important to emphasize, in closing, that such exercises do not claim to provide the sort of practice that will necessarily improve grammatical or sociolinguistic competence on the part of the learner. Alternative classwork will probably be required for improvement in these other areas. However, the teacher may find the framework presented in this paper, and the suggestions for classwork included here, to be helpful as models in designing class materials that will enable students to be more effective in using the target language for the transmission of information in interactions both inside and outside of the classroom.

NOTES

I would like to thank Eric Nelson for his valuable comments on an earlier version of this paper.

1. The Canale and Swain framework described here has subsequently been revised to include a fourth component, discourse competence. See Swain in this volume, Canale (1983), and Savignon (1983).

2. These teaching strategies were suggested by Eric Nelson.

REFERENCES

Canale, M. 1983. "From communicative competence to communicative language pedagogy." In J. Richards and R. Schmidt (eds.). *Language and communication*. London: Longman.

Canale, M. and M. Swain. 1980. "Theoretical bases of communicative approaches to second-language teaching and testing." *Applied Linguistics* 1: 1–47.

Faerch, C. and G. Kasper. 1983. *Strategies in interlanguage communication*. New York: Longman.

Paribakht, T. 1982. "The relationship between the use of communication strategies and aspects of target language proficiency: a study of Persian ESL students." Unpublished Ph.D. dissertation, University of Toronto.

Savignon, S. 1983. *Communicative competence: theory and classroom practice*. Reading, Mass.: Addison-Wesley.

Swain, M. and S. Lapkin. 1981. *Bilingual education in Ontario: a decade of research*. Toronto: Ontario Ministry of Education.

Tarone, E. 1977. "Conscious communication strategies in interlanguage." In H. D. Brown, et al (eds.). *On TESOL '77*. Washington D.C.: TESOL.

Tarone, E. 1981a. "Some thoughts on the notion of 'communication strategy.'" *TESOL Quarterly* 15: 285–295. Also in Faerch and Kasper. 1983. 61–74.

Tarone, E. 1981b. "Decoding a nonprimary language: the crucial role of strategic competence." Paper presented at the British Association of Applied Linguistics Seminar Interpretive Strategies in Language Learning, University of Lancaster, September 1981.

Tarone, E. and G. Yule. 1983. "Communication strategies in east-west interactions." Paper presented at the Conference on English as an International Language: Discourse Patterns Across Cultures, Honolulu, Hawaii (June 1–8, 1983).

Yule, G., G. Brown & A. Anderson. 1982. "Communicative effectiveness in speaking." Paper presented to the Fifth International Symposium on Educational Testing, University of Stirling.

Chapter 9

Teacher-Made Videotape Materials for the Second-Language Classroom

Tony Silva

Tony Silva is presently a Teaching Associate at the University of Illinois Intensive English Institute. He has also served as a Teaching Fellow at Harvard University's Summer EFL Program. His main interests are ESL teaching and materials development. In addition to having presented numerous papers on these topics at state, regional and international TESOL conferences, he has served some of the major ESL publishers as a manuscript reviewer, consultant and/or materials writer.

INTRODUCTION

As more communicative approaches to second-language teaching are explored, the use of videotape (VT) instructional materials is becoming a subject of great interest. Unlike written dialogs, and even audio recordings, videotape is capable of capturing a communicative act in its entirety. This medium thus provides an excellent means for the presentation, analysis, and discussion of authentic oral discourse. Not surprisingly, therefore, VT programs for second-language (L2) instruction have begun to proliferate. These materials, both commercial and in-house productions, have appeared in a variety of formats: videotaped lecture series, off-air recordings (taped TV broadcasts), and dramatic and informational series, to mention only a few; and their very presence has served to heighten teacher awareness of VT as an instructional medium. An additional factor not to be overlooked in the current interest in VT instructional materials is, of course, the increasing accessibility of the facilities, equipment, and technology needed for their production and/or use. Today, for the first time, a great number of L2 classroom teachers can avail themselves of a technology heretofore limited to only a very few experimental programs.

Though VT has provoked much interest and is widely recognized as a viable and effective medium for L2 instruction, its actual use in L2 classrooms remains rather limited. There seem to be three significant causes for this limited use: (1) many L2 classroom teachers are still uncomfortable with VT technology and equipment; (2) there is a lack of understanding about the possibilities for the exploitation of VT materials; and (3) there exist no standard, widely recognized procedures for the use of VT materials in the L2 classroom.

The first of these problems is perhaps the easiest to solve. It seems likely that time and increased familiarity with video technology will play a large part in lessening L2 teachers' apprehensions about using VT materials. However, time and familiarity cannot be counted on to solve the second and third problems. Only a systematic exploration and demonstration of the potential of VT materials and the teaching/learning activities to accompany them can ensure the successful integration of this new technology into L2 programs.

To illustrate some of the many possibilities for the exploitation of VT materials and to suggest viable classroom procedures for their use, we will examine a sample from an existing teacher-made instructional VT program in some detail. Following a discussion of the considerations that preceded the production of this particular segment, a transcript of the segment will be provided along with an analysis of selected features of the discourse from both linguistic and paralinguistic perspectives. In conclusion, suggestions will be offered for classroom presentation and related follow-up activities.

PRODUCTION OF A
VIDEOTAPE: SOME
PRELIMINARY CONSIDERATIONS

The sample that will be examined and discussed is a VT segment similar to segments from a VT program developed by the author for use in the Intensive English Institute (IEI) of the University of Illinois at Urbana-Champaign (UIUC). The primary audience for these materials were English as a Second Language (ESL) students with high-intermediate to advanced levels of proficiency in English. These particular students comprised a rather heterogeneous group. There was substantial diversity with regard to their age, prior education, linguistic and cultural background, interests, goals and motivation.

What these students had in common (as do most other L2 students in similar situations) was a need to be able to participate effectively in face-to-face communication with native speakers of English. To help them do so, it was felt that what was needed were materials that would familiarize these students with as many aspects of interpersonal oral communication in English as possible.

VT appeared to be a logical choice as an instructional medium for achieving this objective of familiarization. It was chosen primarily because it would expose the students to both the linguistic and paralinguistic features of interpersonal oral communication, and thus provide them with a more complete view and understanding of the communicative act involved. Since, at that time, no commercial materials could be found that could adequately meet this objective, it was decided that the materials should be produced in-house. Fortunately, the necessary facilities, equipment, and technical assistance were available at the Language Learning Laboratory (LLL) of the UIUC.

The next concern was the definition of an approach to guide the development of the materials. The approach chosen contained elements of functional language teaching and discourse analysis. It was decided that particular language functions—e.g., apologizing, inviting (chosen according to their relevance to the students' needs)—would define the parameters of the VT segments, and that the primary focus of the lessons based on these segments would be the analysis of the discourse features contained therein.

Another consideration was the nature of the content of the segments. A fundamental concern here was that the communication presented be as authentic as possible. Therefore, it was determined that the most appropriate format for generating the content of the segment would be a planned, but unscripted role-play. This type of role-play is planned to the extent that the participants are told what language function to execute and what attitude to adopt. For the particular segment that will be dealt with later in this discussion, one participant was told to invite the other to an event; the other participant was instructed to accept the invitation. Both were to act like peers and casual friends. The role-plays are unscripted in the sense that the participants supplied their own language and social context extemporaneously.

Having considered the audience, objective, medium, approach, format, and content, it was necessary to specify a set and participants for the segment. The controlling criterion in choosing the set was simplicity, since it was felt that distractions should be minimized in order to focus attention on the communication taking place. It was decided that the set should include no scenery or props, and that the only visuals on the set should be the two participants, occupying center stage, and a blue curtain as a backdrop.

The main consideration regarding the participants' appearance was that it not unduly distract the viewers' attention from the communicative act. One of the participants (Jean) is female, in her mid-twenties, approximately 5'5", with shoulder-length, wavy, light-brown hair. She wears a brown corduroy jacket over a print blouse and denim skirt. The other participant (Brad) is male, in his mid-twenties, approximately 6'1", with neatly cut, straight, dark brown hair and a full, dark brown beard. He wears a dark green, crew neck sweater and blue jeans. The participants' entrances and exits were likewise planned with simplicity in mind. Jean enters and exits stage right; Brad enters and exits stage left.

The final step in the production process was the actual videotaping. This was done in a small TV studio that is part of LLL of the UIUC, and required only one camera and two technicians (the author and the studio director). The production process[1] for the segment took approximately ten minutes.[2]

Having provided a brief overview of the conceptual and physical aspects of the development of the segment, we now return to the two points that are central to this discussion: the exploitation of VT materials and classroom procedures for their use. These points will be dealt with through (1) the enumeration of possible teaching points/foci that can be drawn from a brief VT segment and (2) the suggestion of procedures for the presentation of these points/foci in the L2 classroom. The discussion of these points will be related to the aforementioned VT segment illustrating the language function "inviting" in an informal context, and will include:

1. a verbatim transcript of the segment;
2. analyses of some of the paralinguistic, functional, sociocultural, affective, grammatical, lexical, and phonological features of the discourse contained in the segment; and
2. considerations and suggestions for the classroom presentation of the data from the aforementioned analyses.

TRANSCRIPT OF THE VIDEOTAPED SEGMENT

The following is a verbatim transcript of the videotaped segment. Note the numbers in parentheses and the letters preceding the lines of the dialog. In the following analyses of this segment, any number in parentheses will refer to that particular line in the transcript. In addition, the letters J and B will be used to refer to the speaker of a given line (B = Brad; J = Jean).

(1) J: Hi, Brad.

(2) B: Hi, Jean. How are you?

(3) J: Oh, I'm pretty good. How about you?

(4) B: Not bad. Busy.

(5) J: Busy. I'm sure. Brad, I'm glad I caught you. We're having a Halloween party at our house next Saturday night. Can you come?

(6) B: A Halloween party?

(7) J: A Halloween party—that means costumes.

(8) B: Oh, a costume. Boy.

(9) J: You have to wear a costume.

(10) B: Sure. That's next Saturday night?

(11) J: That's next Saturday, October 30th.

(12) B: Yeah. That sounds fun.

(13) J: Okay. . . .

(14) B: That sounds fun.

(15) J: Great. I'm glad you can come.

(16) B: Do I need to bring anything?

(17) J: No, I don't think so . . . umm . . . we're going to have beer and wine and some pop. . . .

(18) B: Umm-hmm.

(19) J: . . . so if you want anything else, you'll have to bring that. . . .

(20) B: Any charge?

(21) J: No, absolutely not.

(22) B: Okay.

(23) J: Yeah.

(24) B: That . . . now, it's at your house?

(25) J: It's at my house. Do you know where I live?

(26) B: I'm not sure. You better tell me.

(27) J: Okay, I live at
         905 South Race.

(28) B: 905 South Race.

(29) J: Yeah. It's near you.

(30) B: That's close. . . .

(31) J: Right.

(32) B: . . . I'm at 602. Right.

(33) J: That's right.

(34) B: Okay. That's on
         Saturday, the 30th?

(35) J: At . . . at about 7:30 or 8:00.

(36) B: At about 7:30.

(37) J: Uh-huh.

(38) B: Okay, Jean. . . .

(39) J: Okay. Good.

(40) B: . . . thanks a lot.

(41) J: Umm-hmm. I'll see you then. Bye-bye.

(42) B: Okay. Bye-bye.

ANALYSES OF
VIDEOTAPED SEGMENT

The purpose of the following analyses is to illustrate the variety of features that are relevant to an understanding of the preceding dialog. It is not suggested that analyses of this breadth and/or depth need be done by teachers or students when using VT materials of this type.

(1) Paralinguistic Features

The paralinguistic features of this dialog have been broken down into four categories:
kinesics (gestures), eye contact, proxemics (distance between participants), and kinesthetics (touching).

(a) Kinesics

In the following analysis the participants' gestures are indexed to the lines in which they occur. The remarks in parentheses refer to the probable meaning or significance of the gestures; (?) indicates that the meaning of a particular gesture was not readily apparent.

(2) B brings both arms up from sides—palms of hands face up (greeting; welcome)

(4) B returns hands to hips

(8) B cocks head back
    (thinking)

(16) B brings both arms up from sides—palms of hands face up (questioning); returns hands to hips

(17) J moves head side to side (negation)

(20) B brings right arm up from side—right palm face up (questioning); returns hand to hip

(21) J moves head side to side (negation)

(24) B brings right arm up from side—right palm face up; holds position (questioning)

(26) B moves right hand side to side (?); returns hand to hip

(28) B brings left arm up—left palm face up; strikes left palm with index finger of right hand (?); holds position

(30) B lifts right index finger from left palm; points finger at J (agreeing)

(32) B places index finger of right hand in left palm (?); holds position

(34) B lifts right hand; strikes left palm with back of right hand (?); holds position

(42) B lifts right hand from left palm; waves with right hand (leave-taking)

Throughout the dialog both B and J use nods of the head and facial expressions to emphasize and react to points. J gestures only with her head in this dialog. Throughout the sequence, her right hand (her left hand is not visible) remains in her right jacket pocket.

(b) Eye Contact

Eye contact between B and J is fairly constant throughout the dialog. However, there are significant breaks. These breaks are indicated below and are indexed to the transcript. The comments on the right suggest reasons for these breaks.

(8) B—to consider situation

(11) B—to listen for details

(11) J —to recollect

(17) J —to recollect

(28) B—to take mental notes

(34) B—to take mental notes

(36) J —to recollect

(c) Proxemics

A distance of approximately three feet is maintained between J and B through-out the dialog.

(d) Kinesthetics

J and B do not touch each other at any time during this sequence.

(2) Functional Features

The following is a line-by-line description of the functions of the utter-ances of the participants—that is, what the speakers are *doing* with language.

(1) J greets

(2) B greets, asks perfunctory question

(3) J provides perfunctory answer; asks perfunctory question

(4) B provides perfunctory answer; provides additional information

(5) J acknowledges answer; changes subject; provides background for invitation; invites

(6) B considers invitation

(7) J provides additional information; indicates condition

(8) B comments on condition

(9) J repeats condition

(10) B accepts invitation and condition; requests information/clarification

(11) J provides information/clarification

(12) B comments on situation

(13) J acknowledges comment

(14) B comments on situation (continuation of (12))

(15) J acknowledges acceptance of invitation

(16) B requests information

(17) J provides information requested; adds additional information

(18) B shows understanding

(19) J provides additional information; poses hypothetical question

(20) B requests information

(21) J provides information

(22) B accepts information; shows understanding

(23) J acknowledges acceptance/understanding

(24) B requests information/verification

(25) J provides information/verification; offers additional information
(26) B accepts offer
(27) J provides information
(28) B repeats information
(29) J provides additional related information
(30) B acknowledges and agrees with information
(31) J acknowledges agreement
(32) B provides additional information (continuation of (30))
(33) J acknowledges agreement
(34) B requests verification of information
(35) J verifies information; provides additional information
(36) B repeats additional information
(37) J acknowledges understanding
(38) B signals end of conversation
(39) J acknowledges signal
(40) B shows gratitude
(41) J accepts show of gratitude; takes leave
(42) B acknowledges leave-taking; takes leave

(3) Sociocultural Features

The following is a list of topics drawn from the dialog, whose societal and cultural implications are relevant to understanding the interaction. These topics are *not* indexed to the lines of the dialog.

1. Relative status of the participants
2. Level of formality: Register
3. Relationship between the participants
4. Formulaic questions and responses
5. Halloween: meaning and tradition
6. Costumes: significance/purpose
7. Parties: conventions, procedures, elements
8. Saturday night: significance
9. The invitation of a man by a woman
10. An offer by a guest to bring something
11. A question from a guest about a charge
12. Permission given by a host for a guest to bring something

13. Refusal by a host of payment offered by a guest
14. Distance maintained between participants
15. Absence of touching by either participant

(4) Affective Features

The following list of topics addresses the affective implications of the interaction. These topics are *not* indexed to lines from the dialog.

1. Tone of the interaction: degree of seriousness, friendliness, informality
2. Directness/Indirectness—e.g., the lead-in to the invitation
3. Sincerity of the invitation, acceptance of the invitation, expression of gratitude for the invitation
4. Offers of help by the guest: real or perfunctory, acceptable or insulting
5. The host's reactions to the guest's offers

(5) Grammatical Features

The following grammatical features and constructions appear in the dialog. These features and constructions are indexed to the lines of the dialog in which they appear.

1. Contractions (3, 5, 10, 11, 15, 17, 19, 24, 25, 26, 29, 30, 32, 33, 34, 41)
2. Prepositions: of time (34, 35, 36)
                    of place (5, 24, 25, 27, 32)
3. Modals/Quasi-modals (5, 9, 15, 16, 19, 26, 41)
4. Appositives (11, 34)
5. Fomulaic wh- questions (2, 3)
6. That-clause adjective complements (5, 15)
7. Interrogative noun clause (25)
8. Present progressive tense with future time reference (5)
9. "Going to" future (17)
10. "If . . . then" conditional construction (19)

(6) Lexical Features

The following vocabulary items and idiomatic expressions appear in the dialog. These items and expressions are indexed to the lines of the dialog in which they appear.

1. pretty good (3)
2. not bad (4)

3. caught (5)
4. Halloween (5, 6, 7)
5. costume (7, 8, 9)
6. Boy (8)
7. sounds fun (12, 14)
8. pop (17)
9. charge (20)
10. absolutely not (21)
11. Uh-huh (37)
12. thanks a lot (40)
13. I'll see you then (41)
14. Bye-bye (41, 42)

The following terms appear repeatedly through the dialog. Each occurrence of one of these terms should be dealt with individually because of the major role that context plays in the determination of its meaning and function.

1. Okay (13, 22, 27, 34, 38, 39, 42)
2. Sure (5, 10, 26)
3. Yeah (12, 23, 29)
4. Right (31, 32, 33)
5. Oh (3, 8)
6. Umm-hmm (18, 41)
7. Great (15)
8. Good (39)

(7) Phonological Features

The following is a list of occurrences of fast speech phenomena that appear in the dialog. These phenomena are indexed to the lines of the dialog in which they occur.

1. How about (3) = /hawbawt/
2. about you (3) = /bawčuw/
3. caught you (5) = /kɔčuw/
4. having (5) = /haevin/
5. have to (9) = /haefta/
6. glad you (15) = /glaeǰuw/

Other phonological features for consideration could be the normal and contrastive word and sentence stress and intonation patterns of the utterances of the dialog.

In the foregoing analyses a piece of discourse has been examined from a variety of perspectives. Through this examination, different types of data that are relevant to a fairly complete understanding of the discourse have been isolated.[3]

However, the isolation of discrete bits of information is not the goal of this paper. This isolation was done in order to manifest the amount and variety of knowledge necessary to understand even this rather simple piece of discourse, and to emphasize the rather complicated interrelation of its elements. In addition to providing insights into a particular piece of discourse, the analyses are important in that they provide data that can be dealt with in context. However, the provision of data is only half the task of this discussion. The question of how to present this data in the classroom remains.

SUGGESTIONS FOR
CLASSROOM PRESENTATION

The logical starting point in the presentation of this type of VT material is the in-class analysis of the videotaped segment. This mode of presentation seems to lend itself very well to a teaching strategy that could be labeled "guided induction." This strategy requires the teacher to ask questions that will lead students to an understanding of particular features of the discourse and, consequently, to a fairly complete understanding of the discourse as a whole. This strategy is effective for three reasons: (1) It allows the teacher to pinpoint aspects of the discourse that cause problems for the student as well as those that do not. Thus, the teacher can concentrate more attention on the former than on the latter. (2) It allows for an optimum level of student participation in the analytic process. (3) This participation, more often that not, serves to increase student curiosity and motivation. However, like all strategies, this one has limitations on its applicability; therefore, the teacher should not hesitate to provide clarification or explanation when the need arises.

When the teacher is satisfied with the level of understanding of the segment that the students have attained, it is advisable to allow the students to apply what they have learned through the use of follow-up activities.

FOLLOW-UP ACTIVITIES

The in-class analysis of a functionally-based VT segment can easily lead to numerous and varied types of follow-up exercises. The following are some of the possibilities.

Analysis of Alternative Dialogs

The in-class analysis mentioned above was done on a dialog in which an invitation was offered and accepted. To broaden the students' functional range, the teacher might present an alternative dialog(s) for analysis that deals with the same function (in this case, inviting), but whose outcome is different—for example, non-acceptance of the invitation—or whose participants are different—for example, two men rather than a man and a woman. These dialogs could then be analyzed in much the same way as the initial dialog.

Role-plays

Role-plays are excellent vehicles for reinforcing knowledge gained in the above-mentioned analyses. At least three role-play formats can be effectively used: scripted, partially scripted, and unscripted. In a scripted role-play, pairs of students using a verbatim transcript of one of the previously presented dialogs try to duplicate, as nearly as possible, the taped performance of the native speakers. In a partially scripted role-play, students also work from a transcript, but are encouraged to adopt different attitudes—for example, invite someone grudgingly, refuse an invitation even if the inviter is extremely persistent. To do this the students need to alter the dialog substantially and improvise when necessary. In an unscripted role-play, the students are told which function to execute and which register to use. It is their responsibility to provide the language and situational context. Though students can create a dialog for this type of role-play in class, the results tend to be better if they are given this type of assignment as homework.

Viewing and Discussing Videotaped Student Dialogs

Any of the aforementioned student role-plays can be videotaped and played back immediately or at a later time. At the time of playback, they can be discussed, commented on, and constructively criticized by the class with guidance provided by the teacher.

Scrambled Dialogs

In this type of exercise the students are given the lines of a dialog, functionally similar to the original videotaped segment but not in their correct order. The students' task is to reorder these lines correctly into a piece of coherent discourse through the use of overt and covert discourse features. This type of exercise can be done in or out of class by individual students, pairs, or small groups. It can also be done by the entire class in strip-story fashion by putting each line of the dialog on a separate index card or slip of paper; the entire class then works as a group to find the correct order.

Register Change Exercise

In this type of exercise the students are instructed to change the register of a dialog they have previously analyzed from informal to formal or vice-versa. This, of course, requires changing the sociocultural and situational context as well as the language. This type of exercise works equally well when done in or out of class by individuals, pairs, or small groups.

Written Analysis Exercise

This type of exercise consists of a written transcript of an alternative dialog, which the students have not previously seen, followed by written questions that deal with specific features of the dialog. This type of exercise can be done with or without prior exposure to the VT segment from which the transcript was made, and thus, can work equally well as an in-class or out-of-class assignment. If done individually by students, this exercise can perform an evaluative function.

SUMMARY COMMENTS

The reader should note three important points regarding these materials and procedures. First, the foregoing suggestions are in no way hypothetical. They are based on the results of actual classroom use of this type of VT material in ESL programs at the UIUC and at Harvard University. Second, though the materials were designed with high-intermediate to advanced students in mind, it has been found that this type of VT material can be successfully adapted for students at all proficiency levels by adjusting the scope and depth of the analysis and the length, complexity, and focus of the follow-up exercises. Third, though the stated purpose of the materials is to familiarize students with as many aspects of interpersonal oral communication as possible so that they can function meaningfully in this context, this does not imply that the material could not be used as a contextualized point of departure for the further exploration of a particular feature, like contractions, or class of features, like grammar.

Thus, the examples that have been presented here illustrate but one possible means by which a particular type of VT material can be exploited by a teacher for use in the L2 classroom. This discussion has not been included as a "how-to" guide for the use of VT materials, nor has it sought to promote any particular approach to the use of video in L2 teaching. Its main purpose has been to show that it is possible for an L2 classroom teacher to conceive and produce viable and effective VT materials as well as put them to good use in the classroom. It is hoped that discussions of this type will encourage L2 teachers to further explore the possibilities of this medium.

NOTES

1. The "studio production process" refers to the actual videotaping of two takes and the pre- and post-consultation between the author and the participants. It does not include set-up time (lighting and sound checks, camera warm-up and adjustment, etc.).

2. One of the reasons for including this section on the production process was to demonstrate that making a tape of this type is (1) not an extremely complicated and burdensome task, and (2) not beyond the capabilities of classroom teachers who are willing to take the little time necessary to familiarize themselves with the necessary equipment. Furthermore, I believe this type of tape (which is not of the slickest professional quality) to be as effective, if not more so, than slickly produced commercial tapes, which are often quite expensive and not necessarily well-suited in terms of content and/or focus for use in a given classroom situation.

3. There are, of course, more classes of features that could be analyzed than are presented here. And certainly more features could be included in the classes than are analyzed here. However, the analyses done in this paper are meant to point out features that might be useful in the classroom, not to discover and categorize all of the possible features.

. . .

I am indebted to the "actors" in this production, Jean Svacina and Brad Reed, for their time, help, and suggestions; to Netta Gillespie, the LLL studio director, for her time, interest, expertise, and encouragement in this and many other productions; and to Sandra Savignon and Margie Berns for their encouragement, support, and editorial insights.

Chapter 10

Computer-Aided Instruction: Language Teachers and the Man of the Year[1]

Fernand Marty

Fernand Marty came to the United States from France in 1946. In his efforts to better understand the nature of second-language acquisition, he has conducted research projects in applied linguistics, educational psychology, and the use of technology. His many publications include teaching materials for French as a second language as well as research articles. For the last twelve years, he has held a joint appointment in the Department of French and the Computer-Based Research Laboratory at the University of Illinois at Urbana-Champaign.

I have been teaching French in the United States since 1946; in my efforts to improve my teaching, I have depended on applied linguistics, educational psychology, and —to some extent—on technology. I began using tape recorders at Middlebury College in 1948, and in the workshops and NDEA institutes in which I participated in the '50s and early '60s, I emphasized that tape recorders were only devices that could provide out-of-class practice with audio materials (just as books provide practice with written materials). In situations where high accuracy in the spoken language was one of the objectives, the students who, for their "homework," had access[2] to audio equipment were *obviously* able to reach higher levels of performance than those who did not have any equipment—provided, of course, that the exercises were properly designed to fit the objectives of the course and that the students did want to attain those objectives.

I now have about fifteen years of experience with the PLATO computer system at the University of Illinois.[3] In this brief article, I would like to discuss some of the problems that language teachers face when they consider using computers for language instruction.

I will not try to "prove" that computers can facilitate the process of learning a language. Obviously students who *want to learn* will learn faster or reach higher levels of accuracy when they have access to a computer that provides immediate feedback and detailed error analysis, that stores information about their performance, and that—on the basis of that data—supplies them with individualized exercises.[4] I believe that the gains made by such students using such exercises are worth the expense. (Of course, I do not take into consideration the computerized language lessons now commercially available for use on microcomputers and which, generally, are hardly any better than a pack of index cards or a programmed textbook.)

As was the case some twenty years ago with language laboratories, much of what is now written in magazines about the use of computers for instruction is nonsense.[5] Research in the instructional uses of computers has been going on for over twenty years and there is no solid indication that we are about to witness a revolution in our educational system. However, since evidence suggests that computers, under certain conditions, can facilitate the learning process, language teachers should know as much as possible about the available equipment and the results that can be expected today. Three aspects need to be considered: (1) the computer features that we need; (2) the types of installation that are available, and (3) the courseware (lessons) that we need.

(The following comments apply only to language teaching; our colleagues in mathematics, physics, chemistry, etc. have different requirements and, indeed, their requirements may be less demanding than ours; thus, if a computer laboratory is to be installed in a school, the language teachers should make sure their voices are heard.)

FEATURES TO LOOK FOR IN
A COMPUTER SYSTEM

Good language lessons require substantial amounts of computer memory. A typical twenty-sentence exercise with several levels of feedback, a good error analysis, and a complete set of grammar statements that can be used for review requires about three million bits of information or, in computer talk, 375 kilobytes (a byte equals 8 bits); 375 kilobytes is usually written as 375K.

In a computerized lesson, speed is of the essence. The basic justification for using computers in education is that a given set of objectives can be attained and retained in substantially less time than without computers; this goal, obviously, will not be reached if the machine needs several seconds to decide whether the student's response is acceptable, several seconds to find the appropriate feedback, several seconds to display the next question, etc.

In a central (time-sharing) system, a large number of terminals can be attached to a computer; the speed depends on the processing power of the computer and the number of terminals active at a particular time. On the Illinois PLATO system, even when the maximum number of terminals are active (600), the speed of execution is less than one second and can be considered excellent.

In stand-alone microcomputers (APPLE, TRS, IBM PC, etc.), the speed depends on the amount of memory the lesson itself requires *and* the amount of internal memory that the computer has. When the student uses a microcomputer, she must have a floppy disk (or diskette) that contains the language lesson she wants to use.[6] She must place this disk into the disk drive of the microcomputer. There are several kinds of disks (single-sided or double-sided, single-density or double-density, 3-inch disks, 3.5-inch disks, 5.25-inch disks, etc.); thus, the amount of information that can be stored on a disk can vary considerably, and you will find that not all disks can store a language lesson that requires 375K of memory. After the student has placed the disk into the disk drive, the computer copies from the disk into the computer's internal memory as much information as possible.

Let's suppose that you have a 48K microcomputer; this means that the internal memory of your machine can store only 48,000 bytes of information at a time; keep in mind also that part of that memory (the ROM or Read Only Memory) is permanently loaded in the computer; without that permanent memory, the computer could not run. What is left over (RAM or Random Access Memory) can be used to store your lesson.[7] If your lesson requires only about 30K, all of it will be stored in the internal memory and the speed of execution will be very fast (sellers of microcomputers tend to demonstrate only that kind of lesson). But if you have a lesson requiring 375K, most of it will be left on the disk, and the computer will have to go to the disk drive to copy the information necessary to judge the student's response, then to provide feedback, then to display the error analysis, etc. That constant exchange of information between the computer and the disk drive slows down the execution of the lesson to such an extent that, in my opinion, microcomputers with less than 512K of internal memory are unacceptable for effective language teaching.[8]

The computer language (the language that the programmer uses to communicate with the computer) should be so structured that a linguistic analysis of the student's answers is relatively easy; we need to be able to separate affixes from roots, judge the word order, distinguish lexical errors from spelling errors, etc.

The screen should be able to display at least 1920 characters (e.g., twenty-four lines of eighty characters each). This is necessary because, in a language exercise, the instructions, the stimulus, the student's answer, the error analysis and review, etc. will require that many characters. In civilization lessons, you will require detailed maps and various other graphic displays which require a high resolution screen. Diacritics (accents, cedilla, etc.), italics, all alphabets (e.g., Cyrillic) should be available. It should also be possible to type from right to left. The characters on the screen should be as clearly legible as in a textbook; they should be sharply defined and should not flicker. Color is desirable. If color is available, the displays should be as sharp as in black-and-white mode.

The keyboard should be easy to use. The alphanumeric keys ("a" through "z" and "0" through "9") should be arrayed in the same order as on a regular typewriter; the function keys (those providing editing facilities, feedback, help pages, etc.) should be grouped separately and be clearly labeled. The keys, when pressed, should feel "solid" (not "mushy") so that the students will be able to type as rapidly as they can. The keys should not "bounce," that is, type two characters when the student feels he has pressed the key only once.

An edit key is essential; the student must be able to make corrections in any part of his answer without having to retype the whole sentence. Alphanumeric characters and graphic displays should plot and erase rapidly. An alphanumeric statement should plot at a speed of at least 500 characters per second; erasing a line or a group of lines should be instantaneous. Fast plot and erasure of drawings allows animation (for example, a person crossing a street).

It should be possible to communicate with the computer by touching the display screen; this can be useful, for example, in word order exercises.[11] It should be possible to activate external devices such as slide selectors, tape recorders, video tape players, etc. The students should not be exposed to dangerous radiation levels even if they sit very close to the screen.

TYPES OF INSTALLATION

As of February 1983, there are two basic types of installation.

A star or central system: In this installation a powerful computer (mainframe) serves several hundred terminals (time-sharing system). The terminals are usually connected to the main computer with phone lines and can be thousands of miles away from the building that houses the computer.[12] However, since the communication costs depend on the distance, most schools can afford this type of installation only when the central computer is on their campus.

Individual microcomputers: In this type of installation, a school has a number of microcomputers in a room and these machines can be used by students in various disciplines; each machine is independent of all the others. This kind of installation may be acceptable in a temporary, experimental situation, but it has so many drawbacks that, I believe, it should not be generalized. The most serious drawbacks are:

1. You need to prepare as many diskettes of a lesson as you have students using the lesson at the same time. Thus, if you expect to have twenty students using lesson 10 simultaneously, you have to prepare twenty copies of that particular lesson. That takes much time and money.

2. The diskettes require careful handling and must be kept clean. Personnel are needed to distribute the diskettes and to ensure they are properly inserted into the disk drives and that they are returned undamaged.

3. Maintenance is expensive. In this installation, each microcomputer must have a disk drive. Those mechanical disk drives are the most fragile parts of the installation; repairs can be slow and costly.

4. The most serious drawback concerns the storage of each student's performance data ("restart" information so that the next study session will begin at the precise point at which the previous session ended, lists of exercises that have been done, various scores, language areas that need to be reviewed, etc.). In a central system, that information is kept by the main computer and can be accessed by the student at any time from any of the terminals connected to the computer. With stand-alone microcomputers, that data could be stored on the lesson diskettes only if each student had his or her personal set of diskettes (a very expensive solution) and only if his or her performance data could be transferred from one diskette to another as he or she moved from lesson to lesson. Another solution is to provide each student with an individual diskette (to be inserted in a second disk drive); the computer would write the student's performance data on that second diskette. To avoid loss or damage, it would probably be necessary to keep those individual diskettes in the computer laboratory, which would further complicate the work of the laboratory personnel.

Neither of those installations is really satisfactory for school systems. Research is now being done in various places to develop cluster or network systems. The cluster system being developed at the University of Illinois uses a minicomputer with a high speed disk drive; it can operate about 100 terminals all located in the same building. As in the central system, the students have only a terminal and a keyboard in front of them (*no* diskettes to handle) but there are *no* communication costs. In my opinion, this will be the most efficient and cheapest installation for a school.[13]

COURSEWARE

The term *hardware* designates the physical components of a computer; *software* designates the command that can be understood by that computer. The term *courseware* is used for the set of instructional lessons that can operate on that particular type of computer. Good courseware requires a powerful computer and a software that includes all the commands necessary to perform an effective presentation of the lesson and execute a detailed analysis of the students' responses.

How good can computerized lessons be? This subject is difficult to discuss because so many people believe in "magic" and see in computers the solution to all problems.[14] We cannot predict the state of technology twenty or fifty years from now, but there is no indication that artificial intelligence will even come close to duplicating all the functions of human intelligence. As far as language teachers are concerned, I do not see any possibility that we will ever have a computer program that, for example, would judge *free* written expression, would perform a phonemic analysis of a student's oral response, or would understand oral free expression and respond coherently.[15]

I am often asked why I do not make my computerized language lessons as exciting as the computer games that fascinate people in arcades and keep them entranced for hours. It is obviously possible, for example, to design a game in which the alien invaders cannot be destroyed unless the player plans his strategy in French; the problem is that, under such conditions, the amount of learning per hour is so small that it would take much too long to reach satisfactory objectives. Furthermore the game approach is far more feasible with vocabulary and morphology than with syntax. I have yet to see a complete language course (e.g., a four-semester college course) which is exciting, amusing, and efficient (in terms of time needed to reach its objectives).

Computerized lessons can be easily copied on tape or disks and distributed to other systems (of the same type). Making those copies is inexpensive, but the cost of preparing the lesson itself can be very high if it is a lesson with precise cues, detailed error analysis, record keeping, remedial exercise, etc.[16] In order to provide a student with about one hour of language work on the computer, a language teacher and a programmer may have to work for fifty or even one hundred hours—determining the objectives of the exercise, writing the computer code to judge the students' answers and provide the error analysis, checking that the lesson operates properly and catches all the errors the students might make, etc. Thus, to develop a set of exercises for a two-year language course, it might be necessary to spend over $100,000 in salaries alone (not counting computer time, supplies, etc.). However, since the cost of duplicating the course is trivial, this amount, although large as an initial expense, would be quite reasonable if the course were to be used by 200 schools (about $500 per school). Since there are about 2000 colleges and many thousands of secondary schools in the United States, finding 200 buyers does not seem unduly difficult. However, the following points should be kept in mind.

Several computer languages are in use: BASIC, FORTRAN, PASCAL, LISP, COBOL, TUTOR, etc.; some of those languages (e.g., BASIC) exist in several forms ("dialects"). A program written in PASCAL will work only on machines that "understand" PASCAL. There are programs that convert lessons from one language into another, but usually the conversion is not complete and must be finished manually. A solution to this problem will probably be found, but meanwhile, in order to achieve maximum distribution, the author of a course would need to prepare as many versions of her course as there are computer languages in use.

Some terminals can display a maximum of 960 characters (24 lines of 40 characters each), some can display 2048 characters (32 lines of 64 characters each), some can display 1920 characters (24 lines of 80 characters each), etc. Thus, a language lesson written in BASIC and that requires a 64×32 screen will not run on machines that understand BASIC but have a 80×24 screen. The dissemination of computerized materials will remain difficult until a standard is adopted (possibly 24 lines of 80 characters).

The computerized materials will probably have to be of a general nature. Too many different textbooks are in use and each edition is used for too short a time to make it profitable to prepare a computerized version of the exercises of each edition of each textbook. At the University of Illinois, we have prepared a large number of exercises (about 700 in French, about 500 in Spanish); the number is large enough to allow the students to find exercises corresponding to their needs whatever textbook is used.

It is easy to examine textbooks and workbooks and decide which one is preferable for a particular class. It is far more time-consuming to examine a computerized course; in addition to evaluating the contents, one must ascertain that the computer program will not "bomb out" leaving, for example, the student with a blank screen and unable to proceed. It will probably be necessary to establish review boards composed of language teachers and students to "go through" the programs in order to evaluate them and verify that the code performs correctly.

At present, language teachers can easily prepare materials to supplement their textbooks, but it is unlikely that they will have enough free time and/or training in computer programming to prepare their own computerized materials. It is even more unlikely that they will be able to modify/improve the courses they might purchase. The code for good language lessons is so complex that even expert programmers hesitate to change programs written by other programmers.

Audio-visual components are desirable. It is fairly easy to add color slides to a computerized lesson since there are machines that can be connected to a terminal and that can access *any* picture (on a microfiche, a tray, or a carousel) in less than one second. The problem is that we must prepare a number of slide sets or microfiches as large as the maximum number of students likely to use the lesson at a particular time. We also need personnel to check out the slides, make sure that they are used properly, returned undamaged, etc. The cost in time and money is very high.[17]

It is also easy to connect an audiotape machine and/or a videotape player to a computer terminal and write a program that can access any part of the tape. The problem is that in a good, individualized lesson, the needed segments will not occur in a linear fashion, for example, a particular student might need segment 1, then segment 20, then segment 12, then segment 45, etc. The tape is wound or rewound automatically, but it takes far too much time. And, of course, we have the same problems as with color slides (number of copies, personnel, etc.).

Currently, the only way to obtain immediate random access to any part of an audio and/or video recording is to place the recording on a disk or a cylinder; for example, on the random access audio device developed at the University of Illinois, the disk and the playback/record head move jointly in such a way that any part of the disk can be accessed in less than half a second.[18] Some video disc machines can provide practically immediate access to any audio, slide, or moving picture segment, but the cost of manufacturing a video disc master is still very high and the number of potential users is not sufficient to bring the cost of the copies to an affordable price. In any case, the use of such audio or video devices suffers from the limitations already mentioned (number of copies to be made or bought, personnel, etc.).

Another possibility is to convert the needed recordings into digital information and store it in the computer memory with the code for the lesson but, because of restrictions in the available amount of memory and/or the transmission rate of information between the computer and the terminal, the speech needs to be compressed. This process of removing nonessential information keeps the speech intelligible to natives, but it is hardly satisfactory for language teaching.

One might also use synthetic speech. Instead of recording the needed sentences, we can type phonemic strings with their pertinent prosodic features into the computer program for the lesson, and a synthesizer, incorporated into the terminal used by the student, changes that information into speech. It is also possible to use a computer program to convert the graphemic strings into phonemic strings[19] that can be sent to the synthesizer; this presents the advantage of allowing the students to hear the sentences they have typed or of allowing audio feedback based on the student's response (Sherwood and

Sherwood 1982). At present, the quality of the voice produced by such synthesizers is not good enough for language teaching, but progress is being made.

CONCLUSION

At the University of Illinois, many of my students have profited from the computer programs I have written and have reached levels of accuracy they could not have attained without the programs; for those students, the expense of time and money was clearly justified. But my purpose in writing this article was not to convince you that all forward-looking language departments should use computerized lessons. It may well be that this world would be a better world, with happier people, if cars, television, computers, etc. had never been invented or if wisdom had governed their development and their use. But, for better or for worse, language teachers and their students are part of a society that has been deeply affected by technology, a technology that is omnipresent and cannot be ignored. Computers will not go away; their influence in our daily lives and education will continue to grow. It is up to us, in the Humanities, to understand that technology, to evaluate its potential (for good or for bad), and to be among those who decide how it will be used.

NOTES

1. For those who have already forgotten and those who never knew, *Time*'s Man of the Year for 1982 was the computer.

2. Access to technology can also take place at home; students whose parents can afford tape machines, shortwave radio receivers, dish antennas to receive foreign television programs, computers, etc., have a marked advantage over students whose access to instructional technology is limited to the school. It can be argued that technology at present is helping mostly the students already lucky enough to have educated parents who can devote their own time and money to the education of their children and who can afford to pay for private lessons, for trips abroad, etc. Our rapidly deteriorating school system can no longer offset that growing imbalance in educational opportunities.

3. The PLATO system was conceived at the University of Illinois (Urbana-Champaign) and began to function in 1960; it has been under constant development and improvement since that time. Control Data Corporation, by virtue of an agreement with the University, has installed PLATO systems in Minnesota, Delaware, Florida, California, Maryland, and several foreign countries (Canada, England, France, Belgium, Korea, Australia, South Africa, etc.).

4. For a discussion of language lessons, see Marty 1981, 1982.

5. For example, *Time* magazine (February 20, 1978) writes: "The computers provide an intensely visual, multisensory learning experience that can take a youngster in a matter of a few months to a level he might never reach in less than many, many

years of study by conventional methods" and . . .'these magical beasts,' as they have been called, are revivifying soporific students, dangling and delivering challenges beyond the ken of most educators."

6. The program can also be on a cassette and loaded into the computer's memory with a cassette player. This takes more time and is used only with programs short enough to fit entirely into the computer's memory.

7. Some advertisements state the amount of Random Access Memory (e.g., 64K RAM or 64K User Memory); the buyer then knows how much memory is really available for his or her programs.

8. Few microcomputers today have 512K of internal memory, but more are becoming available.

9. The PLATO system uses a square display panel consisting of 262,144 (512×512) dots which can be turned on or off individually.

10. Most computer terminals use cathode-ray tubes (like television). The terminals used at the University of Illinois have a plasma panel. Plasma panels display orange dots on a black background; they have no flicker at all and cause much less eye fatigue than CRTs. Unfortunately, the manufacturers of microcomputers have shown little interest in plasma panels and, because the demand has been so small, the cost has remained high. At present, plasma panels do not have color.

11. There are two types of touch panels. The cathode-ray tubes can be covered with a pressure-sensitive film that determines which area of the screen is touched by the student. Around the screen of the terminals equipped with a plasma panel, there are light-emitting diodes (LEDs) that generate vertical and horizontal infrared light beams; when the student touches the screen, two light beams are interrupted and the location is determined.

12. Most of the terminals connected to the University of Illinois PLATO system are in Illinois, but there are terminals in Arizona, Hawaii, Connecticut, Florida, and some other states.

13. The current estimate is that a 40-terminal cluster system will cost $100,000—$20,000 for the minicomputer and $2000 for each of the 40 color terminals.

14. See, for example, Jean-Jacques Servan-Schreiber's "Le Défi mondial," (Fayard, 1980), in which the author claims that microcomputers can solve the problems of the Third World. For example, he writes (1980:373):

> Le moment arrive, indique «le mémoire», où nous n'aurons qu'à parler aux ordinateurs pour qu'ils enregistrent nos instructions, nos messages, ou l'expression de nos pensées, et où ils auront appris, par l'intermédiaire de la voix synthétique, à nous transmettre leur réponse, une fois leur travail accompli. Les échanges dans les deux sens se feront, et bien plus rapidement, par la parole.
>
> Ainsi l'abîme qui sépare encore les populations des continents industrialisés des populations illettrées est appelé à perdre son caractère d'obstacle infranchissable au développement du Tiers-Monde.

This passage shows a total lack of understanding of the difficulties posed by natural speech processing. The search for "magical solutions," which require little or no intellectual effort, is also apparent in an article published by *L'Express* (February 25,

1983). The article claims that under hypnosis one can learn to speak a foreign language in one month.

15. Articles in journals or demonstrations in "computer fairs" tend to be deceiving. It is true that there are computer programs that judge free expression if the "writer" limits his "free expression" to a short list of syntactic constructions and a given vocabulary. It is also true that computers can understand human speech if the speaker uses the vocabulary and syntax already stored in the computer and if the speaker's voice (distribution of the formants, pitch, rate of delivery, etc.) matches the voice(s) that the computer has been trained to recognize. Understanding *totally free* oral and written expression is quite another matter.

16. Other possible uses of the computer are:

    In culture and civilization courses, we could provide the students with simulation lessons. For example , in a course on contemporary France, the student could pretend he was born in France; he could choose his place of birth, his family and friends, his profession, or could get married, etc., thus assuming a "French" identity. Since he could enter the program as many times as he wanted and could make different choices, he would get to know contemporary France from many different angles: *un O.S chez Renault, un instituteur dans un village de Lozère, un docteur dans le 16e arrondissement*, etc.

    Another powerful use of computers is to detect the weak points in a student's knowledge and to have the computer present the student with remedial work. For example, a student who wants to resume his study of French after a lapse of a few years would be given a general test. He would be told what his weak points are, and the computer would put together exercises that would bring the student to the desired level.

    In literature, a student about to enter a course on the Renaissance could be told that he needs to take a computerized test designed to determine whether he has acquired the knowledge necessary to take the course with profit; if not, the computer program would provide the necessary remedial training.

17. I used microfiches with 256 color slides for my "culture" lessons (geography, etc.) for several years. I had to discontinue the use of those microfiches because of the cost of updating them and replacing them.

18. The random access audio devices are manufactured by Education and Information Systems in Champaign, Illinois.

19. A grapheme-to-phoneme program for French is being developed at the University of Illinois by Fernand Marty and Robert Hart.

REFERENCES

Marty, F. 1981. "Reflections on the use of computers in second-language acquisition—I." *System* **9**: 85–98.

———. 1982. "Reflections on the use of computers in second-language acquisition—II." *System* **10**: 1–11.

Servan-Schreiber, J-J. 1980. *Le défi mondial*. Paris: Fayard.

Sherwood, B. A. and J. N. Sherwood. 1982. "Computer voices and ears furnish novel teaching options." *Speech Technology*. Sept/Oct.: 46–51.

Chapter 11

Immersion and Other Innovations in U.S. Elementary Schools

Helena H. Anderson
Nancy C. Rhodes

Helena Anderson is Foreign Language Curriculum Specialist for the Milwaukee Public Schools, Wisconsin, and is on the Board of Directors of the Central States Conference on the Teaching of Foreign Languages. She is a frequent presenter at regional and national conferences on the topics of bilingual education and U.S. immersion programs.

Nancy C. Rhodes is Project Coordinator for the elementary school foreign language project at the Center for Applied Linguistics in Washington, D.C. Since the project's beginning in 1980, she has acted as the national liaison for elementary schools that have immersion or other types of innovative language programs. She is currently completing research comparing language proficiency of immersion and FLES students with second year high school students.

"Es facil. Es facil!" were the cries heard from the first-graders learning a complex mathematical task. The teacher was at the board demonstrating how to draw a three-dimensional box and the children were eagerly reproducing the geometric figure on their own slates. *"Miren me. Hagan una caja, y una linea asi. . . . Eschuchen—no es facil!"* cautioned the teacher, making sure that they watched her and drew their lines carefully.

A typical first-grade math lesson was being taught in a public school, La Ballona Elementary in Culver City, California . . . but there was a difference. These American-born English-speaking children were being taught math *in Spanish*, and were learning all their other subjects in the foreign language as well. With little extra effort, they were becoming fluent in Spanish as well as learning all the regular class material.

How can this be? Children learning a new language during their regular classes? Of course! It has long been known that young children approach second-language learning with an ease and naturalness not found in older learners. So why not take advantage of this asset? Without detracting from their regular school work, children can acquire a second language while learning other subject matter taught in that language. At least thirteen school systems across the United States have adopted this idea and have started their own language immersion classes.

Immersion programs are not the only type of elementary language programs in which there is currently a wave of renewed interest. The Center for Applied Linguistics (CAL), with funding from the U.S. Department of Education, has become the unofficial clearinghouse for information on the types of foreign-language classes that are being offered in elementary schools across the country.

The CAL investigators first surveyed elementary schools in eight states to find out how much early language instruction was going on and what teaching methods were being used. The survey covered 1237 schools in California, Illinois, Maryland, Massachusetts, New York, Ohio, Pennsylvania, and Wisconsin. Of the 453 schools that responded, 18 percent reported that foreign language was being taught.

Investigators then visited schools with successful programs to gather information to develop step-by-step guidelines for parents, teachers, and administrators interested in starting foreign-language classes in their elementary schools. The innovative programs observed could generally be classified according to three categories: language immersion, revitalized foreign language in the elementary school, and foreign language experience (FLEX).

LANGUAGE IMMERSION

The most dramatic approach to teaching languages in the elementary schools can be found in the immersion programs where children do learn to understand, speak, read, and write in two languages, the second language and English. U.S. immersion programs are modeled after the extremely successful French immersion programs that have been operating in Canada for the past fifteen years. Immersion simply means a program in which the usual curriculum activities are conducted in a second language which is the *medium* of instruction rather than the object of instruction. It can begin at any level—the kindergarten or the primary grades where it is called early immersion, or in the middle grades where it is called late immersion. In different kinds of immersion programs the amount of time spent each day in the second language may also vary. In total immersion programs, the second language is used for the entire school day during the first two or three years of the program. In partial immersion programs, instruction takes place in the second language for part (usually at least half) of the school day. It is important to remember that slight variations in immersion program design can occur depending upon the needs or desires of an individual school district. However, even though there may be variations in the amount of time spent in the second language or the grade level at which formal English instruction is introduced, the basic concept and methodology remain the same.

From the minute the children arrive at school in the morning, they hear only the second language from the teacher. All classroom conversation and instructions are in the new language. In this way, children acquire the second language in natural situations: "I have hot lunch today," "Can we go out for recess?" "Give me the ball!" "I want to be first!" "May I go to the bathroom?" The language instruction does not exist in a vacuum, but is an integral part of the students' daily lives. During the first few months students answer in English when the teacher speaks to them in the second language. Gradually, as their second-language skills improve, they start speaking the language with their teacher and friends.

Children show little anxiety about learning in another language, because the things they learn are within their experience. They learn to speak and read about things they understand: in kindergarten, a visit to the zoo; in second grade, a lesson on magnets; in fifth grade, a lesson on United States geography.

The curriculum in an immersion program is basically the same as the curriculum in any elementary school. Students have reading, mathematics, language arts, science, social studies, art, music, and physical education. After two or three years in a total immersion program, when children have acquired comprehension and can easily generate needed speech in the second language, English is introduced as a language arts subject for thirty minutes to an hour each day in the second or third grade. As the students progress through the middle grades, the amount of English is gradually increased until in grades five or six there is a balance of both the second language and English. The end result is that upon leaving a total immersion program, students have not only completed the regular elementary curriculum, but are able to begin middle school or junior high school with bilingual skills sufficient to take subject content classes in either language.

Questions about achievement have been a common concern among parents who fear that children in immersion programs would fall behind the traditional English-only classes. Many research studies from Canada, a country with many years of experience with French immersion programs, have shown that immersion pupils achieve as well as or better than their monolingual peers in their content subjects, even though they have learned those subjects through the second language. The children do show a temporary lag in the development of their English language skills, but this lag is quickly made up once English language arts instruction is introduced. The research on early immersion not only is reassuring about achievement, but also indicates desirable side effects. Merrill Swain (1979) summarizes the research related to immersion programs in Canada for the past ten years:

> *Effects on English Skills*—By the end of grade four, the immersion students and their English-educated peers perform equivalently. By the end of grade five the immersion students often outperform the comparison groups on several aspects of measured English skills—for example, reading comprehension and vocabulary knowledge.
>
> *Effects on Second Language Skills*—The results reveal consistently superior performance in French skills as compared to students who have had a traditional program of French instruction. The results also show that the immersion students score as well on French proficiency instruments as 30 percent of the native-speaking students.
>
> *Effects on the Learning of Subject Content Material*—On standardized tests given in English, science, social studies, and mathematics, the immersion students who had been taught the subject matter in French, perform as well as their monolingual peers.
>
> *Other Effects of Immersion Programs*—Many studies show that bilingualism can positively influence aspects of cognitive and linguistic growth (Cummins 1976).

Parents become very enthusiastic when they see these research findings reflected in the achievement of their own children. They are proud of their children's abilities in a new language. Consequently, immersion schools have a very high degree of parent involvement. Parents choose this type of program for many reasons, but most often the reason given is that parents felt unsuccessful in learning a second language themselves and wanted to make sure that their children had a better chance of success. For example, Milwaukee's immersion program has become so successful that there are long waiting lists for admission.

In response to questions about the kinds of children who enroll in immersion programs, the answer, based on immersion experiences in cities such as Milwaukee, San Diego, and Cincinnati, is very simple—all kinds. Only a very small percentage of the students come from bilingual homes; close to half are members of racial or ethnic minority groups. The magnet immersion programs draw students from every geographical sector and every socioeconomic group in the cities in which they are located. Parent interest is the only criterion for entrance into these programs.

Test scores from United States immersion programs have consistently shown the same good results as the research from Canada. For example, in Milwaukee's program, standardized achievement tests administered in English to students who have been taught in French, German, or Spanish show that Milwaukee's immersion students score well above local and national averages in both language arts and mathematics. In the 1981 Metropolitan Achievement Test results, students did so well that no students in the program scored in the "low" category in any subject area. The 1982 and 1983 results on the Iowa Test of Basic Skills showed the same excellent results.

Teachers for immersion programs are not always easy to find. Staffing has been difficult because prospective teachers interested in second-language learning have traditionally gone into secondary education. What is required is an elementary teacher with native or near-native ability in the second language. No special certification is needed in the second language, but the teacher does need to have demonstrated proficiency in all aspects of the language.

Learning materials have also not always been easy to obtain. Curriculum materials in Spanish can be adapted from materials intended for bilingual education programs. French materials can be obtained from Canadian sources. Materials in German have proven to be most difficult to find, but Milwaukee's immersion program has made a good start in developing materials for grades kindergarten through six.

The question of costs of immersion programs is vitally important in these times of budgetary constraints. It would be difficult to implement any new program or methodology that appears to generate new costs. However, the experience of schools that have begun immersion programs has shown that the costs of immersion and non-immersion classes are similar. For example, curriculum materials (textbooks, workbooks, maps, etc.) are reordered each year, and the costs, whether for English or second-language materials, are comparable. No additional staff is required because the regular classroom teacher is also the "language teacher." The point is that a teacher and new books and materials are provided for every classroom, whether the teaching that goes on there is

TABLE 11.1 IMMERSION AND PARTIAL IMMERSION LANGUAGE PROGRAMS IN U.S. ELEMENTARY SCHOOLS, 1982
INFORMATION COMPILED BY THE CENTER FOR APPLIED LINGUISTICS
ELEMENTARY SCHOOL FOREIGN LANGUAGE PROJECT
3520 PROSPECT STREET, N.W.
WASHINGTON, D.C 20007
(202) 298-9292

School District/City	Comments	No. of Schools	No. of Pupils
Alpine (UT) School District	Started 1978 Total immersion Local funding only Grades 1–5	1	104
Baton Rouge, LA	Started 1980 Total immersion	1	60
Cincinnati (OH) Public Schools	Started 1974 Partial immersion Total immers. in K Local funding only Articulation w/junior and senior high	4 Spanish 3 French 1 German 1 Middle Sch. ——— 9 total	900 Spanish 480 French 580 German 430 Middle Sch. ——— 2390 total
Culver City, CA	Started 1971 Total immersion Magnet school Local funding only	1	149 total
Holliston, MA	Started 1979 Total immersion Grades K–4 Spanish partial immersion offered in middle school	1	99
Milwaukee (WI) Public Schools	Started 1977 Magnet schools Begins with 4-yr-old kinder. Total immersion Articulation w/junior and senior high	2 total German K–6 French K–5 Spanish K–3	174 German 199 French 190 Spanish 30 Jr. High ——— 593 total
Montgomery County (MD) Public Schools	French total immersion started at Four Corners Elementary and now continuing at Oak View Small outside funding	1 French	172

No. of Teachers	Languages	No. of Aides	Contacts
4	Spanish		Janet G. Spencer, Principal Cherry Hill Elementary School 250 East 1650 South Orem, UT 84057 801/225-3387
4	Spanish French		Mrs. Ben Peabody, Sr. Principal La Belle Aire Elementary 12255 Tams Drive Baton Rouge, LA 70815 504/275-7480
80 (approx. total)	Spanish French German	German−1 Spanish−½	Mimi Met, Supervisor Cincinnati Public Schools 230 East 9th Street Cincinnati, OH 45202 513/369-4937
5 (full-time)	Spanish	Some parent volunteers	Eugene Ziff, Principal La Ballona Elementary School 10915 Washington Boulevard Culver City, CA 90230 213/839-4361 Ext. 229
3	French	1 full-time 1 part-time	James Palladino, Principal Miller Elementary School Woodland Street Holliston, MA 01746 617/429-1601
20	German French Spanish	10	Helena Anderson, Foreign Language Curriculum Specialist Milwaukee Public Schools P.O. Drawer 10K Milwaukee, WI 53201 414/475-8305
7	French	1 position (college volunteers, occasionally parents), high school interns	Gabriel Jacobs, Principal Oak View Elementary School 400 East Wayne Avenue Silver Spring, MD 20901 301/589-0020

School District/City	Comments	No. of Schools	No. of Pupils
	Articulation with junior high: one subject course per year for former immersion pupils		
	Spanish total immersion Magnet school Local funding only	1 Spanish	45–50
Rochester, NY	Started 1981 Total immersion (except for English reading) Grades 1–2 Local funding only	2	48
San Diego (CA) City Schools	Started 1977 Total immersion for students who begin in grades K–2, partial for those who begin in grades 3–6 Partial immersion for grades 7–12 Magnet schools Special funding in initial years; regular funding now	5 (includes two secondary schools)	850 total
Tulsa (OK) Public Schools, Independent School District #1	Started 1981 Total immersion	1	26
Washington, DC	Started 1966 Independent Partial immersion, English/French, English/Spanish Nursery through grade 12 Pupils 85 nationalities; staff 35 nationalities International baccalaureate	1	550
Washington, DC	Started 1971 Partial immersion Local funding only	1	330

No. of Teachers	Languages	No. of Aides	Contacts
2 (Grades 1, 2, 3) (Grades 4, 5, 6)	Spanish		Louise Rosenberg, Principal Rock Creek Elementary School 8330 Grubb Road Chevy Chase, MD 20815 301/589-0005
2	Spanish		Alessio Evangelista Director, Foreign Language Dept. City School District 131 W. Broad Street Rochester, NY 14608 716/325-4560 Ext. 2315
35 total	French Spanish	35 (native speakers)	Harold B. Wingard Curriculum Specialist, Second Language Education San Diego City Schools Linda Vista Elementary, B-8 2772 Ulric Street San Diego, CA 92111 714/569-9640
1	Spanish	1	Jack Griffin Tulsa Public Schools Assoc. Supervisor for Instruction P.O. Box #45208 Tulsa, OK 74145 918/743-3381 Ext. 485
60 full-time equivalents	French Spanish		Dorothy Bruchholz Goodman, Director Washington International School 3100 Macomb Street, N.W. Washington, DC 20008 202/966-8510
11 Spanish 11 English	Spanish	1 (Pre-k)	Frank Miele, Principal Oyster Elementary School 29th and Calvert Streets, NW Washington, DC 20008 202/673-7277

in English or a second language. Library books for second language students do, however, constitute a "new" expense, and collections may need to be acquired gradually, over a number of years.

Of the three types of programs identified at the beginning of this discussion of innovations in U.S. elementary school foreign-language programs, immersion programs set the highest goals in terms of language proficiency. Students are expected to master the regular curriculum and also to become "functionally proficient" in the foreign language. This means that fifth- and sixth-graders should be able to communicate in the foreign language (on topics appropriate to their age) almost as well as ten- and eleven-year-olds for whom the language is native. It must be noted, however, that even though the children develop a functional proficiency, their second-language skills are not native-like with respect to all characteristics of grammar and vocabulary. In a report of research findings for immersion programs in Canada, Swain (1981) summarizes the distinction: "This does not mean that the children were unable to say what they wanted to, but they used numerous strategies or techniques to say what they did not have the grammatical means to say." Further development of their second-language skills depends on interaction with native speakers of the language, either in or out of school.

The first immersion classes in the U.S. were started in Spanish in the Culver City Unified School District, with assistance from the University of California at Los Angeles, in the fall of 1971. A group of nineteen five-year-old monolingual English speakers were taught the kindergarten curriculum completely in Spanish. This program was modeled after the St. Lambert project in Montreal, Canada, in which English Canadians were immersed in French instruction from kindergarten (see Lambert and Tucker 1972). Definite patterns have emerged from the Culver City program. As in the case of the St. Lambert study, the English-speaking students acquired competence in understanding, speaking, reading, and writing Spanish, while maintaining English language proficiency. These students also performed on a par with their English-speaking age group in content subjects such as mathematics and science. (Cohen 1974)

Since the Culver City program began in 1971, other school systems have followed the lead in Baton Rouge, Louisiana; Chevy Chase and Silver Spring, Maryland; Cincinnati, Ohio; Holliston, Massachusetts; Milwaukee, Wisconsin; Orem, Utah; Rochester, New York; San Diego and Davis, California; Tulsa, Oklahoma; and Washington, D.C. Table 11.1, detailing immersion programs in the United States, shows languages offered, size of the program, type of program, and type of school. Some of the immersion schools came about as a result of desegregation efforts and became "magnet" schools designed to attract students from every part of the community because of the quality of the program being offered.

REVITALIZED FLES PROGRAMS

The second type of program popular today includes foreign languages taught before, during, or after school for a specific number of days per week. Instruction is begun in the elementary school and the opportunity is provided for continuing study of the same language through grade 12. Today's revitalized language classes emphasize spoken language more than such programs used to.

Foreign language in the elementary school (FLES) is a concept whose time has come . . . again. Popular in the 1960s, those years saw great public and government support of language learning at all levels of instruction, especially in primary and middle grades, a reaction due in large part to the shock of Sputnik and the sudden awareness that linguistic isolation had played a role in that technological setback. By the early 1970s, however, national attention and federal funding had clearly shifted to new priorities. FLES programs that had been developed at the peak of public enthusiasm declined abruptly for several reasons. Heading the list was the fact that foreign languages had been, in many cases, simply added to the elementary curriculum and never fully grafted onto it (Pesola 1982). Other contributing factors included a lack of qualified teachers, a shortage of quality instructional material, a failure to create specific goals, parent demands for a return to the "basics," and the problem of articulation between elementary and secondary schools.

Despite the failures of some FLES programs, other programs remained viable and functioning. The climate of the 1980s, which sees language competence in the United States as crucial, has created an opportunity for a renewed and sounder rationale for languages in the elementary school. In this climate, revitalized FLES programs are becoming increasingly popular. These new programs carry with them a new set of goals—an emphasis on developing second-language speaking and listening skills and on developing each student's cultural awareness. The following guidelines (Pesola 1982) give an indication of the new directions in FLES.

1. The FLES student learns most effectively when language is presented in a meaningful communicative context: social/cultural situations, games, songs and rhymes, experiences with arts, crafts, sports.

2. Although grammar should not be ignored in FLES instruction, it is not the most useful organizing principle for instruction, and should not be the object of instruction for its own sake.

3. Elementary and middle school children need to work with *concrete* experiences as the starting point of learning; thus considerable planning should go into the use of visuals, props, and realia in the FLES classroom.

4. Planning should incorporate opportunity for physical movement and activity.

FLES classes are usually taught by a language specialist teacher who meets students three to five days per week for twenty to thirty minutes per day. Such a specialist must have excellent language skills, especially in speaking, as well as skills in working with elementary children. Some FLES classes are taught by the classroom teacher with the support of a language specialist. Budget restrictions are a problem that must be overcome with language specialists, because the salary of the language teacher is an additional cost.

Traditional FLES programs did not necessarily emphasize speaking skills, and parents were frequently disappointed if they had expected their children to speak the language fluently after only three years of classes given twice a week. Parents are now told that the level of fluency their children will attain in a FLES program is a direct result of the amount of time spent using the foreign language. They are advised to set their expectations accordingly.

Interesting instructional material is an important part of today's FLES programs, and the lack thereof is still a problem that needs to be solved. The best solution to date has been teacher-prepared or school-district-prepared materials that meet the varying individual needs. Publishers of foreign language textbooks need to become more aware of this market.

FOREIGN LANGUAGE EXPERIENCE (FLEX)

A third innovative approach, foreign language experience (FLEX), has also become popular in the 1980s. FLEX programs are self-contained, nonarticulated programs designed to introduce elementary school students to language study on an informal basis. This approach usually has the following goals and purposes (Strasheim 1982):

1. An improved foreign language program with increased strength at the beginning and reduced attrition throughout the sequence

2. The development of motivation for language study through building a readiness for language learning and giving the student an intelligent basis for the selection (or nonselection) of a language to study

3. The mastery of a limited amount of language material, including all the major facets of language learning (i.e., grammar, pronunciation, vocabulary)

4. The development of greater interest in the world and its peoples, encompassing increased sensitivity to cultural similarities and decreased ethnocentrism as better preparation for life in a pluralistic society and world

5. Awareness of the career uses for foreign-language skills

Fluency in the target language is clearly not an objective in FLEX programs, and this must be explained at the outset. However, because of the limited objectives of FLEX, many schools offer a sequence of short FLEX courses in different languages during one year. It is hoped this varied experience gives students a strong basis for choosing which language to study in the future.

One possible difficulty of this approach is that qualified FLEX instructors need not be fluent in the second language. In fact, in some school districts FLEX instructors with limited foreign-language study learn the foreign language right along with the students. This is possible because the program strives only to *introduce* foreign languages and to make the initial learning experience pleasurable. Again, the program does not aim for student fluency but for an enthusiastic response to language learning in general, together with the mastery of a limited body of material. It would seem that if the FLEX instructor has a positive, enthusiastic attitude toward language and language teaching, this might compensate for a lack of language proficiency.

The state of Indiana currently has a program in which classroom teachers learn the language right along with their students and begin to implement the program after a two-day training session. New FLEX self-instructional materials and tapes developed by the Indiana Department of Public Instruction are intended as an experiential enrichment component for the primary grades curriculum and are currently being tested in several school districts. The materials, in French, Spanish, and German, introduce the children to numbers, colors, parts of the body, and clothing. While some administrators may initially question classroom teachers' willingness to learn a language along with their students, Stockwell Elementary School administrators in Evansville, Indiana, found overwhelming enthusiasm for the program.

In many school districts, FLEX is taught by high school or college students, parents, or other community members who have a background in foreign language and who will often volunteer their services. Usually, instructors and prospective instructors attend a short training program.

While results of the survey in these eight states indicate there is not yet total commitment to foreign-language study at the elementary school level, visits to schools were very encouraging. Foreign-language programs that do exist are successful and have a promising future. The enthusiasm of the parents, students, and administrators for these programs is overwhelming.

The trend toward clearly stating program goals should help alleviate some of the proficiency-expectation problems that plagued educators in the past when goals were not spelled out. Once the goals of the program are understood, increased satisfaction and less criticism should result. Now parents and administrators can expect, for example, that children participating in a FLEX program will experience a basic exposure to the language being studied and to the corresponding culture. Children enrolled in a FLES program will be introduced to the basics of language, with emphasis on oral communication (and attention to reading and writing skills, in some programs). If the children are participating in a language immersion program, they should be expected to become functionally proficient—to be able to communicate in the foreign language on topics appropriate to their age, and perform appropriately in all of the basic subjects of the curriculum.

Those who, as of a few years ago, felt that elementary foreign-language study was dead should take another look at what is currently going on in elementary schools. Immersion, revitalized FLES programs emphasizing spoken language, and foreign-language experience programs are setting a new trend for the future. Schools that currently do not offer foreign languages need to recognize that learning a foreign language enriches a child's life. In today's world, every child can profit by learning the language and culture of other countries, and effective instruction in these two areas should be a basic goal in our elementary schools.[1]

NOTE

1. For a free copy of the booklet *Foreign Language in the Elementary School: A Practical Guide*, please write Elementary School Foreign Language Project, Center for Applied Linguistics, 3520 Prospect St. NW, Washington, DC 20007, or call (202) 298-9292.

REFERENCES AND SUGGESTED READING

Adcock, D. 1976. "Foreign languages in elementary and emerging adolescent education." In G. Jarvis (ed.). *An integrative approach to foreign-language teaching: choosing among the options.* ACTFL Foreign Language Education Series, vol. 8. Skokie, Ill.: National Textbook Co.

Anne Arundel County (MD) Public Schools. 1980. *Foreign language in the elementary school: German* FL 013 099. Program guide includes objectives, teaching guidelines for classroom teachers and volunteers, and a nine-unit FLEX curriculum. (Also available for French: FL 013 101 and Spanish: FL 013 100.)

Canadian Parents for French. 1979. *So you want your child to learn French! A handbook for parents.* Ottawa, Ontario: Canadian Parents for French.

Cohen, A. 1974. "The Culver City Spanish immersion program: the first two years." *The Modern Language Journal* **58:** 94–103.

Cummins, J. 1976. "The influence of bilingualism on cognitive growth: a synthesis of research findings and explanatory hypotheses." *Working Papers on Bilingualism* **9:** 1–43.

Donoghue, M. 1968. *Foreign languages and the elementary school child.* Dubuque, Iowa: Wm. C. Brown Co.

Grittner, F. 1974. "Foreign languages and the changing curriculum." *NASSP Bulletin* **58:** 71–78.

Indiana Department of Public Instruction. 1981. *Introduction to French: numbers, colors, and body/clothing.* ED 207 342. (Introductory French materials intended for experiential or enrichment component of primary grades curriculum.) (Also available for Spanish: ED 207 343 and German: ED 207 344.)

Krashen, S., R. Scarcella, and M. Long (eds.). 1982. *Child-adult differences in second-language acquisition.* Rowley, Mass.: Newbury House.

Lambert, W. and G. Tucker. 1972. *Bilingual education of children: the St. Lambert experiment.* Rowley, Mass.: Newbury House.

Pesola, C. 1982. *A source book for elementary and middle school language programs.* Minneapolis: Minnesota State Department of Education.

Rhodes, N. and A. Schreibstein. 1983. *Foreign language in the elementary school: a practical guide.* Washington, D.C.: Center for Applied Linguistics.

Rhodes, N., G. Tucker, and J. Clark. 1981. *Elementary school foreign-language instruction in the United States: innovative approaches for the 1980's. Final Report.* Washington, D.C.: Center for Applied Linguistics. ED 209 940.

Strasheim, L. 1982. "FLEX: the acronym and the entity." *Die Unterrichtspraxis* **15:** 60–62.

Swain, M. 1981. "Linguistic expectations: core, extended and immersion programs." *The Canadian Modern Language Review* **37:** 486–497.

Swain, M. 1979. "What does research say about immersion education?" *So you want your child to learn French!* Ottawa: Canadian Parents for French.

Section III

Evaluation

Chapter 12

Large-Scale Communicative Language Testing: A Case Study

Merrill Swain

Merrill Swain has been involved over the last ten years in the evaluation of French immersion programs in Canada. In this context, she has participated in the development of language tests, culminating in the preparation of the communicative language testing units discussed in the present paper. Her other interests include second language acquisition, bilingualism and bilingual education. She is currently Professor in the Department of Curriculum and Director of the Modern Language Centre at the Ontario Institute for Studies in Education. She also holds an appointment in the Department of Linguistics at the University of Toronto.

INTRODUCTION

In Canada we are experiencing an increasing demand from English-speaking communities for schooling that will produce bilingual individuals. The motivations for this demand are varied, but minimally they include both social and economic reasons. Recent political events in Canada have heightened awareness of the needs and demands of Canada's French-speaking peoples. As a result, a genuine desire has developed on the part of some English-Canadians to learn French in order to be able to interact with French-Canadians in their own language. These same political events have also resulted in establishing bilingual proficiency in French and English as a highly desirable or, in some cases, a required qualification for employment. Clearly, then, what was needed in these circumstances were school programs that could provide students not only with a formal knowledge of the second language, characteristic of traditional second-language teaching programs, but also with the ability to *use* the second language as a communicative tool.

Over the last decade in Canada a variety of programs have been initiated aimed at turning out English-French bilingual students. Although these programs differ with respect to the grade level at which they begin, the length of the program, and the proportion of the school day taught in each of the two languages, they all have in common the exclusive use of the second language, French, as a medium of instruction for all or most of the school day for several years. These programs referred to in Canada as immersion programs and considered as experiments in bilingual education, have been monitored to evaluate the students' first- and second-language development, as well as their academic achievements in content subjects taught to them through the medium of the second language (see Lambert and Tucker 1972; Swain and Lapkin 1982).

Assessments of the immersion students' second-language proficiency have included the use of French achievement tests standardized on native speakers of French, word association tests, cloze tests, tests of general listening and reading comprehension, as well as oral and written production tests. However, with the exception of several isolated and small-scale studies (Genesee, Tucker and Lambert 1975; Harley 1982; Harley and Swain 1977; Szamosi, Swain and Lapkin 1979), little attempt has been made to assess the immersion students' ability to use French as a communicative tool through directly engaging them in communicative activities. With the intent of filling this gap, several of us[1] in the Modern Language Centre of the Ontario Institute for Studies in Education have undertaken the development of "testing units" to be used in provincial-wide assessments of the communicative performance of immersion students.

The purpose of this paper, then, is to describe the testing unit we have developed for students at the secondary school level—that is, for students who are fifteen years of age or older. I intend to describe the testing unit in the following way: first, by outlining several general principles of communicative language testing that guided our test development; and secondly, by discussing briefly the process we are following in developing scoring procedures for the test's large-scale administration. Overall, this paper describes aspects of the development of valid and viable communicative language tests, using one specific example of a test that we have developed to assess the communicative performance of immersion students at the ninth-grade level in order to illustrate this process. My intent is to provide an educational/pedagogical viewpoint to the development of communicative language tests rather than a measurement point of view. Having said this, I would add that I see no necessary long-run incompatibility of the two approaches.

Before turning to a discussion of the general principles of communicative language testing that guided our test construction, it will be useful to describe briefly the actual components of our testing unit. The central component is a twelve-page student booklet titled *A Vous la Parole*, which can be roughly translated as "the floor is yours." The booklet presents information about two summer employment possibilities for youth. Included in the booklet is information about job qualifications, the nature of each job, the location of each job, remuneration, working and leisure time, and living conditions. The student booklet also contains a list of government offices that offer, or organize, special programs for the summer employment of youth, and it encourages interested students to write for more information.

The second component consists of a series of six communicative tasks commonly required of a native speaker of the language; four involving writing, two involving speaking. The four writing tasks consist of writing a letter, a note, a composition, and a technical exercise. The two speaking tasks consist of an informal discussion among three or four students at a time, and a formal job interview with an adult. More details about the nature of these tasks will be given below.

The third component consists of a *Teacher's Guide*, which outlines the objectives of the testing program, explains how to organize and administer the test unit, and instructs on scoring procedures appropriate to each communicative task. We are in the process now of completing the writing of the *Teacher's Guide*.

GENERAL PRINCIPLES
OF COMMUNICATIVE
LANGUAGE TESTING

A considerable literature now exists on communicative language teaching and on communicative language testing. I have no intention of reviewing that literature here. Rather, I would like to highlight four general principles that we found highly relevant when faced with the practical problems of developing a communicative test of speaking and writing that could be administered on a large scale, and that could be sensitive to a wide range of proficiency levels. The four principles are:

1. Start from somewhere
2. Concentrate on content
3. Bias for best
4. Work for washback

Start from Somewhere

The first principle, start from somewhere, is intended to suggest that from both a theoretical and practical viewpoint, test development should *build from* existing knowledge and examples. Practically, of course, starting from somewhere saves reinventing the wheel. But much more is at stake in this principle than the somewhat superficial interpretation of simply saving time and energy— namely, the gradual and systematic growth in our understanding of the nature of communicative competence.

Several years ago, Michael Canale and I had the opportunity of reading much of the then existing literature on communicative language teaching and testing. We found that the literature contained quite different conceptions of communicative language teaching (Canale and Swain, 1980a). We attempted to bring together the various viewpoints into a coherent, linguistically-oriented, and pedagogically useful framework, arguing that communicative competence minimally includes four areas of knowledge and skills: grammatical competence, sociolinguistic competence, discourse competence, and strategic competence (Canale and Swain 1980b). The assumption is that learners may develop competence in any of these areas relatively independently, that learners and native speakers will differ in their relative mastery of these skills, and that the skills are involved in different degrees in specific language tasks.

Grammatical competence is understood to reflect knowledge of the language code itself. It includes knowledge of vocabulary and rules of word formation, pronunciation/spelling, and sentence formation. Such competence focuses directly on the knowledge and skills required to understand and express accurately the literal meaning of utterances.

Sociolinguistic competence addresses the extent to which utterances are produced and understood appropriately in different sociolinguistic contexts, depending on contextual factors such as topic, status of participants, and purposes of the interaction. Appropriateness of utterances refers to both appropriateness of meaning and appropriateness of form.

Discourse competence involves mastery of how to combine grammatical forms and meanings to achieve a unified spoken or written text in different genres such as narrative, argumentative essay, scientific report, or business letter. Unity of a text is achieved through cohesion in form and coherence in meaning. Cohesion deals with how utterances are linked structurally to facilitate interpretation of a text. For example, the use of cohesion devices such as pronouns, synonyms, ellipsis, conjunctions, and parallel structures serves to relate individual utterances and to indicate how a group of utterances is to be understood logically or chronologically as a text. Coherence refers to the relationships among the different meanings in a text where these meanings may be literal meanings, communicative functions, or social meanings.

Strategic competence refers to the mastery of communication strategies that may be called into action either to enhance the effectiveness of communication or to compensate for breakdowns in communication due to limiting factors in actual communication or to insufficient competence in one or more of the other components of communicative competence. (For further discussion of the nature of these components, see Savignon 1983).

The point of briefly reviewing these four proposed components of communicative competence is not to argue for or against them, but rather to indicate our starting point for the development of the *A Vous la Parole* testing unit. Other theoretical frameworks might have equally well provided a starting point for our test development.

Having a theoretical framework to start from is crucial. In a practical sense, its constructs guide the development of the stimulus material, the tasks to which the test-taker must respond, the scoring procedures, and the subsequent analyses and interpretation of the data. However, even more is at stake. Regarding accomplishments in standardized testing from 1927 to 1977, Buros states: "Except for the tremendous advances in electronic scoring, analysis, and reporting of test results, we don't have a great deal to show for fifty years of work" (1977:10). Shoemaker (1980:38—39) argues that:

> . . . improvements will not be brought about by further refinements of what generally has been done in achievement testing to date, nor in the development of more elaborate statistical procedures for analyzing data, nor in the expanded use of computer systems . . . advances in the state of the art of achievement testing are directly related to advances in the conceptualization of the skill domains on which student achievement is assessed.

We think there is merit to Shoemaker's claim in the area of communicative language testing, and that only through the specification of a theoretical framework will, as Michael Canale (1983) has stated, "the current disarray in conceptualization, research, and application in the area of communicative language pedagogy" disappear. Competing claims about the efficacy of communicative language teaching programs, for example, cannot be verified unless we can agree upon what is meant by communicative competence and performance. In proposing the constituent components of communicative competence (Canale and Swain 1980a) and a general outline of communicative skills involved within each component (Canale and Swain 1980b), we were proposing a starting point. What has been proposed are constructs that need to be validated. In fact, in a separate study on the development of bilingual proficiency being undertaken at the Ontario Institute for Studies in Education,[2] we are specifically testing the model using a multi-method, multi-trait design. (See Bachman and Palmer 1981; 1982 for discussions of this approach to language test validation.) Although the data from *A Vous la Parole* will not be sufficient for a complete trait-method analysis, they can, however, provide a separate, albeit limited, validation of the theoretical constructs. Starting from somewhere assumes that a "scientific" rather than an "evaluation" model underlies test design and implementation. Starting from somewhere allows one to build and refine one's concepts; starting from nowhere may mean another fifty years of little progress.

Concentrate on Content

The second principle, concentrate on content, refers to both the content of the material used as the basis of communicative language activities and the tasks used to elicit communicative language behaviours. The content of the material used as the basis for generating communicative activities—the *A Vous la Parole* booklet in our case—must be sufficient to generate each component of communicative performance. Similarly, the specific tasks—the composition, letter, note, technical exercise, informal peer discussion, and formal interview—must in their entirety provide the opportunity to use each component of communicative language behavior. The necessity of the first principle, start from somewhere, becomes all the more obvious in this context: the "somewhere" provides the framework that guides material and task development.

　　To ensure that our materials and tasks are capable of generating language that includes sociolinguistic, discourse, grammatical and strategic performance, we considered that the content needed to reflect at least four characteristics: it needed to be motivating, substantive, integrated, and interactive in nature. These are essential characteristics from the learners' point of view; that is, the materials need to be motivating, substantive, integrated, and interactive for the testee. For example, what is motivating in content for the learner may not be for the test-maker.

　　I would like now to illustrate how these characteristics are reflected in our testing unit of *A Vous la Parole*.

Motivating in Content.　In order to provide content that would be motivating for the target student population, we could have carried out a needs assessment-type survey. But we had neither the time nor the resources to do so. Instead we contacted several high school students from immersion and francophone programs for input into the topic of the materials. In informal sessions with these students, which took place both within and beyond the school walls (over lunch in a restaurant, in fact), project staff explored topics of greatest personal relevance and interest to these students. Recurrent themes in these discussions included travel, summer employment, care of animals, camping, bicycle riding, and music. Such topics as roller-skating and student exchange programs were considered too boring, too old hat.

After these consultations with students, the project staff went to work on a booklet that would incorporate as many of these themes of interest as was feasible. Development of the materials focused on two possible summer employment opportunities: one was to work on a rock-concert series to be organized in one francophone locale, Sudbury, in the province of Ontario; and the other was to tend vegetable gardens and farm animals in the historic francophone park of Fort Louisbourg in the province of Nova Scotia.

Early drafts of the *A Vous la Parole* booklet and tasks were pretested in classes containing some of the same students who had provided input in the design stages. Most students were thrilled to see their opinions in print. Since then the materials have been pilot-tested with a number of students who had not provided input to the content of the materials, and their feedback has been overwhelmingly positive. Thus, while we cannot claim to have hit on two topics of interest to all youths of this age, it is clear that the themes are interesting and relevant to the large majority of the students we have tested.

A second aspect to the provision of content that would motivate the students is in the actual presentation of the materials. We therefore tried to present the material in as attractive a format as possible, subject to budgetary restrictions. As a result, the *A Vous la Parole* booklet includes a comic strip, cartoons, drawings, maps, photos, and the use of bright, cheerful colors.

A third aspect to the provision of motivating content is in the nature of the communicative tasks the students are required to undertake based on the stimulus material. We felt the tasks should reflect contexts for writing and speaking that do not end with the end of education—that is, activities that would represent real uses of French by those who may or may not be continuing their studies. For this reason, the tasks of writing a letter, a note for a bulletin board, a factual paragraph, an opinion composition, and of conversing with peers and participating in an interview were used. Thus, although the tasks were not truly authentic in the sense that they were performed in school rather than in the actual setting, they represented tests of the students' ability to use their second language in situations reflecting real situations of interest to them.

Substantive in Content. A second characteristic of the content is that it be substantive. By this is meant not only that information be presented to the students, but that some of it be new to them. There are several reasons for presenting substantive content, some of which is new to the learner. In part, the presentation of new information should contribute to the motivation of the learner to read the materials carefully. Already known content can be boring and provide little incentive to consider the content thoughtfully. Additionally, the presentation of new information ensures that "real" communication can occur. That is to say, real communication frequently occurs as a function of an *information gap*.

For this reason, the *A Vous la Parole* booklet contains information about the two locales of the job opportunities being proposed. In the case of Sudbury, the students are informed that approximately a third of the population speak French; that a bilingual university is situated there where some courses taught are unique in Canada; that there is a rich and dynamic cultural life with theaters, orchestras, choirs, festivals, museums, and an art gallery; that Sudbury is in the northeast part of Ontario close to a lake offering exceptional facilities for swimming and water skiing; and so on.

In the case of Louisbourg, the students are given a brief history of it as a French fort set up to protect French possessions, which later became an important fishing port and active commercial center. The fort was later destroyed by the British and the town was abandoned. In 1961 the Canadian government decided to reconstruct Louisbourg, and in so doing relieved some of the hardships of unemployment caused by the closing of the coal mines in Cape Breton. Today the fort stands as a monument to the life and times of the eighteenth century; during the summer approximately 200 people are employed to live as the colonists did, growing and preserving their own food, making their own clothes, etc. In the case of both Sudbury and Louisbourg, maps, photos, and illustrations support the text.

This information, much of which will be new to many students, provides the context of the tasks they will be required to carry out. In order that the students consider this new information without feeling anxious or threatened by the test situation, we begin *A Vous la Parole* by indicating to the students that "the authors of this booklet have tried to propose some new ideas to you in a form that pleases you and will encourage you to learn and think about them."

From our point of view, then, presenting content that is substantive fulfills three criteria for communicative language tests. First, it provides a context for the tasks the students will be required to carry out. Secondly, it is potentially one of the few means by which the students' attention can be focused on content rather than form, which represents one way of approximating real communication in a test situation. Thirdly, to the extent that some of the content is new for the learner, the test material fulfills a genuine communicative function by responding to an information gap between the learner and the materials.

Additionally, and perhaps more an issue of pedagogy or ethics than of communicative language testing, by presenting substantive content, some of which is new, the test-taker will not go away empty-handed—or should I say, empty-headed. He or she should have gained some new ideas or knowledge, or even some new linguistic insight by having taken the test. To put it another way, in taking a communicatively-oriented test, the testee should have the experience of being communicated to, and of being able to communicate. The "meta-test" of this is that the testee has learned something from the experience of being tested.

We have discovered that translating these criteria into practice means being prepared to spend considerable time collecting relevant and accurate information, and translating this information into age-appropriate textual material. In fact, this phase of test development was equivalent to the development of curriculum materials for use in schools by our target population. I will return to this point below in the discussion of the principle of work for washback.

Integrated in content.   Neither the characteristic of being motivating in content nor of being substantive in content implies that the content be integrated—integrated, that is, in the sense of dealing with one theme around which *all* information and activities are centered. In the case of *A Vous la Parole*, the central theme is summer employment for youth. This theme provides the focus for all the tasks the students are asked to do. As the criterion for substance in content implies, the test resembles a lesson the students might encounter in class.

Although integrated content may not seem particularly radical for those who have been working on communicative language test development, when one compares the text and tasks of *A Vous la Parole* to a typical language test, the differences are profound in this respect. Even in the communicative test items that we developed several years ago as part of an item bank for the Ontario Ministry of Education to test French as a second-language communicative skills (Ontario Ministry of Education 1980), the contexts established were minimal—limited to sentences or short paragraphs. And to a large extent, each test item involved a new context. In traditional discrete-point tests of language proficiency, little attention was paid to context, let alone to integrated situational contexts.

Integrated content is essential to communicative language testing because it gives clues to meaning—the more context, the more clues. When a test item can be responded to correctly on the basis of the immediate linguistic environment alone, to that extent the task is unlikely to be reflective of the communicative aspects of language behavior.

Interactive in content.   The fourth characteristic of the content of a communicative test is that it should foster interaction. This can be accomplished in part by providing new substantive content so that the learners may be stimulated to ask questions. Perhaps more important, though, in fostering interaction is the provision of content that includes opinions or controversial ideas. This offers the possibility of an exchange of opinions, or of the expression of one's own ideas and opinions on the topic.

For example, to start the students thinking about the topic of *A Vous la Parole*, we reproduced a letter written by Eric Martin, a Montreal student of the same age as the students tested. The letter reads roughly as follows:

Dear friends,

I would like to give you my point of view on the subject of the life of today's adolescents. I am 15 years old and I am shocked to see the ignorance and the lack of respect that is shown us by adults. For adults, we are inferior beings and of little importance. For example, in stores and restaurants, adults are served before us even if we were there long before them.

What I find the most annoying is that adults also have priority over adolescents in the work world. It's always difficult for students between the ages of 15 and 17 to find a summer job, or a full-time job after graduation, and this will be even more serious this year. Contrary to what most adults think, adolescents are more conscientious and open than those of the same age in the 1960s and '70s. We have a big contribution to make to the work world.

The preoccupations of the adolescent of the '80s are not only the threat of nuclear war, the depletion of our energy sources, and the political divisions in our country. There is also a problem we don't talk much about at school: unemployment. It turns out that we are not well-prepared for the labor market. What a shame! So much money and time wasted.

Adults judge our situation and make decisions for us without asking our advice. Then, when these decisions don't meet our needs, they ask why! Since they don't want to consult us . . . let's speak for ourselves . . . à nous la parole!

Eric Martin

In the associated task, the learners are asked to write a letter to Eric, giving their opinions about what Eric said. The students are specifically asked to say whether they agree or disagree and why, giving examples from their own experiences or those of their friends. In order to indicate the tone and style in which their letter is to be written, they are reminded that Eric is also a student of their age.

Similarly, the *A Vous la Parole* booklet describes, among other aspects of the summer jobs, the living conditions for the students: seven to ten students will live together in a large house along with two adults. Each one will have his or her own bedroom, but will share bathroom, kitchen, and living room. In the associated task, the students, in groups of three or four, are asked to discuss such questions as: What difficulties might occur when living together like this with others they don't know? What solutions might be sought in face of these difficulties? What would they do if two people in the house didn't get along at all? and so on.

Thus the content of the stimulus material can set the stage for some form of interaction, and the tasks provide the opportunity for the interaction to occur. Together they help the student to determine the tone, the style and even the format of the interaction. This is important if one is to be able to judge the learners' sociolinguistic competence.

Bias for Best

The third principle we used in guiding our communicative test development is bias for best. This means do everything possible to elicit the learners' best performance. There is a good reason for this from the point of view of test interpretation: if the testee does well, then it can be said with some confidence that the learner can do what is expected of him or her when given the opportunity. However, if the testee does not do well, then it is not clear whether this occurs because the testee cannot do what is expected, or is prevented from doing it because of distracting factors, or whatever. In other words, it is important to minimize the effect of the measurement technique on the test-taker's performance.

In *A Vous la Parole*, we introduced several procedures into the testing situation to bias performance positively. Recognizing that individuals work at varying paces, the testees are given more than adequate time to complete the task assigned for the day. In addition to being allowed to work at their own speed on the written tasks, they are given an opportunity each day to review the work they have previously completed and are encouraged to make any changes they wish (Odell 1977). Furthermore, they are given access to such reference materials as dictionaries, and are explicitly encouraged to use them. While the task is being done, the test administrator is expected to check that everyone is following the task instructions correctly.

In addition to these procedures, we decided that we could bias results for best performance by, in some cases, informing the students of what was being tested. Thus, in the introduction to *A Vous la Parole*, the students read that "this short booklet serves as a basis for a series of exercises in order to evaluate your written and spoken French." In the technical exercise, where the students are required to take the point form description of the tasks to be performed in the summer jobs and write them up in a paragraph in the same style as the rest of the text, it is explicitly stated that "the goal of this exercise is to be able to evaluate your ability to produce complete sentences."

In a similar vein, students are given suggestions about how to proceed with the task as, for example, in writing the composition, where they are advised "to express their ideas clearly." In some cases the students are given suggestions of points to include in their written work or discussion, and are explicitly told who their audience is and therefore the style, or level of formality, they should adopt. For example, in the note-writing task of *A Vous la Parole*, the students who choose the Louisbourg project are given the following instructions:

> In this exercise, we are asking you to write a note to other young people your age. *The style should therefore be informal.*
>
> In order to do this exercise, you must imagine that you are already a participant in the Louisbourg project.
>
> Imagine the following situation: you have been in Louisbourg for several weeks now and you would like to visit Halifax next weekend. You decide to post a note in French in the cafeteria in order to find someone who can drive you to Halifax at that time. In your note, mention that you will share expenses for the trip and that you have a driver's license. Leave your telephone number or indicate where you can be easily met. Don't forget that you are writing to *someone your own age.*

Thus, to bias for best is to provide the test-takers with useful suggestions as to what and how to respond, to provide adequate time to complete the task, and in the case of written work, to have access to dictionaries or other reference material as well as to have the opportunity to review and revise their work.

Work for Washback

The fourth and final principle guiding our test construction is to work for washback. Washback refers to the effect a test has on teaching practices. It has frequently been noted that teachers will teach to a test; that is, if they know the content of a test and/or the format of a test, they will teach their students accordingly. This is not particularly surprising, given the frequency with which educational administrators use tests, legitimately or not, to judge teacher effectiveness.

Recognizing that neither teacher nor administrative behavior is likely to change in this regard, and believing that teaching practices, especially in the higher grade levels of immersion programs, could profit from some changes, we have tried to build teacher involvement into the development of the test, into its administration, and eventually into its scoring. Before discussing how we have done this, I would like to digress briefly to comment on the suggestion that some changes in teaching practices might be appropriate in the higher grades of immersion education.

Immersion education has two goals—to foster the development of high levels of second language proficiency; and to do this at no expense to mother-tongue development, cognitive growth, or academic achievement. These goals are accomplished essentially through the teaching of academic content in the second language. Although at later grade levels more class time is used for the teaching of French *per se* (Swain 1981), the emphasis is on teaching content. The result, typical of many classroom settings, is that the teacher talks and the students listen. Student responses are typically short and elliptical. In other words, individual students are given relatively infrequent opportunities to use their second language, especially in extended discourse or in sociolinguistically variable ways. As might be expected in this situation, the students develop native-like *comprehension* skills (Swain and Lapkin 1982), but their *spoken* French has many non-native features in it (Harley and Swain 1978; Harley 1982). We think that the sorts of materials and related activities that form the *A Vous la Parole* testing unit exemplify teaching units that may help students to overcome these weaker aspects of their second-language proficiency. Incidentally, no suggestion is being made that *all* teaching be activity-oriented and student-centered. Rather the implication is that communicative activities form a legitimate and significant part of the teaching-learning process for both the acquisition of language and content knowledge.

To return to the main point, that of working for washback, we have for this reason involved teachers in the development of *A Vous la Parole*, first by establishing an advisory panel that includes teachers, as well as Department of Education (Saskatchewan) officials, to comment on this and other test units we are producing, while still in the development stage; secondly, by holding a workshop to explain the test and its purposes to teachers whose classes were involved in the pilot-testing of *A Vous la Parole*; thirdly, by asking these same teachers to help supervise the students being tested; and fourthly, by informally discussing with these teachers their reactions to the test unit and their perceptions of the students' reactions to it. In general, their reactions have been both positive and thoughtful, and many excellent suggestions have been made for revisions, which have been incorporated in the present version of the testing unit.

For practical reasons, in order to administer a test like *A Vous la Parole* on a large scale, teachers must be involved in its administration and scoring. It is simply too time-consuming and therefore too expensive to hire the additional personnel necessary for its administration. Moreover, for the very reason of working for washback, we consider it advantageous that teachers be involved in test administration and scoring. To this end, we have begun writing a *Teacher's Guide* which explains the purposes of the testing unit, a step-by-step guide of how to administer the test, including the specific wording of the information and instructions that the teachers will give to the students, and a description of how to score the exercises, including a brief theoretical and empirical rationale for the scoring criteria as well as many illustrative examples.

Through these means of involving teachers in the development and/or administration and scoring of the test, we hope not only to change aspects of what is taught, but also to suggest alternative teaching-learning strategies.

SCORING

Although *A Vous la Parole* was developed for use in a large-scale, summative evaluation of immersion education, it could also be used for formative program evaluation or for evaluating individual student performance. The scoring procedures developed should reflect the use or uses for which test is intended and the theoretical framework that initially guided the test's construction.

We began the development of scoring criteria with the view that each task would reveal aspects of communicative language performance; that is, each task could be scored for grammatical, sociolinguistic, discourse, and strategic aspects of communicative language performance. We did not, however, attempt to predetermine the specific aspects of each component that would be scored. Rather, we worked from the data gathered during the pilot-testing phase to determine what specifically would be scored in each task and what scoring criteria would be used. By proceeding in this way, the scoring scheme was able to reflect the most salient aspects of each task response, and the full range of responses observed for any specific aspect. Neither could have been fully known before the data were examined.

Our approach in developing scoring procedures has been to begin comprehensively, using a mixture of objective counts and subjective judgments. Scoring the note to be posted on the bulletin board, for example, included counting the number of word order errors, anaphora errors and omissions, homophonous and non-homophonous morphological errors, and the points of information provided. Additionally, judgments were made on a three-point scale about the use of attention-getting devices, the overall appropriateness of lexical register used, the persuasiveness of the note, and the physical organization and appearance of the note as a note.

For purposes of large-scale testing, our intention is to reduce the number of aspects scored based on analyses carried out with the pilot data. Several factors will determine the final set of features to be scored.

One factor will be the ways the data cluster in correlational and factor analytical analyses. We anticipate, for example, that the analyses of the written data will reveal clusters of variables that correspond to the theoretical constructs of sociolinguistic, grammatical, and discourse competence. (Strategic performance was not scored in the written data.) Preliminary analyses on a partial data set are suggestive of these three components, but also revealed a fourth cluster of variables having largely to do with vocabulary knowledge. Our plan is to select several variables from each cluster of variables.

Which variables are selected will depend in part on the face validity of the variables. Additionally, however, their selection will depend on patterns of systematic and interesting variability. For example, the data suggest systematic differences between early immersion students (those starting an immersion program at age 5 or 6) and late immersion students (those starting an immersion program around age 13) in their ability to write homophonous morphology correctly. Early immersion students tend to make more homophonous morphological errors (e.g., tu *a* dit; les enfants *pense*) than late immersion students, reflecting perhaps the stronger oral base of the early immersion students' language-learning experiences.

Thus the steps we pursued in developing scoring procedures for large-scale testing—a task that is not yet complete for us—involves the selection of variables from a much larger set, the larger set being determined by the nature of the responses to each task. By proceeding in this way, the criteria reflect the range of possible responses, and the task responses will have been exploited to their fullest in contributing to theory and practice.

SUMMARY AND CONCLUSIONS

To sum up, four principles useful in guiding the development of communicative language tests have been discussed using the testing unit of *A Vous la Parole* as illustrative material. The four principles—start from somewhere, concentrate on content, bias for best, and work for washback—assume a pedagogical function to language testing as well as a scientific approach to language test design and implementation. Although some may foresee inherent conflicts between these assumptions and those of measurement theory, I do not see any necessary long-run incompatibility.

The process followed in developing scoring procedures and criteria has also been discussed. The process has involved moving from maximum detail and comprehensiveness to the selection of key variables that still permit comprehensiveness in the measurement of the components of communicative performance. It has also involved working from the testees' responses to each task. This has ensured that the scoring criteria reflect the range of possible responses and that the salient component features elicited by each task are considered. What is still not known, however, is the feasibility of large-scale administration and scoring of *A Vous la Parole*. We, as well as Departments of Education, think it is possible for purposes of *program* evaluation. Its feasibility for individual student assessment on a large scale remains uncertain, primarily because of the testing time involved. The testing unit is well suited, however, for use by classroom teachers as a teaching unit through which communicative language performance of individual students can be assessed.

NOTES

I would like to thank Michael Canale, Daina Green, Jill Kamin, Sharon Lapkin, Sandra Savignon, Nina Spada, and Peter Tung for their time and thoughtfulness in commenting on an earlier version of this paper, which was presented at the International Symposium on Language Testing, University of Hong Kong, Dec. 18–21, 1982. This paper will be published in *Language Learning and Communication*, Vol. II, no. 2, and permission to include it here is gratefully acknowledged.

1. Actively participating in this project are Valerie Argue, Suzanne Bertrand, Jim Cummins, Daina Green, Gila Hanna, Jill Kamin, Sharon Lapkin, Laurette Levy and Merrill Swain.

2. The principal investigators of this project are Patrick Allen, Jim Cummins, Raymond Mougeon, and Merrill Swain.

REFERENCES

Buros, O. K. 1977. "Fifty years in testing: some reminiscences, criticisms, and suggestions." *Educational Researcher* **6**: 9–15.

Bachman, L. and A. Palmer. 1981. "Basic concerns in test validation." In J. Read (ed.). *Directions in language testing.* Singapore University Press.

———. 1982. "The construct validation of some components of communicative proficiency." *TESOL Quarterly* **16**: 449–465.

Canale, M. 1983. "From communicative competence to communicative language pedagogy." In J. Richards and R. Schmidt (eds.). *Language and communication.* London: Longman.

Canale, M. and M. Swain. 1980a. "Theoretical bases of communicative approaches to second-language teaching and testing." *Applied Linguistics* **1**: 1–47.

———. 1980b. "A domain description for core FSL: communication skills." In *The Ontario assessment instrument pool: French as a second language, junior and intermediate divisions,* Ontario Ministry of Education, pp. 27–39. Toronto: Ontario Ministry of Education.

Genesee, F., G. R. Tucker, and W. E. Lambert. 1975. "Communication skills of bilingual children." *Child Development* **46**: 1010–1014.

Harley, B. 1982. *"Age-related differences in the acquisition of the French verb system by Anglophone students in French immersion programs."* Unpublished Ph.D. dissertation, University of Toronto.

Harley, B. and M. Swain, 1977. "An analysis of verb form and function in the speech of French immersion pupils." *Working Papers on Bilingualism* **14**: 31–46.

Harley, B. and M. Swain. 1978. "An analysis of the verb system used by young learners of French." *Interlanguage Studies Bulletin* **3**: 35–79.

Jones, R. L. 1977. "Testing: a vital connection." In J. K. Phillips (ed.). *The language connection: from the classroom to the world.* Skokie, Ill.: National Textbook Co.

Lambert, W. E. and G. R. Tucker. 1972. *Bilingual education of children.* Rowley, Mass.: Newbury House.

Odell, L. 1977. "Measuring changes in intellectual processes as one dimension of growth in writing." In C. R. Cooper and L. Odell (eds.). *Evaluating writing.* Urbana, Ill.: NCTE.

Ontario Ministry of Education 1980. *The Ontario assessment instrument pool: French as a second language, junior and intermediate divisions.* Toronto: Ontario Ministry of Education.

Savignon, S. 1983. *Communicative competence: theory and classroom practice*. Reading, Mass.: Addison-Wesley.

Shoemaker, D. M. 1980. "Improving achievement testing." *Educational Evaluation and Policy Analysis* **2 (6):** 37−49.

Swain, M. 1981. "Immersion education: applicability for non-vernacular teaching to vernacular speakers." *Studies in Second Language Acquisition* **4:** 1−17.

Swain, M. and S. Lapkin. 1982. *Evaluating bilingual education: a Canadian case study.* Clevedon, Avon: Multilingual Matters.

Szamosi, M., M. Swain, and S. Lapkin. 1979. "Do early immersion pupils 'know' French?" *Orbit* **49:** 20−23.

Chapter 13

Testing Performance in Oral Interaction

Keith Morrow

Keith Morrow is Director (Education) of the Bell Educational Trust. While working at the Centre for Applied Language Studies at the University of Reading, he undertook a research project to explore the feasibility of developing notional-functional syllabuses. This project led to the creation of the Royal Society of Arts CUEFL examinations referred to in the contribution, for which he is now Chief Examiner.

The testing procedures described in this paper are employed in the Oral Interaction examination, set by the Royal Society of Arts in the "Examination in the Communicative Use of English as a Foreign Language." This examination is now becoming widely established in the United Kingdom, and increasingly overseas, as a measure of what candidates can actually do when using English as a foreign language. It measures the candidates' performance on a range of pre-specified tasks in terms of its relationship to established criteria. It is thus an examination based on performance as a reflection of underlying competence. The definition and description of the levels of performance appropriate to the different levels of the examination proved to be one of the most challenging and rewarding aspects of the examination development.

The examinations are offered twice a year at three levels (Basic, Intermediate, Advanced) in four areas (Reading, Listening, Writing, Oral Interaction). The candidate is free to enter any combination of areas at any combination of levels—except that for administrative reasons the same area may not be entered at more than one level at one session. The advantage of this is that it

	Basic
Accuracy	Pronunciation may be heavily influenced by L1 and accented though generally intelligible. Any confusion caused by grammatical/lexical errors can be clarified by the candidate.
Appropriacy	Use of language broadly appropriate to function, though no subtlety should be expected. The intention of the speaker can be perceived without excessive effort.
Range	Severely limited range of expression is acceptable. May often have to search for a way to convey the desired meaning.
Flexibility	Need not usually take the initiative in conversation. May take time to respond to a change of topic. Interlocutor may have to make considerable allowances and often adopt a supportive role.
Size	Contributions generally limited to one or two simple utterances are acceptable.

Figure 13.1.   Tests of Oral Interaction: Degrees of Skill

allows a candidate to build up a profile of performance, which corresponds to his or her own actual strengths and weaknesses in English. Thus, for example, an Arab student may enter Listening and Oral Interaction at Advanced level, while taking Intermediate level Reading and perhaps only Basic level Writing; a Japanese student, on the other hand, may take Reading at Advanced level, Writing at Intermediate, Oral Interaction at Basic level, and Listening not at all. Every candidate receives a certificate showing exactly what he or she has passed, at what level and, crucially, a brief statement of what it means to have obtained this result.

This notion of "knowing what it means" to achieve a given level of task-performance is crucial to the whole concept of the examinations. It is defined along three parameters. The first of these is *operation*, which delineates the tasks that the candidate is expected to perform at different levels of the examination. For example in Reading at Basic level, one of the operations is "Searching through a text to locate a specific piece of information," while at Intermediate level the candidate may be asked to "Skim through the text to

Intermediate	Advanced
Pronunciation still obviously influenced by L1 though clearly intelligible. Grammatical/lexical accuracy is generally high, though some errors which do not destroy communication are acceptable.	Accurate in pronunciation, though some residual accent is acceptable. Grammatical/lexical accuracy is very high.
Use of language generally appropriate to function. The overall intention of the speaker is always clear.	Use of language entirely appropriate to context, function and intention.
A fair range of language is available to the candidate. He is able to express himself without overtly having to search for words.	Few limitations on the range of language available to the candidate. Little obvious use of avoidance strategies.
Is able to take the initiative in a conversation, and to adapt to new topics or changes of direction—though neither of these may be consistently manifested.	Contributes well to the interaction and will take the initiative. Little strain is imposed on the interlocutor.
Most contributions may be short, but some evidence of ability to produce more complex utterances and to develop these into discourse should be manifested.	Candidates should be able to produce lengthy and developed responses and contributions.

© RSA 1982. Reprinted with permission.

establish the gist." The listing of operations is cumulative, so that those appearing at Basic level may also be tested at Intermediate and Advanced levels. The higher levels will differ from the lower, however, in requiring the candidate to display a higher *degree of skill* in performing these operations on a wider range of *text-types*. This last is a familiar concept to language teachers and testers. It is easy to accept that reading a popular newspaper report is "different" from reading an academic textbook, and that performance on one does not necessarily imply performance on the other. But it is the *degree of skill* that is perhaps the most innovative and the most practically useful criterion, especially in the productive tests of Writing and Oral Interaction. The *degree of skill* specification for Oral Interaction tests is set out in Fig. 13.1. As should be clear by now, this shows *how well* the candidates must perform; *what* they must do, and in terms of what *text-types*, is specified elsewhere.

So far this paper has been concerned with general statements of principle and intent. Let us now look in more detail at the Oral Interaction examination to see how these are applied in practice.

The examination is in three parts. In Part I, the candidate talks alone with an interlocutor; in Part II a pair of candidates discuss a "problem" together and decide on an appropriate course of action; in Part III the candidates report back to the interlocutor (who has been absent during Part II) what they have been doing and the decision they have reached. They must explain and justify their proposed course of action to the interlocutor. During the whole of Parts I, II, and III, the candidates' performance is observed by an assessor, who judges whether or not each candidate reaches the required performance (as specified in Fig. 13.1) for the level. Samples of the tasks set in Part I and Parts II/III of the examination at Basic level in 1981 are shown in Figures 13.2 and 13.3.

A number of points emerge from this bald summary. First, the roles of interlocutor and assessor are separated. This reflects a deliberate attempt to give the examination a "human face" and to lessen the inevitable anxiety that candidates feel. The interlocutor is normally a member of staff from the school or college at which the candidate is studying, and is hopefully a familiar figure. The assessor plays no part in the actual conduct of the examination as far as the candidate is concerned. He/she observes as unobtrusively as possible what is happening and stays on the sidelines. In fact the conduct of these examinations requires a third person, the usher, whose role is to explain their tasks to the candidates before they go into the examination room. This is our solution to the difficulty, especially at basic level, of conveying complex written instructions to candidates whose English may be defeated by them. Even translation, which is not possible given the unpredictable L1 background of our candidates, would not, we feel, be as helpful as this procedure.

Secondly, the orientation of the examination is "educational" rather than "administrative." It is undoubtedly uneconomic to split the role of assessor and interlocutor; it is equally "complex" to organize proceedings with single

THE ROYAL SOCIETY OF ARTS EXAMINATIONS BOARD

EXAMINATIONS IN THE COMMUNICATIVE USE OF
ENGLISH AS A FOREIGN LANGUAGE
TEST OF ORAL INTERACTION
BASIC/INTERMEDIATE/ADVANCED LEVEL
1981
CANDIDATES' PAPER
PART I

You must talk with a teacher for about 5 minutes. While you are talking, an Assessor will be listening to what you and the teacher say.

You now have a few minutes to study the programme of evening classes before discussing it with the teacher. You should choose 3 activities that interest you and that are suitable for your level of English. If you need advice on the different activities, the teacher will be able to help you.

RSA SCHOOL OF ENGLISH

In addition to your general English classes, you should choose 3 activities from the programme of evening classes below.

Please note that the activities marked with an asterisk (*) are only suitable for students with an Intermediate or Advanced level of English.

	Monday	Tuesday	Wednesday	Thursday	Friday
19.00 to 20.30	Conversation Practice or Study Skills* (If you choose this class, give your teacher as much information as you can about your future study plans)	Translation* (Ask your teacher which languages are available) or Language Games	Handwriting or English Literature* (If you choose this class, tell your teacher what kind of Literature you are most interested in)	Business English* (Tell your teacher which areas of Business Studies you are interested in) or Language Teaching Film	Language Learning Songs or Technical English* (Tell your teacher what technical subjects you are interested in)

© RSA 1981. Reprinted with permission.

Figure 13.2.   Samples of Basic Level Tasks for Part I, and Parts II, III

THE ROYAL SOCIETY OF ARTS EXAMINATIONS BOARD

EXAMINATIONS IN THE COMMUNICATIVE USE OF
ENGLISH AS A FOREIGN LANGUAGE
TEST OF ORAL INTERACTION
BASIC LEVEL
1981
CANDIDATES' PAPER
PART II/III

For part II of the examination you must do one of the tasks on this sheet with a fellow-student. When you go into the examination room, the examiner will tell you which task you must do and will explain anything you do not understand. When you have completed the task, a teacher will come into the room. You must explain to him/her what you have done in your task and what you have decided to do. This is part III of the test.

Task 1:   You have been invited to take part in a radio programme in which foreign students are asked for their views on life in Britain. To prepare you for the programme, the examiner will give you a list of points to consider. Discuss these with your fellow student and compare your opinions.

Task 2:   You and your fellow student have won first prize in a competition. The prize is a weekend for two in London with all expenses paid. The examiner will give you a list of suggestions to help you plan your weekend. Discuss these with your fellow student and decide how you would like to spend your time.

Figure 13.3.

candidates and then pairs; and it poses unfamiliar problems for test centers to "pair" students in such a way that each has the chance to perform to his or her best. But our conviction is that these practical problems are outweighed by the positive educational advantages of a test format whose "washback" effect on the classroom is so clearly in line with current thinking about good pedagogy.

It is perhaps at this point that experienced test constructors will sigh deeply and raise questions about reliability, validity, and other aspects of the real world designed to deflate euphoria. Happily, our experience is that face validity is high; both teachers and students agree readily that these tests are a good approximation to what is involved in "real" language use in the "real" world. Interesting work remains to be done on the investigation of concurrent validity between these tests and other oral tests, and of correlations between these tests in different areas. At the moment, however, our main attention is focused on reliability in terms of variability between different applications of the same test in different settings. This hinges crucially on the role of the interlocutor, and we are now putting considerable effort into the production of detailed guidelines for interlocutors and the holding of briefing and standardization meetings. Our greatest help is the fact that the role we are asking interlocutors to adopt is essentially that of a good teacher, being supportive and constructive, and we are able to build on this classroom practice.

The question of marker-marker (inter-rater) reliability, which has traditionally haunted "subjective" tests, causes us very few problems, and it is perhaps worth briefly considering why. The assessor is asked to evaluate the candidate's performance in terms of the criteria set out in Figure 13.1. This may seem at first sight a daunting task, but in fact it turns out to be much more straightforward. Firstly, all the candidates presenting themselves in a given session are entering at the same level, so the assessor need only be concerned with one column of the chart at a time. Secondly, the question to be answered is not an open one ("How good is the candidate?") but a closed one ("Is the candidate good enough to meet these criteria?"). And the answer is to be based on a global consideration of *all* the criteria. If they are all met, the candidate passes; if not, the candidate fails.

Of course, the criteria themselves are subjective. What is a "fair" range? What are "more complex" utterances? How much is "little" strain? But it is in terms like this that communication operates and we find that teachers have no difficulty in working within this framework as assessors with very high reliability.

Language in use is a qualitative, not essentially a quantitative, phenomenon. In testing as in teaching we need to break away from the idea that a language is merely the sum of its parts. This represents the road that we are following; we're enjoying the journey.[1]

NOTES

1. The full specifications, and sample papers, for these examinations can be obtained from: Royal Society of Arts Examinations Board, Murray Road, Orpington, Kent, BR5 3RB. Price: £1.00 + £1.20 airmail.

Chapter 14

Proficiency in Context: The Pennsylvania Experience

Barbara F. Freed

Barbara Freed trains and supervises teaching assistants in foreign languages in the College of Arts and Sciences at the University of Pennsylvania. Her primary interests have been in the area of L2 acquisition research, with particular reference to input phenomena and the effects of communicative curricula. She has worked actively in the language attrition project at the University of Pennsylvania and is Director of the Regional Center for Language Proficiency which was initiated at the University of Pennsylvania in 1983.

Every ten years or so a new movement seems to take hold of the language teaching profession. Each movement promises better and more rapid learning of a second language and brings with it new approaches, methods, techniques, and materials. A brief retrospective glance identifies the era of grammar-translation, that of audiolingual teaching, another focused on communicative/interactional learning, and in the recent past, that of the notional-functional syllabus. (For discussion see, among others, Brown 1980; Clarke 1982; Richards and Rodgers 1982.) Most recently, the term *proficiency* has come into popular usage. We are barraged with information about proficiency-based language instruction, proficiency standards, proficiency requirements, and proficiency tests. While proficiency-oriented teaching cannot be equated with a method but should be regarded, rather, as an organizing principle or system (ACTFL 1982), the notion of proficiency-based instruction has already had an indisputable effect on the language teaching profession.

On a national level, recognition of the need to establish commonly understood and accepted proficiency standards is not new. The Report of the Modern Language Association—American Academy of Learned Society's (MLA—ACLS) Language Task Forces, completed in 1978 (Brod 1980), and that of the President's Commission on Foreign Language and International Studies (1979) emphasized the need to set clearly defined, realistic proficiency goals for each level of study and to develop tests to measure such proficiency. Response to these recommendations was generated by a grant to the American Council on the Teaching of Foreign Languages (ACTFL) to provide a "Design for Measuring and Communicating Foreign Language Proficiency" (ACTFL 1982). This project resulted in the ACTFL Provisional Proficiency Guidelines, which provide a series of "generic" and language-specific (French, Spanish, German) functionally defined proficiency standards for speaking, listening, reading, writing, and culture. These guidelines identify sequential stages of development in language proficiency.

On a more personal level, we have long felt the need for a common and absolute set of standards against which we could meaningfully measure and identify the abilities of individual students. We are well aware of the meaninglessness of course grades and units of study, at least so far as basic language learning is concerned. We know that one school's "A" is another school's "C"; four semesters at one institution may be equal to two somewhere else. MLA Cooperative or College Entrance Examination Board (CEEB) language achievement test scores tell us little about what students are able to *do* with the language. Efforts to place new students into the appropriate level of a language course serve to underscore the vagueness of a number of years of study as a measure of ability to use the language. (For detailed discussion see Hagiwara 1983.)

The purpose of this paper is to illustrate how proficiency-based language instruction has operated within the context of one university's experience. The discussion will include background information regarding the perceived need to establish a proficiency requirement, details of that requirement for one language section at the university, and a preliminary evaluation of the effects this requirement has had on language learning.

THE NEED TO ESTABLISH A PROFICIENCY REQUIREMENT

The College of Arts and Sciences at the University of Pennsylvania has maintained a foreign language requirement in one form or another since the mid 1800s. While the number of hours and even the languages required to satisfy the requirement have changed over the years—Latin and Greek in the mid- and late-nineteenth century with a switch to modern languages at the turn of the century—the basic catalogue description has changed very little in that time and essentially not at all in the twelve year period from 1968 to 1980. The 1980–81 *University of Pennsylvania Course of Study* described the foreign language requirement as follows:

> Every student is required to attain a certain competence in a foreign language. Such competence may be demonstrated either by passing a foreign language course numbered 4 (or equivalents) . . . or by the student's score in the Advanced Placement Test or the College Entrance Examination Board (CEEB) Achievement Test or on a departmental placement examination.
>
> Students who are placed in an intermediate or advanced level language course upon entrance to the University may not receive credit for a lower level course in the same language. Students are admitted to first, second or third year courses in language according to the amount of work they have had in high school and their score in the CEEB test.
>
> Foreign language courses taken to fulfill the foreign language requirement as well as foreign language electives not being used in a major may be taken on a pass/fail basis.

The description may be disturbingly familiar to many readers. The problem, of course, is that what is in reality a "time" requirement is couched in other terms. At the University of Pennsylvania, as at many other institutions with language requirements, language competence has been evaluated primarily in terms of length of study. The catalogue descriptions have traditionally begun by invoking such admirable goals as "competence," "performance," or even "proficiency," yet such competence or proficiency has tended to be measured by semester hours at worst and by scores on standardized multiple-choice discrete-point tests at best (Freed 1981a).

In 1979 the Advisory Committee on Language Instruction began what was to be a two-year examination of this long-standing foreign language requirement. In the course of this two-year period many aspects of the language learning experience at Pennsylvania were analyzed. As a result of their findings the committee decided to investigate the feasibility of redefining the requirement as a proficiency requirement. Among the first facts that the committee considered were the following:

1. Only thirty-three percent (33%) of all College of Arts and Sciences matriculants at the University of Pennsylvania present CEEB language achievement test scores upon entrance. Because students are placed into language classes according to their CEEB scores, this means that some sixty percent (60%) of all incoming freshmen have to be tested during or before the first week of classes. (A small percentage are exempt by virtue of Advanced Placement.)

2. Only one-third of those who present CEEB language scores upon entrance receive scores high enough (650 or above) to exempt them from further language study. Even if the minimum score were lowered to 600, no more than half of those students who present CEEB scores would be exempt from further study. In other words, some seventy-five to eighty percent (75%−80%) of all entering freshmen have to take course work to satisfy the foreign language requirement.

These data were both surprising and disturbing. We had anticipated that those who felt confident enough to take the CEEB language achievement tests would achieve relatively high scores. We would also have liked to believe that those who had spent valuable years of foreign-language study at the secondary level would have developed skills that would have exempted them from elementary- and intermediate-level language courses at the university level. Such was clearly not the case. These findings did not mean that college expectations were necessarily too high, or that secondary school achievement was too low. (Proponents of one or the other view are often all too quick to reach such conclusions.) They suggested, rather, that college and secondary levels of instruction lacked common goals or standards of evaluation.

The results of an internal testing program further convinced us of the inadequacy of a system that evaluates language learning almost exclusively in terms of length of study. The CEEB language achievement tests were administered to all students enrolled in levels 1−4 French, Spanish, Italian, German, Russian, and Latin at the end of the Spring and Fall semesters, 1980. (These are the levels that constitute the four-semester language requirement.) Mean scores for students who were completing the fourth semester of study are shown in Table 14.1.[1] These data showed that, at the end of the required four semesters of study, our own students were not achieving the 650 minimum score that incoming freshmen needed for exemption from further language study. They also established the fact that a high correlation existed between CEEB scores and grades awarded. CEEB scores for "A" students were in almost all cases higher than those scores for "B" students, which in turn were higher than those for "C" students, etc., and they increased with level of study. This correlation, then, told us something about the nature of the skills we were teaching and testing.

TABLE 14.1   MEAN SCORES ON CEEB LANGUAGE ACHIEVEMENT TESTS FOR STUDENTS COMPLETING A LEVEL 4 LANGUAGE COURSE.

French	Spanish	Italian	German	Russian	Latin
558	533	561	575	593	580

Beyond this we had learned little about our students' abilities. We knew before we began our study that students were dissatisfied with what they were learning. They continually told us that they wanted to learn to speak, that relevance for them meant the development of oral proficiency. However, the results of these two studies provided little information as to the functional oral proficiency of our students. For this we looked to the second part of our internal testing project.

To evaluate the oral skills of our students, we administered the Foreign Service Institute (FSI) Oral Proficiency Interview to a subset of the larger group. This oral interview was given to ten percent (10%) of students who were completing French 3 during the 1980 academic year. These students were selected at random from those who volunteered to be interviewed. The FSI Interviews were given by those of us who were trained in the use of the standard FSI procedure at a 1980 FSI Testing Kit Workshop.

The results of this study were again disappointing, but not surprising in view of what we already knew about the language skills of our students. The mean FSI score for this group of students was slightly more than 1+, or an *Intermediate-High* as defined by the *ACTFL Provisional Proficiency Guidelines*. (ACTFL 1982).[2] Moreover, this 1+ was a *mean* score that represented a range of from 0+ to 2+, or from a *Novice-Low* to *Intermediate-High*.

This information further convinced us of the futility of a requirement based almost exclusively on length of study. It had become clear that many students who fulfilled the four-semester requirement remained unable to use the language in any meaningful way. While they had in fact satisfied a university requirement, they had experienced no personal satisfaction nor had they developed a useful skill.

Consideration of these data as well as the prevailing attitude toward the language requirement at the University of Pennsylvania led to a decision on the part of several language departments, or sections within a department, to change the nature of the language requirement. It is important to clarify that not all language departments have made this decision.

September 1981 brought the first major change. At that time the French section of the Department of Romance Languages instituted a proficiency requirement based on a set of functionally defined proficiency standards. In September 1982 the German, Russian, and Arabic Departments also replaced the time requirement with a proficiency requirement. While the details of the requirements vary from department to department, the principle remains the same: students must demonstrate proficiency in a variety of functional skills as measured by departmental language proficiency tests in order to meet the college language requirement. While most students take this test upon completion of the level 4 course, some choose to take it earlier, for example, after completing the level 3 course. Some, who are unable to pass the test after four semesters of study, are obliged to continue their study of the language until they earn a passing score. It is not within the scope of this paper to present a detailed description of the proficiency requirement as it exists in each department. For purposes of illustration the standards and policies adopted by the French section of the Department of Romance Languages follow.

THE PROFICIENCY REQUIREMENT IN THE FRENCH SECTION OF THE DEPARTMENT OF ROMANCE LANGUAGES[3]

The proficiency categories, listed in the left-hand column of Table 14.2, are as follows: Oral Interaction, Listening Comprehension, Reading Comprehension, Writing, and Culture. Temporarily, the CEEB language achievement tests are included with this set of five proficiency standards. The numbers 5, 10, 15, and 20 across the top of the table represent the numerical scores for performance at each of the described levels.

The capsule descriptions corresponding to a score of 10 represent the performance levels needed to satisfy the proficiency requirement. For example, students must demonstrate oral language skills as described by an FSI rating of 1+ and listening comprehension skills that permit partial comprehension of factual news broadcasts and/or partial comprehension of native-speaker conversation. To demonstrate reading comprehension, they have to answer questions that require factual and inferential responses to literary texts and to provide a summary with the most salient features of a non-literary text correctly represented. To test writing proficiency, students are given guided composition tasks that require adequate vocabulary and some use of complex sentences beyond subject-verb-object organization. The standards for measuring competence in culture are still to be determined. In addition, students must achieve a score of 500 on the CEEB language achievement test in French.

Proficiency is determined by computing a composite score for all six portions of the test. A student is thus able to compensate for weakness in one area

TABLE 14.2. DESCRIPTION OF FUNCTIONAL PROFICIENCY STANDARDS FOR FRENCH
UNIVERSITY OF PENNSYLVANIA

Skill and Method of Testing	5	10	15	20
Oral Interaction: [FSI interview] (Adams and Frith 1979, p. 13–15)	S-1 "able to satisfy routine travel needs and minimum courtesy requirements. Can ask and answer questions on very familiar topics; can understand very simple questions and statements, allowing for slowed speech, repetition, or paraphrase; vocabulary inadequate to express anything but the most elementary needs, errors in pronunciation and grammar are frequent, but can be understood; should be able to order a simple meal, ask for shelter, ask and give simple directions, make purchases and tell time. —linguistic elements usually limited to the present tense—*avoir*, *aller*, *être*; might have pidginized forms, and/or phrases without verbs"	S-1+ "Exceeds S-1 primarily in vocabulary, can meet more complex travel and courtesy requirements; grammar weak and usually can't cope with social conversation; fluency may vary. —linguistically has a notion of the past tense but confuses uses and may occasionally fail to use; can use *futur proche*"	S-2 "—able to satisfy most routine social demands and limited work requirements. Can handle with confidence most social situations including introductions and casual conversations about current events, work, family, autobiographical information, can get the gist of most conversations on non-technical subjects, speaking vocabulary sufficient to respond simply with circumlocutions; does not have thorough or confident control of grammar but distinguishes the future tense even if he doesn't fully control, uses the passé composé and l'imparfait although with error, may have negative, "depuis" with present, present and infinitive"	S-2+ "exceeds 2 in grammar or vocabulary; better comprehension —has control of the future; still makes mistakes with the passé composé and l'imparfait. —usually no command of the conditional or subjunctive; must use passé composé correctly"

(Continued)

217

TABLE 14.2. *(Continued)*

Skill and Method of Testing	5	10	15	20
Listening Comprehension (Review in writing radio broadcasts just heard—topic identification and salient features]	a few key words of factual news broadcasts; tour guide; —partial comprehension of slow careful simplified telephone speech	partial comprehension of factual news broadcast; partial comprehension of native speaker conversation; partial comprehension of normal phone conversations; partial comprehension of lectures or formal presentations on a subject with which he/she is familiar	—reasonably complete comprehension of phone speech, can detect affective components of speech —very good comprehension of factual news broadcasts, partial comprehension of news commentary and analysis; partial comprehension of movie sound tracks; can catch some words of popular songs, can get the gist of native speaker conversation	—complete comprehension of phone speech, can detect affective components of speech —very good comprehension of factual news broadcasts, partial comprehension of news commentary and analysis, partial comprehension of movie sound tracks; can catch some words of popular songs; can get the gist of conversation
Reading Comprehension (Questions and summary of literary and non-literary texts)	—ability to interpret a) literary and b) non-literary texts: a) questions requiring factual responses b) summary of non-literary text in which the topic is correctly identified but which contains gross misstatement of information presented	—ability to interpret a) literary and b) non-literary texts: a) questions requiring factual and inferential responses b) summary of non-literary text in native language	—ability to interpret a) literary and b) non-literary texts a) questions requiring factual, interpretive and inferential responses b) summary of non-native text in native language	—ability to interpret a) literary and b) non-literary texts: a) questions requiring factual, interpretive, inferential and stylistic responses b) summary of non-literary text in native language

	450	500	550	600
Writing (Guided composition)	deficient vocabulary —can only write the most simple sentences; frequent spelling errors, many grammatical errors, lack of idiomatic usage	—adequate vocabulary for writing about familiar topics, some use of complex sentences beyond SVO organization, morphological problems remain but basic control of past, present and future evident, some idiomatic usage evident	—varied basic vocabulary, varied but somewhat limited syntactic patterns, fewer morphological problems, good use of idioms	—extensive vocabulary, well developed use of various syntactic patterns, natural and well formed transition frequent use of idioms
Culture (To be determined)				
CEEB Language Achievement Test	450	500	550	600

219

by excellence in another. To pass the proficiency test, students must achieve a minimum composite score of 10. (See Appendix II for a detailed description of the scoring procedure.)

Policies for implementing the requirement are as follows:

1. Students must receive a composite score of at least 10 on the proficiency test in order to be eligible for a grade in French 4. No letter grade is assigned for the test itself. Results are recorded as either pass or fail.

2. Students who have passed the test are given a course grade based on their cumulative performance throughout the semester. This grade is based on quizzes, homework, hour exams, etc. The content of many of these tests and assignments is similar to areas tested in the proficiency test.

3. Any relationship between the scoring system and A, B, C, D grades has been eliminated by using the categories 5, 10, 15, 20.

Students who fail the proficiency test are counseled on an individual basis. They are required to improve their performance on the portions of the test they failed, or raise their score on passed portions to achieve a composite average score of 10. Students in French 3 who believe they are eligible are also permitted to take the proficiency test.

PRELIMINARY IMPRESSIONS OF THE EFFECTS OF A PROFICIENCY-BASED LANGUAGE REQUIREMENT

At the conclusion of almost two years experience with the revised language requirement, we have attempted to evaluate the effects it appears to have had on the language learning environment at Pennsylvania (Freed 1982). With the exception of student scores on the proficiency test, the evaluation is preliminary and largely impressionistic. It is based on personal observations, on discussions with those responsible for language instruction at this level, and on a questionnaire distributed to teaching assistants and to students completing the fourth semester of French in December 1982. Even at this early date, a number of important effects and ramifications are already evident. They may be divided into four general categories: effects on the faculty; effects on teaching assistants, including their training and attitudes; effects on the curriculum: materials and methods; and effects on students, test scores, attitudes, and motivation. Test scores are reported for French only; all other comments pertain to all language groups. Each will be discussed in turn.

Effects on the Faculty

The most obvious effect on the faculty with respect to instituting a proficiency requirement is that it has promoted their involvement in decisions regarding elementary and intermediate language instruction. The decision to change the nature of the requirement and to implement specific standards required the consideration and participation of many faculty members who in recent years had not been called upon to think about the goals of language instruction at this level. While this new requirement does not involve senior faculty in the teaching of these courses, it has involved them in the testing of oral skills as one part of the comprehensive proficiency exam. In at least two departments senior faculty now share the responsibility of interviewing hundreds of students using the ACTFL oral proficiency test.

A less positive feature of the proficiency requirement from a faculty perspective is the enormous amount of detailed organizational work that its implementation entails. This includes scheduling oral interviews, tabulating total proficiency scores, and dealing with apprehensive students before the test as well as with indignant failing students afterwards. This work typically falls not to senior faculty, but to untenured assistant professors. However, the reaction to date of those concerned has been not to doubt the wisdom of moving from a time to a proficiency requirement, but rather, to search for more efficient ways of handling the bureaucratic details.

Effects on Teaching Assistants

Seen from the vantage point of language supervisors, the implementation of proficiency standards seems to have instilled in graduate teaching assistants a better sense of what is important at this level. Teaching assistants appear to be more realistic about goals for student achievement and less likely to think that grammar and grammatical exercises supplemented by a few reading and writing activities constitute a well-taught course. Those responsible for training teaching assistants have incorporated the notion of proficiency standards and proficiency testing into all aspects of their training; and subsequent observation of classroom instruction has shown that in preparing exercises and activities, TAs do tend to think more in terms of what speakers actually do with a language.

Responses of several teaching assistants to a questionnaire pertaining to the effect of the proficiency requirement corroborates the impression of faculty supervisors. Statements such as the following were frequent: "The proficiency requirement has had a positive effect on my own language teaching experience. I find that it motivates students and helps me develop proficiency-oriented teaching and testing materials." "Proficiency-oriented programs carry both the student and instructor beyond concern with sentence-level production to focus on more comprehensive language skills such as sustained conversation and listening comprehension. I've noticed in my classes that I teach not only language but extralinguistic strategies for dealing with the real problems that one is confronted with in using a foreign language." "Proficiency makes students, even at the lowest level, aware of their own progress. Materials are designed to help students handle everyday situations."

Effects on the Curriculum: Materials and Methods

Commitment to a proficiency requirement has brought with it visible changes in course content. However, this observation should not be interpreted to mean that one has been the direct result of the other. Rather, recognition of the need for one has prepared the way for the other. In some instances a department had changed textbooks, adopted new methods, replaced the emphasis on literature with one on oral skills, and revised testing techniques just prior to implementing the proficiency requirement. In such cases recognition of the need for curricular changes prepared the way for a somewhat radical transition from a long-standing time requirement to a proficiency requirement. In other cases, the decision to revise basic language instruction by adopting standards of functional proficiency has resulted in curricular changes that demand different materials, adjustments in course emphases, and more rigorous evaluation.

Regardless of which changes came first, language courses in these departments are now frequently characterized by a greater diversification of teaching techniques. These include techniques and materials that emphasize various types of listening comprehension, those that give students the opportunity to develop functional oral skills in context, more practical types of writing assignments, and a decreased emphasis on formal grammatical manipulation drills. There is general, if not absolute, recognition that it is each instructor's responsibility to provide appropriate materials and techniques to help students develop the requisite functional skills.

In addition to greater emphasis on the more practical aspects of language use, the implementation of a proficiency requirement has resulted in a more integrated sequence of courses and improved articulation between elementary and intermediate courses. It is anticipated that this integration will ultimately lead to improved articulation between the secondary and college level.

Effects on Students: Test Scores, Attitude, and Motivation

The most important data, those that can confirm or dispel our belief that a proficiency requirement will result in improved performance in foreign-language study, are not yet available. It will be a number of years until we are able to determine with certainty whether or not proficiency-based language instruction has improved language learning at the University of Pennsylvania. The only available data that suggest a positive effect on learning attributable to the proficiency requirement is the effect it has had on pass/fail enrollments. As mentioned earlier, the university has traditionally permitted students to take a number of courses, including foreign languages, on a pass/fail basis. A pilot study on pass/fail in French has yielded two positive facts. First, fewer students are enrolled in these courses on a pass/fail basis and second, the letter grade value of a P (passing) grade has increased. In 1976, prior to the proficiency requirement, twenty-three percent (23%) of all "P" grades would have been "A"s or "B"'s had letter grades been awarded; and well over seventy percent (70%) of all "P" grades would have been a "C" or lower. By contrast, in the fall of 1981, fifty-five percent (55%) of all "P" grades would have been "A" or "B" with a rough forty-five percent (45%) at the "C" or lower level.

The following progress report on the first three administrations of the proficiency test in French are encouraging. At the conclusion of the fall semester 1981, when the proficiency test was first administered, 214 students took all five portions of the test. Eleven percent (11%), or twenty-four students, failed the test. Of these, three were failing the course, seventeen were borderline students whose final grade was D, and four were C students. No student with a final grade of A or B failed the test. The area most frequently failed was the oral interview followed by listening comprehension. All students who failed were required to improve their performance in order to satisfy the language requirement. At the conclusion of the spring 1982 semester, 232 students were tested, and twenty-one, or nine percent (9%), failed. Of these, eleven received a final grade of D and ten a final grade of C. Again, no A or B student failed the test. As in the preceding semester, more students had difficulty with the oral interview than with any other portion of the test. The results at the end of the fall 1982 semester were roughly comparable: of 200 students tested, twenty-six (13%) failed to receive a passing composite score of 10.

The only section of the test for which a mean score has been computed is the CEEB. For both spring and fall 1982 semesters the mean CEEB score was 582. This compares favorably with the mean CEEB score of 558 established during the pre-proficiency evaluation period in 1980. While we did not expect to see a significant increase in CEEB scores, we were encouraged to learn that the reorientation of language teaching with an emphasis on functional proficiency did not adversely affect student performance on this test.

The curricular changes previously described have not gone unnoticed by students enrolled in these courses. To gather a sample of student opinion, students registered in level 4 French were asked to describe the effect of the proficiency requirement on their language learning experience. They were asked to consider classroom methods, materials, course emphases, tests, motivation, and anything else they deemed relevant. Of the 170 students who responded, many reported that they were more motivated than in the past because of the emphasis on the spoken language. Others commented that their increased motivation was due to more lively and varied classes. To our surprise, a note of regret was expressed by some that they were not being asked to read a literary text.

Many students have also attributed increased motivation and seriousness of purpose not to classroom activities *per se*, but rather to the prospect or, as they perceive it, the *threat* of a proficiency test. A good deal of resentment was expressed toward the concept of a proficiency test. This view notwithstanding, enrollment in those language programs that have adopted a proficiency requirement has not decreased. However, students do tend to be more outspoken about what they believe they are not getting in class. In retrospect they also state that they find the *prospect* of the exam far worse than the experience itself.

Not surprisingly, along with the good news there is also some bad. The most discouraging, yet perhaps the most useful outcome of this evaluation has been the revelation of student attitudes. The best summary of student opinion would be simply to say that for them "a language requirement by any other name is still a language requirement." Roughly one-third of those who responded to the questionnaire vehemently expressed their dissatisfaction at the mere idea of a proficiency examination. It was clear from their responses that these students were reacting not to the value of a proficiency as opposed to a time requirement, but rather to the need for a requirement in the first place. That is, these students were addressing the issue of a foreign language requirement rather than that of proficiency standards. This expression of student attitudes was instructive in itself. It clearly showed us that the implementation of a proficiency requirement must be accompanied by a thoroughgoing presentation of the concept of functionally defined proficiency standards and their place in the curriculum.

CONCLUSION

The experience at the University of Pennsylvania has provided a context in which we can evaluate both the need for proficiency-based language instruction and its potential success. A review of the experience points to several reasons for adopting proficiency standards and a proficiency requirement.

The first relates to the need for absolute standards, absolute in the sense that they relate to the competence of native speakers, the knowledge such speakers have which enables them to use language correctly and appropriately within ever varying communicative contexts. Such proficiency standards do not correspond to length of study; acquisition time will vary from student to student, school to school, and semester to semester. But the understanding of what the second-language learner should be able to do with language, in terms of content, function, and degree of accuracy, should remain constant.

This might be the appropriate place to suggest that we must resist slogans. We have survived the audiolingual era and have learned to contend with numerous misrepresentations of the concept of communicative competence. It is clear that language use and language learning are multifaceted and cannot be neatly compartmentalized into a restricted set of skills. Some research suggests that if we teach only communicative survival skills we risk producing students who can satisfy basic survival needs but who have difficulty progressing beyond this minimal level to acquire control of increasingly complex syntactic and stylistic features (Higgs and Clifford 1981). By contrast, students who learn to do grammatical drills and transformations and fill-in-the-blanks are good at just that; but, as we all know, that has precious little to do with using language correctly and appropriately (Savignon 1972).

Secondly, proficiency standards based on content, function, and form facilitate articulation between levels, whether from high school to college or within each of these programs. At the same time that articulation is improved, placement procedures should become easier. If we establish a common set of standards, recognized and accepted by teachers and students at all levels, it will be far easier to place new students at the appropriate level of study. Moreover, the definition and common use of such standards should serve students and the community beyond the educational sector. If we adhere, more or less, to what has been called a "common yardstick," future employers will be able to evaluate students' skills in a sensible way that cannot be communicated in a transcript filled with "A"s, "P"s for Pass, or even "C"s.

Finally, proficiency-based language instruction should prepare students to use language in an unlimited number of contexts that will include but not be limited to literary study.

The observed effects of the proficiency requirement on language study at the University of Pennsylvania suggest that important changes have begun to take place. There is increased faculty awareness of, interest and involvement in, decisions concerning basic language instruction. There is more cooperation between the teaching assistants who teach these courses, as well as evidence of more creative teaching with increased emphasis on language use, both written and oral. We have also observed articulation in the sequence of elementary and intermediate courses.

There is also evidence that the proficiency examination looms as a threat to many students. To the extent that this is true, the resultant learner anxiety may in fact be a negative influence on language learning. Only time, and close monitoring of student attitudes and achievement, will tell. In the meantime, it is clear that the emphasis must be on the creation of proficiency standards and on the understanding of these standards by *all* those involved in the language learning process. To the extent that the emphasis is on tests and testing, real changes will not necessarily occur. In fact, the terms proficiency standards or proficiency requirements could easily become as empty as were the former catalogue descriptions that invoked the term "competence," but really meant "time." Perhaps more than ever before, we must provide for and maintain an intimate connection between training, teaching, and testing.

NOTES

1. It should be understood that all students did not necessarily study language at Pennsylvania during four consecutive semesters. Many students had been placed into language levels 2, 3, or 4 upon entrance. The results for students completing

one, two, and three semesters of study in each of these languages are reported in Freed (1981b).

2. The 1+ designation is a rating used by the U.S. government (see Adams and Frith 1979). It has been redefined by the *ACTFL Provisional Proficiency Guidelines* (ACTFL 1982) for academic use as an *Intermediate-High* on a (9 level) scale which progresses from *Novice-Low* to *Advanced*. See Appendix I for descriptions of these levels.

3. The proficiency standards described herein were adopted by the French section in the spring of 1981. It is anticipated that they will be revised at the end of the Spring 1983 academic term. The intention is to make the standards for satisfying the language proficiency requirement in French consistent with the *ACTFL Provisional Proficiency Guidelines*. The revised requirement will require students to speak at the level described by an Intermediate High and will most likely require them to write at the same level. In all likelihood the minimal level for reading will be that described as Advanced. For a description of the ACTFL guidelines see Appendix I.

REFERENCES

ACTFL. 1982. *ACTFL provisional proficiency guidelines*. Hastings-on-Hudson, N.Y.: American Council on the Teaching of Foreign Languages.

Adams, M. and J. Frith (eds.). 1979. *Testing kit: French and Spanish*. Washington, D.C.: Foreign Service Institute.

Brod, R. (ed.). 1980. *Language study for the 1980s: reports of the MLA—ACLS language task forces*. New York: Modern Language Association.

Brown, H. 1980. *Principles of language learning and teaching*. Englewood Cliffs, New Jersey: Prentice-Hall.

Clarke, M. 1982. "On bandwagons, tyranny, and common sense," *TESOL Quarterly* **16:** 437—448.

Freed, B. 1981a. "Establishing proficiency-based language requirements," *ADFL Bulletin* **12:** 6—12.

Freed, B. 1981b. "Achievement in elementary and intermediate language classes as measured by the College Entrance Examination Board language achievement tests," Unpublished manuscript. University of Pennsylvania, Philadelphia.

Freed, B. 1982. "Preliminary impressions of the effects of a proficiency-based language requirement." Paper presented at the ACTFL Annual Meeting, New York.

Hagiwara, P. 1983. "Student placement in French: results and implications," *The Modern Language Journal* **67:** 23—32.

Higgs, T. and R. Clifford. 1982. "The push toward communication." In T. Higgs (ed.). *Curriculum, competence and the foreign language teacher*. ACTFL Foreign Language Education Series, vol. 13. Skokie, Ill.: National Textbook Co.

President's Commission on Foreign Language and International Studies. 1979. *Strength through wisdom: a critique of U.S. capability*. Washington, D.C.: Government Printing Office.

Richards, J. and T. Rodgers. 1982. "Method: approach, design and procedure," *TESOL Quarterly* **16:** 153–168.

Savignon, S. 1972. *Communicative competence: an experiment in foreign language teaching.* Philadelphia: Center for Curriculum Development.

APPENDIX 1—ACTFL PROVISIONAL PROFICIENCY GUIDELINES

Provisional Generic Descriptions—Speaking

Novice–Low | Unable to function in the spoken language. Oral production is limited to occasional isolated words. Essentially no communicative ability.

Novice—Mid | Able to operate only in a very limited capacity within very predictable areas of need. Vocabulary limited to that necessary to express simple elementary needs and basic courtesy formulae. Syntax is fragmented, inflections and word endings frequently omitted, confused or distorted, and the majority of utterances consist of isolated words or short formulae. Utterances rarely consist of more than two or three words and are marked by frequent long pauses and repetition of an interlocutor's words. Pronunciation is frequently unintelligible and is strongly influenced by first language. Can be understood only with difficulty, even by persons such as teachers who are used to speaking with non-native speakers or in interactions where the context strongly supports the utterance.

Novice—High | Able to satisfy immediate needs using learned utterances. Can ask questions or make statements with reasonable accuracy only where this involves short memorized utterances or formulae. There is no real autonomy of expression, although there may be some emerging signs of spontaneity and flexibility. There is a slight increase in utterance length but frequent long pauses and repetition of interlocutor's words still occur. Most utterances are telegraphic and word endings are often omitted, confused or distorted. Vocabulary is limited to areas of immediate survival needs. Can differentiate most phonemes when produced in isolation but when they are combined in words or groups of words, errors are frequent and, even with repetition, may severely inhibit communication even with persons used to dealing with such learners. Little development in stress and intonation is evident.

Intermediate—Low   Able to satisfy basic survival needs and minimum courtesy requirements. In areas of immediate need or on very familiar topics, can ask and answer simple questions, initiate and respond to simple statements, and maintain very simple face-to-face conversations. When asked to do so, is able to formulate some questions with limited constructions and much inaccuracy. Almost every utterance contains fractured syntax and other grammatical errors. Vocabulary inadequate to express anything but the most elementary needs. Strong interference from native language occurs in articulation, stress and intonation. Misunderstandings frequently arise from limited vocabulary and grammar and erroneous phonology but, with repetition, can generally be understood by native speakers in regular contact with foreigners attempting to speak their language. Little precision in information conveyed owing to tentative state of grammatical development and little or no use of modifiers.

Intermediate—Mid   Able to satisfy some survival needs and some limited social demands. Is able to formulate some questions when asked to do so. Vocabulary permits discussion of topics beyond basic survival needs such as personal history and leisure time activities. Some evidence of grammatical accuracy in basic constructions, for example, subject-verb agreement, noun-adjective agreement, some notion of inflection.

Intermediate—High   Able to satisfy most survival needs and limited social demands. Shows some spontaneity in language production but fluency is very uneven. Can initiate and sustain a general conversation but has little understanding of the social conventions of conversation. Developing flexibility in a range of circumstances beyond immediate survival needs. Limited vocabulary range necessitates much hesitation and circumlocution. The commoner tense forms occur but errors are frequent in formation and selection. Can use most question forms. While some word order is established, errors still occur in more complex patterns. Cannot sustain coherent structures in longer utterances or unfamiliar situations. Ability to describe and give precise information is limited. Aware of basic cohesive features such as pronouns and verb inflections, but many are unreliable, especially if less immediate in reference. Extended discourse is largely a series of short, discrete utterances. Articulation is comprehensible to native speakers used to dealing with foreigners, and can combine most phonemes with reasonable comprehensibility, but still has difficulty in producing certain sounds in certain positions, or in certain combinations, and speech will usually be labored. Still has to repeat utterances frequently to be understood by the general public. Able to produce some narration in either past or future.

Advanced

Able to satisfy routine social demands and limited work requirements. Can handle with confidence but not with facility most social situations including introductions and casual conversations about current events, as well as work, family, and autobiographical information; can handle limited work requirements, needing help in handling any complications or difficulties. Has a speaking vocabulary sufficient to respond simply with some circumlocutions; accent, though often quite faulty, is intelligible; can usually handle elementary constructions quite accurately but does not have thorough or confident control of the grammar.

Advanced Plus

Able to satisfy most work requirements and show some ability to communicate on concrete topics relating to particular interests and special fields of competence. Generally strong in either grammar or vocabulary, but not in both. Weaknesses or unevenness in one of the foregoing or in pronunciation result in occasional miscommunication. Areas of weakness range from simple constructions such as plurals, articles, prepositions, and negatives to more complex structures such as tense usage, passive constructions, word order, and relative clauses. Normally controls general vocabulary with some groping for everyday vocabulary still evident. Often shows remarkable fluency and ease of speech, but under tension or pressure language may break down.

Superior

Able to speak the language with sufficient structural accuracy and vocabulary to participate effectively in most formal and informal conversations on practical, social, and professional topics. Can discuss particular interests and special fields of competence with reasonable ease. Vocabulary is broad enough that speaker rarely has to grope for a word; accent may be obviously foreign, control of grammar good; errors virtually never interfere with understanding and rarely disturb the native speaker.

Provisional Generic Descriptions—Listening

Novice—Low   No practical understanding of the spoken language. Understanding limited to occasional isolated words, such as cognates, borrowed words, and high frequency social conventions. Essentially no ability to comprehend even short utterances.

Novice—Mid   Sufficient comprehension to understand some memorized words within predictable areas of need. Vocabulary for comprehension limited to simple elementary needs and basic courtesy formulae. Utterances understood rarely exceed more than two or three words at a time and ability to understand is characterized by long pauses for assimilation and by repeated requests on the listener's part for repetition, and/or a slower rate of speech. Confuses words that sound similar.

Novice—High   Sufficient comprehension to understand a number of memorized utterances in areas of immediate need. Comprehends slightly longer utterances in situations where the context aids understanding, such as at the table, in a restaurant/store, in a train/bus. Phrases recognized have for the most part been memorized. Comprehends vocabulary common to daily needs. Comprehends simple questions/statements about family members, age, address, weather, time, daily activities and interests. Misunderstandings arise from failure to perceive critical sounds or endings. Understands even standard speech with difficulty but gets some main ideas. Often requires repetition and/or a slowed rate of speed for comprehension, even when listening to persons such as teachers who are used to speaking with non-natives.

Intermediate—Low Sufficient comprehension to understand utterances about basic survival needs, minimum courtesy and travel requirements. In areas of immediate need or on very familiar topics, can understand non-memorized material, such as simple questions and answers, statements, and face-to-face conversations in the standard language. Comprehension areas include basic needs: meals, lodging, transportation, time, simple instructions (e.g., route directions) and routine commands (e.g., from customs officials, police). Understands main ideas. Misunderstandings frequently arise from lack of vocabulary or faulty processing of syntactic information often caused by strong interference from the native language or by the imperfect and partial acquisition of the target grammar.

Intermediate—Mid   Sufficient comprehension to understand simple conversations about some survival needs and some limited social conventions. Vocabulary permits understanding of topics beyond basic survival needs such as personal history and leisure time activities. Evidence of understanding basic constructions, for example, subject-verb agreement, noun-adjective agreement; evidence that some inflection is understood.

Intermediate—High   Sufficient comprehension to understand short conversations about most survival needs and limited social conventions. Increasingly able to understand topics beyond immediate survival needs. Shows spontaneity in understanding, but speed and consistency of understanding uneven. Limited vocabulary range necessitates repetition for understanding. Understands commoner tense forms and some word order patterns, including most question forms, but miscommunication still occurs with more complex patterns. Can get the gist of conversations, but cannot sustain comprehension in longer utterances or in unfamiliar situations. Understanding of descriptions and detailed information is limited. Aware of basic cohesive features such as pronouns and verb inflections, but many are unreliably understood, especially if other material intervenes. Understanding is largely limited to a series of short, discrete utterances. Still has to ask for utterances to be repeated. Some ability to understand the facts.

Advanced   Sufficient comprehension to understand conversations about routine social conventions and limited school or work requirements. Able to understand face-to-face speech in the standard language, delivered at a normal rate with some repetition and rewording, by a native speaker not used to dealing with foreigners. Understands everyday topics, common personal and family news, well-known current events, and routine matters involving school or work; descriptions and narration about current, past and future events; and essential points of discussion or speech at an elementary level on topics in special fields of interest.

Advanced Plus

Sufficient comprehension to understand most routine social conventions, conversations on school or work requirements, and discussions on concrete topics related to particular interests and special fields of competence. Often shows remarkable ability and ease of understanding, but comprehension may break down under tension or pressure, including unfavorable listening conditions. Candidate may display weakness or deficiency due to inadequate vocabulary base or less than secure knowledge of grammar and syntax. Normally understands general vocabulary with some hesitant understanding of everyday vocabulary still evident. Can sometimes detect emotional overtones. Some ability to understand between the lines, i.e., to make inferences.

Superior

Sufficient comprehension to understand the essentials of all speech in standard dialects, including technical discussions within a special field. Has sufficient understanding of face-to-face speech, delivered with normal clarity and speed in standard language, on general topics and areas of special interest; understands hypothesizing and supported opinions. Has broad enough vocabulary that rarely has to ask for paraphrasing or explanation. Can follow accurately the essentials of conversations between educated native speakers, reasonably clear telephone calls, radio broadcasts, standard news items, oral reports, some oral technical reports, and public addresses on non-technical subjects. May not understand native speakers if they speak very quickly or use some slang or unfamiliar dialect. Can often detect emotional overtones. Can understand "between the lines" (i.e., make inferences).

Provisional Generic Descriptions—Reading

Novice—Low   No functional ability in reading the foreign language.

Novice—Mid   Sufficient understanding of the written language to interpret highly contextualized words or cognates within
predictable areas. Vocabulary for comprehension limited
to simple elementary needs such as names, addresses,
dates, street signs, building names, short informative
signs (e.g., no smoking, entrance/exit) and formulaic
vocabulary requesting same. Material understood rarely
exceeds a single phrase and comprehension requires suc-
cessive rereading and checking.

Novice—High   Sufficient comprehension of the written language to interpret set expressions in areas of immediate need. Can
recognize all the letters in the printed version of an alphabetic system and high-frequency elements of a sylla-
bary or a character system. Where vocabulary has been
mastered can read for instruction and directional purposes standardized messages, phrases or expressions
such as some items on menus, schedules, timetables,
maps and signs indicating hours of operation, social
codes, and traffic regulations. This material is read only
for essential information. Detail is overlooked or mis-
understood.

Intermediate—Low Sufficient comprehension to understand in printed form
the simplest connected material, either authentic or specially prepared, dealing with basic survival and social
needs. Able to understand both mastered material and
recombinations of the mastered elements that achieve
meanings at the same level. Understands main ideas in
material whose structures and syntax parallel the native
language. Can read messages, greetings, statements of
social amenities or other simple language containing only
the highest frequency grammatical patterns and vocabulary items including cognates (if appropriate). Misunderstandings arise when syntax diverges from that of the
native language or when grammatical cues are overlooked.

Intermediate—Mid Sufficient comprehension to understand in printed form
simple discourse for informative or social purposes. In
response to perceived needs can read for information

material such as announcements of public events, popular advertising, notes containing biographical information or narration of events, and straightforward newspaper headlines and story titles. Can guess at unfamiliar vocabulary if highly contextualized. Relies primarily on adverbs as time indicators. Has some difficulty with the cohesive factors in discourse, such as matching pronouns with referents. May have to read material several times before understanding.

Intermediate—High Sufficient comprehension to understand a simple paragraph for personal communication, information or recreational purposes. Can read with understanding social notes, letters and invitations; can locate and derive main ideas of the introductory/summary paragraphs from high interest or familiar news or other informational sources; can read for pleasure specially prepared, or some uncomplicated authentic prose, such as fictional narratives or cultural information. Shows spontaneity in reading by ability to guess at meaning from context. Understands common time indicators and can interpret some cohesive factors such as objective pronouns and simple clause connectors. Begins to relate sentences in the discourse to advance meaning, but cannot sustain understanding of longer discourse on unfamiliar topics. Misinterpretation still occurs with more complex patterns.

Advanced Sufficient comprehension to read simple authentic printed material or edited textual material within a familiar context. Can read uncomplicated but authentic prose on familiar subjects containing description and narration such as news items describing frequently occurring events, simple biographic information, social notices, and standard business letters. Can read edited texts such as prose fiction and contemporary culture. The prose is predominantly in familiar sentence patterns. Can follow essential points of written discussion at level of main ideas and some supporting ones with topics in a field of interest or where background exists. Some misunderstandings. Able to read the facts but cannot draw inferences.

Advanced Plus Sufficient comprehension to understand most factual information in non-technical prose as well as some discussions on concrete topics related to special interests. Able to read for information and description, to follow sequence of events, and to react to that information. Is able to separate main ideas from lesser ones, and uses that division to advance understanding. Can locate and interpret main ideas and details in material written for the general public. Will begin to guess sensibly at new words by using linguistic context and prior knowledge. May react personally to material but does not yet detect subjective attitudes, values, or judgments in the writing.

Superior   Able to read standard newspaper items addressed to the general reader, routine correspondence reports and technical material in a field of interest at a normal rate of speed (at least 200 wpm). Readers can gain new knowledge from material on unfamiliar topics in areas of a general nature. Can interpret hypotheses, supported opinions and conjectures. Can also read short stories, novels, and other recreational literature accessible to the general public. Reading ability is not subject-matter dependent. Has broad enough general vocabulary that successful guessing resolves problems with complex structures and low-frequency idioms. Misreading is rare. Almost always produces correct interpretation. Able to read between the lines. May be unable to appreciate nuance of stylistics.

Provisional Generic Descriptions—Writing

Novice—Low   No functional ability in writing the foreign language.

Novice—Mid   No practical communicative writing skills. Able to copy isolated words or short phrases. Able to transcribe previously studied words or phrases.

Novice—High   Able to write simple fixed expressions and limited memorized material. Can supply information when requested on forms such as hotel registrations and travel documents. Can write names, numbers, dates, one's own nationality, addresses, and other simple biographic information, as well as learned vocabulary, short phrases, and simple lists. Can write all the symbols in an alphabetic or syllabic system or 50 of the most common characters. Can write simple memorized material with frequent misspellings and inaccuracies.

Intermediate—Low   Has sufficient control of the writing system to meet limited practical needs. Can write short messages, such as simple questions or notes, postcards, phone messages, and the like within the scope of limited language experience. Can take simple notes on material dealing with very familiar topics although memory span is extremely limited. Can create statements or questions within the scope of limited language experience. Material produced consists of recombinations of learned vocabulary and structures into simple sentences. Vocabulary is inadequate to express anything but elementary needs. Writing tends to be a loosely organized collection of sentence fragments on a very familiar topic. Makes continual errors in spelling, grammar, and punctuation, but writing can be read and understood by a native speaker used to dealing with foreigners. Able to produce appropriately some fundamental sociolinguistic distinctions in formal and familiar style, such as appropriate subject pronouns, titles of address and basic social formulae.

Intermediate—Mid   Sufficient control of writing system to meet some survival needs and some limited social demands. Able to compose short paragraphs or take simple notes on very familiar topics grounded in personal experience. Can discuss likes and dislikes, daily routine, everyday events, and the like. Can express past time, using content words and time expressions, or with sporadically accurate verbs. Evidence of good control of basic constructions and inflections such as subject-verb agreement, noun-adjective agreement, and straightforward syntactic constructions in present or future time, though errors occasionally occur. May make frequent errors, however, when venturing beyond current level of linguistic competence. When resorting to a dictionary, often is unable to identify appropriate vocabulary, or uses dictionary entry in uninflected form.

Intermediate—High   Sufficient control of writing system to meet most survival needs and limited social demands. Can take notes in some detail on familiar topics, and respond to personal questions using elementary vocabulary and common structures. Can write simple letters, brief synopses and paraphrases, summaries of biographical data and work experience, and short compositions on familiar topics. Can create sentences and short paragraphs relating to most survival needs (food, lodging, transportation, immediate surroundings and situations) and limited social demands. Can relate personal history, discuss topics such as a daily life, preferences, and other familiar material. Can express fairly accurately present and future time. Can produce some past verb forms, but not always accurately or with correct usage. Shows good control of elementary vocabulary and some control of basic syntactic patterns but major errors still occur when expressing more complex thoughts. Dictionary usage may still yield incorrect vocabulary of forms, although can use a dictionary to advantage to express simple ideas. Generally cannot use basic cohesive elements of discourse to advantage such as relative constructions, subject pronouns, connectors, etc. Writing, though faulty, is comprehensible to native speakers used to dealing with foreigners.

Advanced

Able to write routine social correspondence and simple discourse of at least several paragraphs on familiar topics. Can write simple social correspondence, take notes, and write cohesive summaries, resumes, and short narratives and descriptions on factual topics. Able to write about everyday topics using both description and narration. Has sufficient writing vocabulary to express himself/herself simply with some circumlocution. Can write about a very limited number of current events or daily situations and express personal preferences and observations in some detail, using basic structures. Still makes common errors in spelling and punctuation, but shows some control of the most common formats and punctuation conventions. Good control of the morphology of the language (in inflected languages) and of the most frequently used syntactic structures. Elementary constructions are usually handled quite accurately, and writing is understandable to a native speaker not used to reading the writing of foreigners. Uses a limited number of cohesive devices such as pronouns and repeated words with good accuracy. Able to join sentences in limited discourse, but has difficulty and makes frequent errors in producing complex sentences. Paragraphs are reasonably unified and coherent.

Advanced Plus

Shows ability to write about most common topics with some precision and in some detail. Can write fairly detailed resumes and summaries and take quite accurate notes. Can write most social and informal business correspondence. Can describe and narrate personal experiences and explain simply points of view in prose discourse. Can write about concrete topics relating to particular interests and special fields of competence. Normally controls general vocabulary with some circumlocution. Often shows remarkable fluency and ease of expression, but under time constraints and pressure language may be inaccurate and/or incomprehensible. Generally strong in either grammar or vocabulary, but not in both. Weaknesses and unevenness in one of the foregoing or in spelling result in occasional miscommunication. Areas of weakness range from simple constructions such as plurals, articles, prepositions, and negatives to more complex structures such as tense usage, passive constructions, word order, and relative clauses. Some misuse of vocabulary still evident. Shows a limited ability to use circumlocution. Uses dictionary to advantage to supply unknown words. Writing is understandable to native speakers not used to reading material written by non-natives, though the style is still obviously foreign.

Superior

Able to use the written language effectively in most formal and informal exchanges on practical, social, and professional topics. Can write most types of correspondence, such as memos and social and business letters, short research papers and statements of position in areas of special interest or in special fields. Can express hypotheses, conjectures, and present arguments or points of view accurately and effectively. Can write about areas of special interest and handle topics in special fields, in addition to most common topics. Good control of a full range of structures, spelling, and a wide general vocabulary allow the writer to convey his/her message accurately, though style may be foreign. Can use complex and compound sentence structures to express ideas clearly and coherently. Uses dictionary with a high degree of accuracy to supply specialized vocabulary. Errors, though sometimes made when using more complex structures, are occasional, and rarely disturb the native speaker. Sporadic errors when using basic structures. Although sensitive to differences in formal and informal style, still cannot tailor writing precisely and accurately to a variety of audiences or styles.

APPENDIX II PROPOSED SCALE FOR FRENCH 4 PROFICIENCY

Examination:	Points:5.00	10.00	15.00	20.00
	↕	↕ LEVEL	↕	↕
A. CEEB Language Achievement Test	450	500	550	600
B. FSI Oral Interaction	S-1	S-1+	S-2	S-2+
C. Listening Comprehension	5	10	15	20
D. Reading Comprehension	5	10	15	20
E. Writing	5	10	15	20
F. Culture	5	10	15	20

Explanation

1. All students will be required to take all six sections of the test as listed above. (See Table 14.2 for a description of the Proficiency Standard at each level for each skill)

2. Performance below 10 on any portion of the exam constitutes failure for that section.

3. *Cumulative performance*, however, is the ultimate criterion for passing. One may accrue from 0 to 20 points on each section but the cumulative average must be equal to 10 or higher (i.e. a student may fail sections of the exam and still pass the proficiency test: see examples a and b below). Those who fall below this average must retake the section which brought the average down, or may retake the entire exam.

4. Sample passing scores:
   a) CEEB   500 (=10.00)
       FSI   1 (= 5.00)
       Listening Comprehension   70% (=10.00)
       Reading Comprehension   85% (=15.00)

Writing	55% (= 5.00)	
Culture	85% (=15.00)	
Total	60.00	÷ 6 = 10.00
b) CEEB	475 (= 7.50)	
FSI	1⁺ (=10.00)	
Listening Comprehension	75% (=11.70)	
Reading Comprehension	85% (=15.00)	
Writing	80% (=13.30)	
Culture	85% (=15.00)	
Total	72.50	÷ 6 = 12.10

Author Index

Abe, Y., 116
Abercrombie, D. 59, **75**
ACTFL Provisional Proficiency
  Guidelines, 212, 215, **226**, 227–239
Adams, J., 58, **75**
Adams, M., 217, 226, **226**
Adcock, D., **180**
Akiyama, C., 13
Anne Arundel County (MD) Public
  Schools, **180**
Asher, J., 40, 50, **50**

Bachman, L., 190, **200**
Bailey, N.C., 37, **50**, 66, **75**
Baldegger, M., 20
Bamgbose, A., 63, 72, **75**
Bédard, E., 74
Berns, M., 29
Bialystok, E., 37, **50**
Bodman, J., 15
Bokamba, E., 62, 75, **75**
Breen, M., 9, 10, **20**, 110, **126**
Brod, R., 212, **226**
Brown, H., 106, **106**, 212, **226**
Brumfit, C., 94, 105, **107**
Bruton, C., 9, **20**
Burling, R., 57, **75**
Buros, O., 189, **200**
Burt, M., 92, 93, **107**
Byrd, D., 18

Calfee, R., 25, **33**
Canadian Parents for French, **180**

Canale, M., 128, 136, **136**, 188, 189, 190,
  200
Candlin, C., 9, 10, **20**, 110, **126**
Carroll, S., 5, **20**
Catford, J., 62, **75**
Center for Applied Linguistics, 173, 180
Chishimba, M., 69, 75, **75**
Chomsky, N., 5, **20**
Clark, J., **181**
Clarke, M., 212, **226**
Clementi, Cabetas, I., 18
Clifford, R., 224, **226**
Cohen, A., 172, **180**
Costo, P., 20
Council of Europe, 10–11
Cummins, J., 170, **180**
Curran, C., 83, **86**, 92

Donoghue, M., **180**
Doyle, L., 125
Duff, A., 81
Dulay, H., 92, 93, **107**
Dustoor, P., 72, **75**

Faerch, C., 130, **136**
Felix, S., 37, **51**
Ferguson, C., 70, 74, **75**
Finegan, E., 74, **75**
Firth, J.R., 5–7, **20**, 67, 68, 71, **75**
Freed, B., 38, **51**, 213, **226**
Frith, J., 217, 226, **226**

241